NATURAL STATE

NATURAL STATE

*A Literary Anthology of
California Nature
Writing*

*Selected and Edited by Steven Gilbar
With a Foreword by David Brower*

UNIVERSITY OF CALIFORNIA PRESS

Berkeley   Los Angeles   London

University of California Press
Berkeley and Los Angeles, California

University of California Press, Ltd.
London, England

© 1998 by
The Regents of the University of California

Library of Congress Cataloging-in-Publication Data

Natural state : a literary anthology of California
nature writing /selected and edited by Steven Gilbar :
with a foreword by David Brower.
    p.   cm.
    Includes bibliographic references and index
    ISBN 0-520-21208-8 (cloth : alk. paper).—
ISBN 0-520-21209-6 (pbk. : alk. paper)
    1. Natural history—California.   2. Nature.
I. Gilbar, Steven.   QH105.C2N425   1998
508.794—dc 21   97-19119

Printed in the United States of America

9 8 7 6 5 4 3 2 1

The paper used in this publication meets the minimum
requirements of American National Standards for
Information Sciences—Permanence of Paper for
Printed Library Materials, ANSI Z39.48–1984.⊚

CONTENTS

THE HILLS AND VALLEYS

EARTH, WIND, RAIN, AND FIRE

Foreword

This book is a feast and requires a celebration. For one thing, I have known, or am almost old enough to have known, so many of the authors: LeConte, Twain, Kerouac, Brewer, Stevenson, London, Steinbeck, Stegner, Abbey, Chase, Powell, Miller (Joaquin and Henry), Muir, and Austin—all of whom preceded me (which isn't easy). I was overwhelmed with serendipity, not to be relieved by the current host of authors who are younger (who isn't?), including John Daniel, who had learned about writing from Wallace Stegner and was fleetingly a student of mine, when as a Berkeley dropout (1931) I briefly became a visiting professor at Stanford (1982). I should take Mr. Daniel to court for overstressing my emotional stability by revealing, in matchless prose, what a desert is all about. It hurts to hold back tears when they have no place else to go.

What John McPhee, from whose *Encounters with the Archdruid* I learned who I was, writes about the seismic cross California bears renews all my old anxieties. I was born in Berkeley so close to the San Andreas that I still find fault too easily and brake for tectonic plates.

But book work, as an editor for the Sierra Club and the University of California Press, informed my Berkeley decades; and I was ready, when Ted Koppel was chairing a Stanford assembly and asked me for a couple of environmental sound bites, to conclude, "We must reform television, which is causing cerebral gridlock across America." The audience loved it. I hope the audience for this book can agree that we must also reform the Internet and Web, where electronics fail to distinguish between data and knowledge, or between surfeit and craft, or between merde (to avoid scatological alliteration) and substance.

There is no such problem with *Natural State*. The book will not cause cerebral problems; it will cure them. Moreover, it can be enjoyed indoors or out; in natural light, unencumbered by power surges; survive splashes of coffee, rain, or chardonnay; comfortably endure thermal changes on a shelf or in a knapsack, never asking to be pointed or clicked. And you can lift your eyes, when you want to, to the hills without suffering painful disintegration of the carpel tunnels or becoming roadkill on the Information Superhighway.

Add a further fussy detail: words written for a book are likely to endure in the mind, rather than perish in a landfill. There are wiser uses for land, considering that the two million Californians here when I arrived have already become thirty-two million. California wildness deserves a chance to recover, and *Natural State* lets us know why.

David Brower
Berkeley, 1997

C alifornia is a land of contrasts. Both the highest and lowest elevations of the lower forty-eight states are in California—and
then only eighty miles apart. The hottest temperatures in the
United States are found there. It has some of the world's greatest wonders, and has had some of its worst natural disasters. Naturally, this
landscape has inspired prose that, like the land itself, is diverse and full
of contrasts. This book aims to corral the best of it.

The special quality of California's landscape has affected all sorts of
writers, not all of whom fall into the category of "nature writer" or
"naturalist." Gretel Ehrlich, Barry Lopez, and David Rains Wallace, for
example, have certainly made nature their special province, but they
also write fiction. Then there are writers known primarily for their
fiction—Henry Miller, Wallace Stegner, and Robert Louis Stevenson,
to name but three—who turned to nonfiction to express their feelings
about California's wild places. Also present are authors who work principally in nonfiction, such as M. F. K. Fisher, John McPhee, and John
Muir. Others yet seem equally at home in both fiction and nonfiction;
these include Edward Abbey, Joan Didion, and Mark Twain. Finally,
there are poets, such as John Daniel, Joaquin Miller, and Gary Snyder,
who have also worked in prose. Not all the pieces rounded up here are

nonfiction, however. Included are selections from works of fiction by Jack Kerouac, Jack London, John Steinbeck, and others. What all the pieces by these authors have in common is good writing, which is what makes this anthology "literary," rather than a historical survey of nature writing in the state.

The constraints of space have regrettably forced the omission of much worthwhile writing. Some of the early European explorers, pioneers, and settlers left wonderfully descriptive journals about a wilder California. Writers as varied as Clarence King, Stewart Edward White, George Wharton James, Page Stegner, Judy Van Der Veer, Galen Rowell, David Wicinas, and Paul McHugh have all written memorably about the outdoors, while others, such as Jaime de Angulo, Gerald Haslam, Maxine Hong Kingston, Roy Parvin, William Saroyan, and Gary Soto, have given life and voice to the people of California, on the land and in their diverse communities. Many other important contributions could be mentioned. In order to strike a balance between classic writers and newer voices, and to provide a consistent focus on the state's natural treasures, hard choices had to be made.

The incredible biodiversity of California has not been mirrored to date by a like diversity in the cultural backgrounds of those who write about nature. Not surprisingly, most such essayists, poets, and fiction writers have been European-Americans, for they had the education and leisure required to trek through the wilderness and record their impressions. Although today some of the best writers in California are of Mexican, African, and Asian descent, these authors have usually chosen to write about their immigrant and urban experiences rather than rhapsodize about the mountains, deserts, and forests. The same is true of Native Californian writers, most of whom write about their people on the land, rather than the land itself. This situation is changing, however, and soon, no doubt, a body of "nature writing" will emerge that better reflects the cultural diversity of California's population.

Women are perhaps more adequately represented in contemporary writings about nature. Although historically they lacked not only rooms of their own, but tents as well, that has changed in the past several decades, and today women are among the best in the field.

Some years ago the Central Valley writer Gerald Haslam claimed that California has four "geo-literary" regions: the greater San Francisco Bay Area, the Heartland, the Southland, and Wilderness California. Most of the places covered in this collection are in the last region—if, that is, "wilderness" can be stretched to embrace the merely rustic and pastoral as well as the truly untamed. It does not mean places where men and women do not dwell. Simply, when we speak of wilderness, our attention is focused not on people, but on the place itself.

The book is organized around the basic landforms: mountains, hills and valleys, deserts, and coast. As a prelude, there are two California Indian myths about how the land was created. The first is an old Cahto narrative, and the second is an A-juma-wi story filtered through the modern sensibility of Darryl Babe Wilson.

Of all California's many mountain ranges, the most imposing is the Sierra Nevada. This four-hundred-mile-long wall of jagged, glacier-sculpted mountains has probably inspired more writers than any other topographical feature in the state. At the top of the list of Sierran natural wonders is surely Yosemite, represented here by Joseph LeConte experiencing its wonders for the first time, Jack Kerouac and a couple of his dharma-bum companions scaling Matterhorn Peak, Daniel Duane climbing Half Dome, and Ann Zwinger delighting in the high country's "trumpets of light." Elsewhere in the Sierra, John Muir relishes a wind storm, and Mark Twain camps out at Lake Tahoe.

Extending north and south between the Central Valley and the Pacific are the Coast Ranges. The Santa Lucia Range, for example, which is visited in a short piece by John Steinbeck, rises abruptly from the ocean to heights of almost 6,000 feet.

Other mountains, too, have heartened writers. Bordering Oregon, the Klamath Mountains (visited here by Joaquin Miller and David Rains Wallace), the Cascade Range, and the Modoc Plateau terminate the Central Valley at its north end. In the south, the valley is closed by the Transverse Ranges—so called because of their east-west lineation, which runs at an oblique angle to the northwest-southwest-trending Sierra Nevada and Coast Ranges. The Transverse Ranges comprise such mountain chains as the San Bernardinos, Santa Monicas, and Santa Ynez, as well as their interior valleys, including San Fernando, San Gabriel, and Ojai. South of the Transverse are the Peninsular Ranges— so called because most of them are in the Baja Peninsula—which include the Santa Ana and San Jacinto ranges. Isolated mountains have captured writers' hearts as well. Mount Tamalpais, for example, whose skyline and trails delight San Francisco Bay Area residents, is described here in closely observed detail by Harold Gilliam.

Wherever there are mountains, there are hills at their feet and valleys in between. Separating the Coast Ranges from the Sierra Nevada is the Great Central Valley, almost five hundred miles in length. The northern portion is known as the Sacramento Valley, and the southern the San Joaquin Valley, after the two rivers that drain them. David Mas Masumoto writes eloquently of the land that he farms near Del Rey, in the San Joaquin. Another prominent valley lies between the Transverse and Peninsular ranges: the populated Los Angeles Basin. Less great, but nonetheless dear to those who live or hike there, are the hundreds of smaller valleys and foothills throughout California. In this collection you will read about Napa Valley (Robert Louis Stevenson), Sonoma Valley (Jack London), Salinas Valley (William H. Brewer), the Altadena foothills (Hildegarde Flanner), Hemet Valley (M. F. K. Fisher), the Santa Barbara foothills (Margaret Millar), the San Rafael Wilderness (David Darlington), the Klamath Basin (Barry Lopez), and the Los Altos hills (Wallace Stegner).

California has three major deserts—the Mojave, the Colorado (or Sonoran), and the Great Basin. Each is unique and thus presents a special challenge to writers who wish to "explain" the desert. Here, the extremes of Death Valley are detailed by Edward Abbey; John Daniel and Sue Zwinger recollect memorable desert treks; Gary Paul Nabhan visits some oases in the Colorado Desert; and Mary Austin writes of the high desert of the Owens Valley.

California is delimited on the west by eight hundred miles of Pacific coastline, with its rocky headlands, bays, beaches, and offshore islands. This collection highlights various faces of this diverse margin. In the northern and central reaches we encounter the "lost coast" as it is walked by John McKinney; Russell Chatham narrates a fishing excursion on Bodega Bay; and Henry Miller describes his beloved Big Sur. Farther south, around Santa Barbara, J. Smeaton Chase and Jane Hollister Wheelwright travel on horseback on the beach, while Kem Nunn surfs the waves and Gretel Ehrlich hikes one of the Channel Islands. In the southland, T. H. Watkins and Lawrence Clark Powell reminisce about Dana Point and Malibu, respectively.

The elements—earthquakes, storms, fire—play a significant role in California. In the last section, the infamous San Andreas Fault is observed by James D. Houston and John McPhee. John Muir and Joan Didion write about the wind—a storm in the Sierra as experienced from the top of a tall tree, and a Santa Ana in Los Angeles—while Mary Austin and Jane Hollister Wheelwright describe the rain as it pours down on the Owens Valley and a Pacific beach. The aftermath of a forest fire is taken up by Margaret Millar.

Finally, in an afterword, Gary Snyder takes a broad look at California's environment and suggests ways in which it can be preserved.

I hope that this book will be kept on a nearby shelf by armchair naturalists and virtual wanderers, and in the backpacks of hikers and trekkers—to refresh and inspire them, like a dip in a cool mountain lake, and as a reminder of the "natural state" of California.

THE CREATION

The Creation

The creation myths of the Native American peoples of California have many elements in common. The following myth of the Cahto (sometimes spelled "Kato"), who inhabited Cahto and Long Valleys in Mendocino County and the upper drainage of the South Fork of the Eel River in Lake County, is a typical example. Collected in 1909 by the University of California ethnologist Pliny E. Goddard (1869–1928), it tells of the great deluge, after which Thunder, the original being, created the landscape, the animals, and humankind.

E very day it rained, every night it rained. All the people slept. The sky fell. The land was not. For a very great distance there was no land. The waters of the oceans came together. Animals of all kinds drowned. Where the water went there were no trees. There was no land.

People became. Seal, sea-lion, and grizzly built a dance-house. They looked for a place in vain. At Usal they built it, for there the ground was good. There are many sea-lions there. Whale became a human woman. That is why women are so fat. There were no grizzlies. There were no fish. Blue lizard was thrown into the water and became sucker. Bull-snake was thrown into the water and became black salmon. Salamander was thrown into the water and became hook-bill salmon. Grass-snake was thrown into the water and became steel-head salmon. Lizard was thrown into the water and became trout. . . .

"What will grow in the water?" he [the creator] asked. Seaweeds grew in the water. Abalones and mussels grew in the water. Two kinds of kelp grew in the ocean. Many different kinds grew there. . . .

"How will the water of the ocean behave? What will be in front of it?" he asked. "The water will rise up in ridges. It will settle back again. There will be sand. On top of the sand it will glisten," he said. "Old kelp will float ashore. Old whales will float ashore.

"People will eat fish, big fish," he said. "Sea-lions will come ashore. They will eat them. They will be good. Devil-fish, although they are ugly looking, will be good. The people will eat them. The fish in the ocean will be fat. They will be good.

"There will be many different kinds in the ocean. There will be water-panther. There will be stone-fish. He will catch people. Long-tooth-fish will kill sea-lion. He will feel around in the water.

"Sea-lion will have no feet. He will have a tail. His teeth will be large. There will be no trees in the ocean. The water will be powerful in the ocean," he said.

He placed redwoods and firs along the shore. At the tail of the earth, at the north, he made them grow. He placed land in walls along in front of the ocean. From the north he put down rocks here and there. Over there the ocean beats against them. Far to the south he did that. He stood up pines along the way. He placed yellow pines. Far away he placed them. He placed mountains along in front of the water. He did not stop putting them up, even way to the south.

Redwoods and various pines were growing. He looked back and saw them growing. The redwoods had become tall. He placed stones along. He made small creeks by dragging along his foot. "Wherever they flow this water will be good," he said. "They will drink this. Only the ocean they will not drink." That is why all drink, many different kinds of animals. "Because the water is good, because it is not salt, deer, elk, panther, and fishes will drink of it," he said. He caused trees to grow up along. When he looked behind himself he saw they had grown up. "Birds will drink, squirrels will drink," he said. "Many different kinds will drink. I am placing good water along the way."

Many redwoods grew up. He placed water along toward the south. He kicked out springs. "There will be springs,'" he said. "These will belong to the deer," he said of the deer-licks.

He took along a dog. "Drink this water," he told his dog. He, himself, drank of it. . . .

Tanbark oaks he made to spring up along the way. Many kinds, redwoods, firs, and pines, he caused to grow. He placed water along. . . . To make valleys for the streams he placed the land on edge. The mountains were large. They had grown. . . .

He threw salamanders and turtles into the creeks. "Eels will live in this stream," he said. "Fish will come into it. Hook-bill and black salmon will run up this creek. Last of all steel-heads will swim in it. Crabs, small eels, and day-eels will come up.

"Grizzlies will live in large numbers on this mountain. On this mountain will be many deer. The people will eat them. Because they have no gall they may be eaten raw. Deer meat will be very sweet. Panthers will be numerous. There will be many jack-rabbits on this mountain," he said.

He did not like yellow-jackets. He nearly killed them. He made blue-flies and wasps.

His dog walked along with him. "There will be much water in this stream," he said. "This will be a small creek and the fish will run in it. The fish will be good. There will be many suckers and trout in this stream."

"There will be brush on this mountain," he said. He made manzanita and white-thorn grow there. "Here will be a valley. Here will be many deer. There will be many grizzlies at this place. Here a mountain will stand. Many rattlesnakes, bull-snakes, and water snakes will be in this place. Here will be good land. It shall be a valley.

"There will be many owls here, the barking-owl, the screech-owl, and the little owl. There shall be many blue jays, grouse, and quails. Here on this mountain will be many wood-rats. Here shall be many varied robins. There shall be many woodcocks, yellow-hammers, and sapsuckers. Here will be herons and blackbirds. There will be many turtle-doves and pigeons. The kingfishers will catch fish. There will be many buzzards, and ravens. There will be many chicken-hawks. There will be many robins. On this high mountain there will be many deer," he said.

. . . The land had become good. The valleys had become broad. All kinds of trees and plants had sprung up. Springs had become and the water was flowing. . . .

"I have made a good earth, my dog," he said. "Walk fast, my dog." Acorns were on the trees. The chestnuts were ripe. The hazelnuts were ripe. The manzanita berries were getting white. All sorts of food had become good. The buckeyes were good. The peppernuts were black. The bunch grass was ripe. The grass-hoppers were growing. The clover was in bloom. The bear-clover was good. The mountains had grown. The rocks had grown. All kinds that are eaten had become good. "We made it good, my dog," he said. Fish for the people to eat had grown in the streams.

"We have come to the south now," he said. All the different kinds were matured. They started back, he and his dog. "We will go back," he said. "The mountains have grown up quickly. The land has become flat. The trout have grown. Good water is flowing. Walk fast. All things have become good. We have made them good, my dog. It is warm. The land is good.

" . . . We are about to arrive. We are close to home, my dog," he said. "I am about to get back north," he said to himself. "I am about to get back north. I am about to get back north. I am about to get back north," he said to himself.

That is all.

Fall River Valley

Grampa Ramsey and the Great Canyon

Darryl Babe Wilson (b. 1939) was born at the confluence of Fall River and Pit River at Fall River Mills in northeastern California, "into two people": Atsuge-wi on his father's side and A-juma-wi on his mother's. He graduated from the University of California at Davis in 1992 with a major in English, and received his Ph.D. from the University of Arizona in 1997. He has spent his life preserving the oral tradition through his speaking and writing. His essays, poetry, and short fiction have appeared in numerous anthologies. This creation story first appeared in the quarterly News from Native California.

It was a summer before I kept track of time. In our decrepit automobile, we rattled into the driveway, a cloud of exhaust fumes, dust, and screaming, excited children. A half dozen ragged kids and an old black dog poured from the ancient vehicle. Confusion reigned supreme. Uncle Ramsey (after we became parents, his official title changed to "Grampa") was standing in the door of the comfortable little pine-board home just east of McArthur. Aunt Lorena was in her immaculate kitchen making coffee.

Just as quickly as we poured from the vehicle, we disappeared. There was a pervading silence. Always the crystal bowl rested on Aunt Lorena's kitchen table. Usually it held exotic, distant, tasty objects: oranges, bananas, store-bought candy! There seemed to be three hundred black, shiny eyes staring at the contents of that bowl, but we knew that we must wait for Aunt Lorena to say "when" before we could have the contents—which we instantly devoured.

I cannot remember if we had any cares. It was before I began the first grade. I didn't care if I had shoes or clothes. I didn't care about anything—except not to allow my brothers and sisters to have something that I couldn't. And when I did not know that they got something more than me, it didn't matter, really.

It seems that my "thoughts" were already focused upon some other objective. I listened to the old people. I remembered what they said, the tone of their voice, the waving of the hands. My mind registered the long silences between their choppy sentences and between their quiet words.

They spoke in our languages, A-Juma-wi and Opore-gee, and they used a very crude and stumbling English. The English words were strange. I preferred the "old language." As our lives moved into the world of the English speakers and our "old" language became less and less important and less and less used, something within the old people hesitated.

His employment as a "cowboy" came to an end when a shying horse threw him and he landed on his neck, nearly breaking it. After his days in the saddle faded, he worked on various ranches in the Fall River Valley until his retirement.

He spoke to us in Opore-gee (Dixie Valley language), giggling when the twins would say the words correctly after he explained them. We would have to go visit him many times before he would tell us a "real, not fake," story of our people and our history. During these times I took notes because a tape recorder "spooked" him; it mattered little what he was trying to say, the "ghost" inside the tape recorder affected him—he was occupied with the "ghost" instead of the lesson.

Close to the time of his "departure," he spoke of being "so old that I no longer think about the end, but think about the beginning again."

As a silent, powerful, unseen ship passing into an endless sea in the darkness, he moved into the spirit world to join his wife and others of our shattered little nation. He departed during the full moon of October 1986. Aunt Lorena preceded him by sixteen years.

Discard the rules of English kings and queens. Suspend logic. Grampa speaks as he learned to around campfires and in a distance so long ago that he claimed, "I didn't have enough good sense to listen good."

Grandfather's story:

HOW THE GREAT CANYON WAS MADE

[This canyon is between Fall River Mills and Barn, California, on the Pit River. Grandfather interchanges the names Qon and Silver-gray Fox occasionally. They are the same being in his thought.]

Qon [Silver-gray Fox] worked to make the world from a mist and a song long ago. He and Makada [Coyote] set to making things on earth. Makada was constantly trying to change things. Qon had the power to create. Makada had the power only to change things. He was always jealous because he could not create—he could only change. Qon created things. Makada always tried to change them. Qon persisted. Makada insisted. Sometimes he made a go of it. Sometimes Makada got his way. He sure was insistent, that Makada. [Smile, twinkle, and gruff giggle.]

His was the time when Qon put his place, his home—maybe you say "office"—on the Pit River/Hat Creek rim near Hogback [a small mountain]. From that place he could watch everything. This was before there was a Great Canyon, so Da-we-wewe and It-Ajuma [streams, including the Fall River and Pit River] could make it to the ocean, so salmon could come up there. Fall River and Dixie Valley are the valley drainage.

It [the office] was like an umbrella that you can look through but you could not see it—like a bubble or something but you can't see him [it]. When it rained, it did not rain in there. When it snowed, snow could not get in. Wind must go around. Storms and lightning bounced off. I don't know just how to say—as if an arch. Like a thinking or a thought or something.

I dunno. You couldn't touch it or see it. Anyhow, it was there so the Power could watch. Qon wanted everything just right. He knew he had to watch old Makada. It was bad. Qon needed help from Makada. Makada was insistent.

Qon molded earth like *wa-hach* [a form of bread made in an iron skillet without grease], flattened here, raised there. Everywhere not the same. It was when Chum-see-akoo was being made [the small area where the Hat Creek and Pit River come together and create a small peninsula in a shape like Argentina; Highway 299 East now runs through it]. Some call it Ya-nee-na. It was made. Qon wanted to name it. Makada wanted to name it. They talked. They argued.

Qon said, "Let's make some other things and get back to this place." So they did. They roamed and made *a-hew* [mountains] and *da-wi-wiwi* [streams] and *a-ju-juji* [springs]. Qon named these places. They returned to Chum-see-akoo/Ya-nee-na. Makada said, "You, brother, have named all of these other places. It is my turn to name this place right here." [A gruff giggle from Grandfather because Coyote called Silver-gray Fox "brother."]

Qon said, "No, you will call it by any name but a real name. Sometimes when you talk you don't make much sense. Let's go and make some more."

So they did. [Silver-gray Fox was in the process of making the Pit River Country into a livable place.]

Watching from a high bluff, Qon saw the insistence of Makada. He waited. Meanwhile, he forgot to make a place for the Pit River to run and drain the upper valley. He forgot to make a canyon. There was a mountain of solid rock. No canyon.

They returned to the small valley. Again they got in an argument. This time Qon give in. He give up. He got tired of arguments.

Makada called it Chum-see Akoo [Mice Valley] because he liked to eat mice. He really liked the taste of fresh mice. Today that is what we call it. Mice Valley. But what about the canyon that was filled with solid rock? The Pit River cannot run through it. The salmon must come so people can eat.

Qon looked and saw a wide spot below rock mountain. Rock mountain must be made into a canyon for Pit River. He spoke to big bass-sturgeon. "You must do this so river can run to the ocean." Sturgeon said, "Okay, but I am not strong enough to break that mountain." Qon said, 'Tomorrow I shall tell you what to do, after I think." Why did Qon have to think? I dunno.

Next day Qon said, "Go to the top of mountain [Mount Shasta] and get power." He went, then he swam back from mountain. He got back and took a run at it and hit it [the rock mountain] with his head. BANG! Again and again, BANG! It hurt. He got tired, and it hurt. Qon said, "Go back to the mountain for more power."

Meanwhile Makada was off doing something. He could not create. He was changing something. Always changing, Makada.

Sturgeon struck the mountain, BANG! again and again. Again and again. Again he got tired. Again it hurt. He went back to the mountaintop and got some more power. BANG! Old mountain rock he began to break. It got weakness. He cracked it! He got more power in a hurry. He broke it! Rocks were everywhere. Later they found some rocks clear up in Dixie [Valley]. Rocks flying everywhere. He broke through. He did it! He came out to Bo-ma-ree [Fall River Valley].

Qon said, "Good."

Meanwhile, Qon found Makada. He was up at the hot springs cooking quail eggs and looking with his head down seeing himself in the water. [Gruff giggle.] Makada always thought he was real cute.

When they came back, Makada noticed the great canyon. Qon looked at Makada. Makada looked away, with his tongue hanging sideways from his mouth, and said, "I didn't do it [make the canyon]. I was gathering quail eggs to boil in hot springs."

Looking to the rim today, you will see power [the "office"] is gone. Qon and Makada ran east up the canyon that was rushing with water [the Pit River]. There were more things to make. Maybe it was then that people were mad, but that is another story. Not for today.

We left Grampa Ramsey in possession of a "real, not fake," story. At times it seemed as if it was a story about creation in general, but it was, for the most part, a story of the Great Canyon. For this time spent with Grampa we are made richer. Richer in knowledge and understanding. Richer in language and the function of that language. Richer in the spiritual connection that binds us to the earth.

THE MOUNTAINS

An Elk Hunt

Joaquin Miller (1837–1913), born Cincinnatus Hiner Miller, was an eccentric, larger-than-life poet, the self-styled "Byron of the West," who achieved great popularity in his day but whose reputation has since melted into the mists. After living in England for some years he retired to an estate he built in the hills of Oakland, California. This hunting account is taken from his autobiography, Memorie and Rime *(1884).*

When the spring came tripping by from the south over the chaparral hills of Shasta, leaving flowers in every footprint as we passed, I set my face for Mount Shasta, the lightest-hearted lad that ever mounted horse. A hard day's ride brought me to Portuguese Flat, the last new mining camp and the nearest town to my beloved Mount Shasta. Here I found my former partner in the Soda Springs property, Mountain Joe, and together we went up to Mount Shasta.

The Indian chief, Blackbeard, gave me a beautiful little valley then known as Now-ow-wa, but now called by the euphonious name of Squaw Valley, and I built a cabin there. As winter settled down and the snow fell deep and fast, however, the Indians all retreated down from out the spurs of Mount Shasta and took refuge on the banks of the

McCloud River. I nailed up my cabin and on snowshoes recrossed the fifteen miles of steep and stupendous mountains, and got down to winter at my old home, Soda Springs. But a new Yankee partner had got his grasp about the throat of things there, and instead of pitching him out into the snow I determined to give it all up and set my face where I left my heart, once more, finally and forever, with the Indians. Loaded down with arms and ammunition, one clear, frosty morning in December I climbed up the spur of Mount Shasta, which lay between me and my little valley of snow, and left the last vestige of civilization behind me. It was steep, hard climbing. Sometimes I would sink into the snow to my waist. Sometimes the snow would slide down the mountain and bear me back, half buried, to the place I had started from half an hour before. A marvel that I kept on. But there was hatred behind, there was love before—elements that have built cities and founded empires. As the setting sun gilded the snowy pines with gold I stood on the lofty summit, looking down into my unpeopled world of snow.

An hour of glorious gliding, darting, shooting on my snowshoes, and I stood on the steep bluff that girt above and about my little valley. A great, strange light, like silver, enveloped the land. Across the valley, on the brow of the mountain beyond, the curved moon, new and white and bright, gleamed before me like a drawn cimeter [*sic*] to drive me back. Down in the valley under me busy little foxes moved and shuttle-cocked across the level sea of snow. But I heard no sound nor saw any other sign of life. The solitude, the desolation, the silence, was so vast, so actual, that I could feel it—hear it. A strange terror came upon me there. And oh, I wished—how devoutly I wished I never shall forget— that I had not ventured on this mad enterprise. But I had burned my ship. It had been as impossible for me to return, tired, hungry, heartsick as I then was, as it had been for me to lay hold of the bright cold horns of the moon before me. With a sigh I tightened my belt, took up my rifle, which I had leaned against a pine, and once more shot ahead. Breaking open my cabin door, I took off my snowshoes and crept down the steep wall of snow, and soon had a roaring fire from the sweet-smelling pine wood that lay heaped in cords against the walls. Seven days I rested there, as lone as the moon in the cold blue above. Queer days! Queer thoughts I had there then. Those days left their impression clearly, as strange creatures of another age had left their footprints in the plastic clay that has become now solid stone. When the mind is so void, queer thoughts get into one's head; and they come and establish themselves and stay. I had some books, and read them all through. Here I first began to write.

On the eighth day my door darkened, and I sprang up from my work, rifle in hand. Two Indians, brave, handsome young fellows, one my best and dearest friend in all the world, stood before me. And sad tales they told me that night as I feasted them around my great fireplace. The tribe was starving over on the McCloud! The gold-diggers had so muddied and soiled the waters the season before that the annual run of salmon had failed. The Indians had for the first time in centuries no stores of dried salmon, and they were starving to death by the hundreds. And what was still more alarming, for it meant the ultimate destruction of all the Indians concerned, I was told that the natives of Pit River Valley had resolved to massacre all the settlers there. After a day's rest these two Indians, loaded with flour for the famishing tribe, set out to return. Again I was left alone, this time for nearly three weeks. The Indians returned with other young men to carry flour back to the famishing, while we who were strong and rested prepared for a grand hunt for a great band of elk which we knew wintered near the warm springs high up on the wood slopes of Mount Shasta. Perhaps I might mention here that this cabin full of provisions had remained untouched all the time of my absence. I will say further that I believe the last Indian would have starved to death rather than have touched one crumb of bread without permission. These Indians had never yet come in contact with any white man but myself. Such honesty I never knew as I found here. As for their valor and prowess, I can only point you to the Modoc battlefields, where the whole United States Army was held at bay so long nearly twenty years after, and pass on.

After great preparation, we struck out steeply up the mountain, and for three days wallowed through the snow in the dense, dark woods, when we struck the great elk trail. A single trail it was, and looked as if a saw-log had been drawn repeatedly through the snow. The bottom and sides of this trail were hard and smooth as ice. Perhaps a thousand elk had passed here. They had been breaking from one thicket of maple and other kinds of brush which they feed upon at such times, and we knew they could not have gone far through this snow, which reached above their backs. We hung up our snowshoes now and, looking to our arms, shot ahead full of delightful anticipation. At last, climbing a little hill, with clouds of steam rising from the warm springs of that region, we looked down into a little valley of thick undergrowth, and there calmly rested the vast herd of elk. I peered through the brush into the large, clear eyes of a great stag with a head of horns like a rocking chair. He was chewing his cud, and was not at all disconcerted. It is possible we were not yet discovered. More likely their numbers and strength gave them uncommon courage, and they were not to be easily frightened. I remember my two Indians looked at each other in surprise at their tranquillity. We lay there some time on our breasts in the snow, looking at them. The Indians observed that only the cows were fat and fit to kill. Some of the stags had somehow shed their horns, it seemed. There were no calves. So the Indians were delighted to know that there was yet another herd. We fell back, and formed our plan of attack at leisure. It was unique and desperate. We did not want one or two elk, or ten; we wanted the whole herd. Human life depended upon our prowess. A tribe was starving, and we felt a responsibility in our work. It was finally decided to go around and approach by the little stream, so that the herd would not start down it—their only means of escape. It was planned to approach as closely as possible, then fire with our rifles at the fattest, then burst in upon them, pistol in hand, and so, breaking their ranks, scatter them in the snow, where the Indians could rush upon them and use the bows and arrows at their backs.

Slowly and cautiously we approached up the little warm, willow-lined rivulet, and then, firing our rifles, we rushed into the corral, pistols in hand. The poor, helpless herd was on its feet in a second, all breaking out over the wall of snow, breast-high on all sides. Here they wallowed and floundered in the snow, shook their heads, and called helplessly to each other. They could not get on at all. And long after the last shot and the last arrow were spent I leisurely walked around and looked into the eyes of some of these fat, sleek cows as they lay there, up to their briskets, helpless in the snow. Of course the Indians had no sentiment in this matter. They wanted only to kill and secure meat for the hungry, and half an hour after the attack on the corral of elk they were quartering the meat and hanging it up in trees secure from the wolves. In this way they hung more than a hundred elk, not taking time to skin or dress them in any way. The tallow was heaped about our camp-fire, to be defended against the wolves at night. And such a lot of wolves as came that night! And such a noise, as we sat there feasting about the fire and talking of the day's splendid work. The next morning, loaded with tallow, my two young friends set out on the long, tedious journey to the starving camp on the McCloud River. They were going to bring the whole tribe, or at least such of them as could make the trip, and the remainder of our winter was to be spent on Mount Shasta. I was once more left alone. But as our ammunition at hand was spent, I was in great fear and in real danger of being devoured by wolves. They drew a circle around that camp and laid siege to it like an army of well-drilled soldiers. They would sit down on their haunches not twenty steps away and look at me in the most appetizing fashion. They would lick their chops, as if to say, "We'll get you yet; it's only a question of time." And I wish to put it on record that wolves, so far as I can testify, are better behaved than the books tell you they are. They snarled a little at each other as they sat there, over a dozen deep, around me, and even snapped now and then at each other's ears; but I saw not one sign of their eating or attempting to eat each other. By day they kept quiet, and only looked at me. But it was observed that each day they came and sat down a little bit closer. Night, of course, was made to ring with their howls both far and near, and I kept up a great fire.

At last—ah, relief of Lucknow!—my brave boys came back breathless into camp. And after them for days came stringing, struggling, creeping, a long black line of withered, starving fellow-creatures. To see them eat! To see their hollow eyes fill and glow with gratitude! Ah, I have had some few summer days, some moments of glory, when the heart throbs full and the head tops heaven; but I have known no delight like this I knew there, and never shall. Christmas came and went, and I knew not when, for I had now in my careless happiness and full delight lost all reckoning of time.

Sierra Nevada

Ramblings in Yosemite

Joseph LeConte (1823–1901) was a popular professor of geology and natural history at the University of California, Berkeley. This excerpt is from A Journal of Ramblings through the High Sierra of California *(1875), written during his first journey to Yosemite as part of a university excursion party.*

JULY 30.— . . . In the afternoon we pushed on, to get our first view of Yosemite this evening, from Sentinel Dome and Glacier Point. . . . About 5 P.M. we passed a high pile of rocks, called Ostrander's Rocks. The whole trail, from Westfall's meadows to Glacier Point, is near eight thousand feet high. From this rocky prominence, therefore, the view is really magnificent. It was our first view of the peaks and domes about Yosemite, and of the more distant High Sierra, and we enjoyed it beyond expression. But there are still finer views ahead, which we must see this afternoon—yes, this very afternoon. With increasing enthusiasm we pushed on until, about 6 P.M., we reached and climbed Sentinel Dome. This point is 4,500 feet above Yosemite Valley, and 8,500 feet above the sea.

The view which here burst upon us, of the valley and the Sierra, it is simply impossible to describe. Sentinel Dome stands on the south margin of Yosemite, near the point where it branches into three canyons. To the left stand El Capitan's massive perpendicular wall; directly in front, and distant about one mile, Yosemite Falls, like a gauzy veil, rippling and waving with a slow, mazy motion; to the right the mighty granite mass of Half Dome lifts itself in solitary grandeur, defying the efforts of the climber; to the extreme right, and a little behind, Nevada Falls, with the Cap of Liberty; in the distance, innumerable peaks of the High Sierra, conspicuous among which are Clouds Rest, Mt. Starr King, Cathedral Peak, etc. We remained on the top of the dome more than an hour, to see the sunset. We were well repaid—such a sunset I never saw; such a sunset, combined with such a view, I had never imagined. The glorious golden and crimson in the west, and the exquisitely delicate diffused rose-bloom, tingeing the cloud caps of the Sierra in the east, and the shadows of the grand peaks and domes slowly creeping up the valley! I can never forget the impression. We remained, enjoying this scene, too long to think of going to Glacier Point this evening. We therefore put this off until morning, and returned to our trail about one and a half miles, to a beautiful green meadow, and there made camp in a grove of magnificent fir trees (*Albies magnifica*).

JULY 31 (SUNDAY).—I got up at peep of day this morning (I am dish-wash today), roused the party, started a fire, and in ten minutes tea was ready. All partook heartily of this delicious beverage, and started on foot to see the sunrise from Glacier Point. This point is about one and a half miles from our camp, about 3,100 feet above the valley, and forms the salient angle on the south side, just where the valley divides into three. We had to descend about eight hundred feet to reach it. We arrived just before sunrise. Sunrise from Glacier Point! No one can appreciate it who has not seen it. It was our good fortune to have an exceedingly beautiful sunrise. Rosy-fingered Aurora revealed herself to us, her votaries, more bright and charming and rosy than ever before. But the great charm was the view of the valley and surrounding peaks, in the fresh, cool morning hour and to the rosy light of the rising sun; the bright, warm light on the mountain tops, and the cool shade in the valley. The shadow of the grand Half Dome stretches clear across the valley, while its own "bald awful head" glitters in the early sunlight. To the right, Vernal and Nevada Falls, with their magnificent overhanging peaks, in full view; while directly across, see the ever-rippling, ever-swaying gauzy veil of the Yosemite Falls, reaching from top to bottom of the opposite cliff, 2,600 feet. Below, at a depth of 3,200 feet, the bottom of the valley lies like a garden. There, right under our noses, are the hotels, the orchards, the fields, the meadows, . . . the forests, and through all the Merced River winds its apparently lazy serpentine way. Yonder, up the Tenaya Canyon, nestling close under the shadow of Half Dome, lies Mirror Lake, fast asleep, her polished black surface not yet ruffled by the rising wind. I have heard and read much of this wonderful valley, but I can truly say I have never imagined the grandeur of the reality. After about one and a half hours' rapturous gaze, we returned to camp and breakfasted. I had left Glacier Point a few minutes before most of the party, as I was dishwash and had, therefore, to help cook prepare breakfast. At breakfast, I learned that two young men, Cobb and Perkins, had undertaken the foolish enterprise of going down into the valley by a canyon just below Glacier Point, and returning by 4 P.M. Think of it! 3,300 feet perpendicular, and the declivity, it seemed to me, about forty-five degrees in the canyon!

After breakfast we returned to Glacier Point and spent the whole of the beautiful Sunday morning in the presence of grand mountains, yawning chasms, and magnificent falls. What could we do better than allow these to preach to us? Was there ever so venerable, majestic, and eloquent a minister of natural religion as the grand old Half Dome? I withdrew myself from the rest of the party and drank in his silent teachings for several hours. About 1 P.M. climbed Sentinel Dome and enjoyed again the matchless panoramic view from this point, and about 2 P.M. returned to camp.

Our camp is itself about four thousand feet above the valley, and eight thousand above sea level. By walking about one hundred yards from our camp-fire, we get a most admirable view of the Sierra, and particularly a most wonderfully striking view of the unique form of Half Dome when seen in profile. I enjoyed this view until nearly time to saddle up.

Our plan is to return to Peregoy's, only seven miles, this afternoon, and go to Yosemite tomorrow morning. It is 3:30 P.M., and the young men who went down into the valley have not yet returned. We feel anxious. Will they return, or remain in the valley? Shall we remain tonight and wait for them, or go on, leading their horses, with the expectation of meeting them in the valley? We are to leave at four; we must decide soon. These discussions were cut short by the appearance of the delinquents themselves, faint with fatigue. They had been down, taken dinner, and returned. We started immediately for Peregoy's, where we arrived, 6 P.M., and camped in a grove on the margin of a fine meadow. At Peregoy's we bought a quarter of mountain mutton. We have been living on bacon and bread for some time. The voracity with which we devoured that mutton may be more easily imagined than described.

Ever since we have approached the region of the High Sierra, I have observed the great massiveness and grandeur of the clouds and the extreme blueness of the sky. In the direction of the Sierra hang always magnificent piles of snow-white cumulus, sharply defined against the deep-blue sky. These cloud-masses have ever been my delight. I have missed them sadly since coming to California, until this trip. I now welcome them with joy. Yesterday and today I have seen, in so many places, snow lying on the northern slopes of the high peaks of the Sierra.

AUGUST 1.—Yosemite today! Started as usual, 7 A.M. . . . Glorious ride this morning through the grand fir forests. This is enjoyment, indeed. The trail is tolerably good until it reaches the edge of Yosemite chasm. On the trail a little way below this edge there is a jutting point, called "Inspiration Point," which gives a good general view of the lower end of the valley, including El Capitan, Cathedral Rock, and a glimpse of Bridalveil Fall. After taking this view we began the descent into the valley. The trail winds backward and forward on the almost perpendicular sides of the cliff, making a descent of about three thousand feet in three miles. It was so steep and rough that we preferred walking most of the way and leading the horses. Poor old Mrs. Hopkins, though a heavy old lady, was afraid to ride, and therefore walked the whole way. At last, 10 A.M., we were down, and the gate of the valley is before us, El Capitan guarding it on the left and Cathedral Rock on the right, while over the precipice on the right the silvery gauze of Bridalveil is seen swaying to and fro.

We encamped in a fine forest on the margin of Bridalveil Meadow, under the shadow of El Capitan, and about one-quarter of a mile from Bridalveil Fall. Turned our horses loose to graze, cooked our midday meal, refreshed ourselves by swimming in the Merced, and then, 4:30 P.M., started to visit Bridalveil. We had understood that this was the best time to see it. Very difficult clambering to the foot of the fall up a steep incline, formed by a pile of huge boulders fallen from the cliff. The enchanting beauty and exquisite grace of this fall well repaid us for the toil. At the base of the fall there is a beautiful pool. Standing on the rocks on the margin of this pool, right opposite the fall, a most perfect unbroken circular rainbow is visible. Sometimes it is a double circular rainbow. The cliff more than six hundred feet high; the wavy, billowy, gauzy veil reaching from top to bottom; the glorious crown, woven by the sun for this beautiful veiled bride—those who read must put these together and form a picture for themselves by the plastic power of the imagination.

Some of the young men took a swim in the pool and a shower-bath under the fall. I would have joined them, but I had just come out of the Merced River. After enjoying this exquisite fall until after sunset, we returned to camp. On our way back, amongst the loose rocks on the stream margin, we found and killed another rattlesnake. This is the fourth we have killed.

Lake Tahoe

Mark Twain (1813–1890) still went by the name Samuel Clemens when he came west in 1861, where he spent a total of seven years, mostly in Nevada and California. His recollection of the period, Roughing It *(1872), has chapters on two lakes, Mono and Tahoe, that lie along the border of the two states. Mono Lake he detested; Tahoe he held to be the "fairest picture" there ever was.*

We tramped a long time on level ground, and then toiled laboriously up a mountain about a thousand miles high and looked over. No lake there. We descended on the other side, crossed the valley, and toiled up another mountain three or four thousand miles high, apparently, and looked over again. No lake yet. We sat down, tired and perspiring, and hired a couple of Chinamen to curse those people who had beguiled us. Thus refreshed, we presently resumed the march with renewed vigor and determination. We plodded on, two or three hours longer, and at last the lake burst upon us—a noble sheet of blue water lifted six thousand three hundred feet above the level of the sea, and walled in by a rim of snow-clad mountain peaks that towered aloft a full three thousand feet higher still! It was a vast oval, and one would have to use up eighty or a hundred good miles in traveling around it. As it lay there with the shadows of the mountains brilliantly photographed upon its still surface, I thought it must surely be the fairest picture the whole earth affords.

We found the small skiff belonging to the brigade boys and, without loss of time, set out across a deep bend of the lake toward the landmarks that signified the locality of the camp. I got Johnny to row—not because I mind exertion myself, but because it makes me sick to ride backward when I am at work. But I steered. A three-mile pull brought us to the camp just as the night fell, and we stepped ashore very tired and wolfishly hungry. In a "cache" among the rocks we found the provisions and the cooking utensils, and then, all fatigued as I was, I sat down on a boulder and superintended while Johnny gathered wood and cooked supper. Many a man who had gone through what I had would have wanted to rest.

It was a delicious supper—hot bread, fried bacon, and black coffee. It was a delicious solitude we were in, too. Three miles away was a sawmill and some workmen, but there were not fifteen other human beings throughout the wide circumference of the lake. As the darkness closed down and the stars came out and spangled the great mirror with jewels, we smoked meditatively in the solemn hush and forgot our troubles and our pains. In due time we spread our blankets in the warm sand between two large boulders and soon fell asleep, careless of the procession of ants that passed in through rents in our clothing and explored our persons. Nothing could disturb the sleep that fettered us, for it had been fairly earned, and if our consciences had any sins on them they had to adjourn court for that night, anyway. The wind rose just as we were losing consciousness, and we were lulled to sleep by the beating of the surf upon the shore.

It is always very cold on that lake shore in the night, but we had plenty of blankets and were warm enough. We never moved a muscle all night, but we waked at early dawn in the original positions, and got up at once, thoroughly refreshed, free from soreness, and brimful of friskiness. There is no end of wholesome medicine in such an experience. That morning we could have whipped ten such people as we were the day before—sick ones at any rate. But the world is slow, and people will go to "water cures" and "movement cures" and to foreign lands for health. Three months of camp life on Lake Tahoe would restore an Egyptian mummy to his pristine vigor and give him an appetite like an alligator. I do not mean the oldest and driest mummies, of course, but the fresher ones. The air up there in the clouds is very pure and fine, bracing and delicious. And why shouldn't it be?—it is the same the angels breathe. I think that hardly any amount of fatigue can be gathered together that a man cannot sleep off in one night on the sand by its side. Not under a roof, but under the sky; it seldom or never rains there in the summertime. I know a man who went there to die. But he made a failure of it. He was a skeleton when he came and could barely stand. He had no appetite and did nothing but read tracts and reflect on the future. Three months later he was sleeping out of doors regularly, eating all he could hold three times a day, and chasing game over mountains three thousand feet high for recreation. And he was a skeleton no longer, but weighed part of a ton. This is no fancy sketch, but the truth. His disease was consumption. I confidently commend his experience to other skeletons.

I superintended again, and as soon as we had eaten breakfast we got in the boat and skirted along the lake shore about three miles and disembarked. We liked the appearance of the place, and so we claimed some three hundred acres of it and stuck our "notices" on a tree. It was yellow-pine timberland—a dense forest of trees a hundred feet high and from one to five feet through at the butt. It was necessary to fence our property or we could not hold it. That is to say, it was necessary to cut down trees here and there and make them fall in such a way as to form a sort of enclosure (with pretty wide gaps in it). We cut down three trees apiece, and found it such heartbreaking work that we decided to "rest our case" on those; if they held the property, well and good; if they didn't, let the property spill out through the gaps and go; it was no use to work ourselves to death merely to save a few acres of land. Next day we came back to build a house—for a house was also necessary, in order to hold the property. We decided to build a substantial log house and excite the envy of the brigade boys; but by the time we had cut and trimmed the first log it seemed unnecessary to be so elaborate, and so we concluded to build it of saplings. However, two saplings, duly cut and trimmed, compelled recognition of the fact that a still modester architecture would satisfy the law, and so we concluded to build a "brush" house. We devoted the next day to this work, but we did so much "sitting around" and discussing that by the middle of the afternoon we had achieved only a halfway sort of affair which one of us had to watch while the other cut brush, lest if both turned our backs we might not be able to find it again, it had such a strong family resemblance to the surrounding vegetation. But we were satisfied with it.

We were landowners now, duly seized and possessed, and within the protection of the law. Therefore we decided to take up our residence on our own domain and enjoy that large sense of independence which only such an experience can bring. Later the next afternoon, after a good long rest, we sailed away from the brigade camp with all the provisions and cooking utensils we could carry off—borrow is the more accurate word—and just as the night was falling we beached the boat at our own landing.

If there is any life that is happier than the life we led on our timber ranch for the next two or three weeks, it must be a sort of life which I have not read of in books or experienced in person. We did not see a human being but ourselves during the time, or hear any sounds but those that were made by the wind and the waves, the sighing of the pines, and now and then the far-off thunder of an avalanche. The forest about us was dense and cool, the sky above us was cloudless and brilliant with sunshine, the broad lake before us was glassy and clear, or rippled and breezy, or black and storm-tossed, according to Nature's mood; and its circling border of mountain domes, clothed with forests, scarred with landslides, cloven by canyons and valleys, and helmeted with glittering snow, fitly framed and finished the noble picture. The view was always fascinating, bewitching, entrancing. The eye was never tired of gazing, night or day, in calm or storm; it suffered but one grief, and that was that it could not look always, but must close sometimes in sleep.

We slept in the sand close to the water's edge, between two protecting boulders, which took care of the stormy night winds for us. We never took any paregoric to make us sleep. At the first break of dawn we were always up and running foot races to tone down excess of physical vigor and exuberance of spirits. That is, Johnny was—but I held his hat. While smoking the pipe of peace after breakfast we watched the sentinel peaks put on the glory of the sun, and followed the conquering light as it swept down among the shadows and set the captive crags and forests free. We watched the tinted pictures grow and brighten upon the water till every little detail of forest, precipice, and pinnacle was wrought in and finished, and the miracle of the enchanter complete. Then to "business."

That is, drifting around in the boat. We were on the north shore. There, the rocks on the bottom are sometimes gray, sometimes white. This gives the marvelous transparency of the water a fuller advantage than it has elsewhere on the lake. We usually pushed out a hundred yards or so from shore, and then lay down on the thwarts, in the sun, and let the boat drift by the hour whither it would. We seldom talked. It interrupted the Sabbath stillness, and marred the dreams the luxurious rest and indolence brought. The shore all along was indented with deep, curved bays and coves, bordered by narrow sand beaches; and where the sand ended, the steep mountainsides rose right up aloft into space—rose up like a vast wall a little out of the perpendicular, and thickly wooded with tall pines.

So singularly clear was the water that when it was only twenty or thirty feet deep the bottom was so perfectly distinct that the boat seemed floating in the air! Yes, where it was even *eighty* feet deep. Every little pebble was distinct, every speckled trout, every hand's-breadth of sand. Often, as we lay on our faces, a granite boulder, as large as a village church, would start out of the bottom apparently, and seem climbing up rapidly to the surface, till presently it threatened to touch our faces, and we could not resist the impulse to seize an oar and avert the danger. But the boat would float on, and the boulder descend again, and then we could see that when we had been exactly above it, it must still have been twenty or thirty feet below the surface. Down through the transparency of these great depths, the water was not *merely* transparent, but dazzlingly, brilliantly so. All objects seen through it had a bright, strong vividness, not only of outline, but of every minute detail, which they would not have had when seen simply through the same depth of atmosphere. So empty and airy did all spaces seem below us, and so strong was the sense of floating high aloft in mind-nothingness, that we called these boat excursions "balloon voyages."

We fished a great deal, but we did not average one fish a week. We could see trout by the thousand winging about in the emptiness under us, or sleeping in shoals on the bottom, but they would not bite—they could see the line too plainly, perhaps. We frequently selected the trout we wanted, and rested the bait patiently and persistently on the end of his nose at a depth of eighty feet, but he would only shake it off with an annoyed manner, and shift his position.

We bathed occasionally, but the water was rather chilly, for all it looked so sunny. Sometimes we rowed out to the "blue water," a mile or two from shore. It was as dead blue as indigo there, because of the immense depth. By official measurement the lake in its center is one thousand five hundred and twenty-five feet deep!

Sometimes, on lazy afternoons, we lolled on the sand in camp, and smoked pipes, and read some old well-worn novels. At night by the campfire, we played euchre and seven-up to strengthen the mind—and played them with cards so greasy and defaced that only a whole summer's acquaintance with them could enable the student to tell the ace of clubs from the jack of diamonds.

We never slept in our "house." It never recurred to us, for one thing; and besides, it was built to hold the ground, and that was enough. We did not wish to strain it.

By and by our provisions began to run short, and we went back to the old camp and laid in a new supply. We were gone all day, and headed home again about nightfall, pretty tired and hungry. While Johnny was carrying the main bulk of the provisions up to our "house" for future use, I took the loaf of bread, some slices of bacon, and the coffeepot ashore, set them down by a tree, lit a fire, and went back to the boat to get the frying pan. While I was at this, I heard a shout from Johnny, and looking up I saw that my fire was galloping all over the premises!

Johnny was on the other side of it. He had to run through the flames to get to the lake shore, and then we stood helpless and watched the devastation.

The ground was deeply carpeted with dry pine needles, and the fire touched them off as if they were gunpowder. It was wonderful to see with what fierce speed the tall sheet of flame traveled! My coffeepot was gone, and everything with it. In a minute and a half the fire seized upon a dense growth of dry manzanita chaparral six or eight feet high, and then the roaring and popping and crackling was something terrific. We were driven to the boat by the intense heat, and there we remained, spellbound.

Within half an hour all before us was a tossing, blinding tempest of flames! It went surging up adjacent ridges—surmounted them and disappeared in the canyons beyond—burst into view upon higher and farther ridges, presently—shed a grander illumination abroad, and dove again—flamed out again, directly, higher and still higher up the mountainside—threw out skirmishing parties of fire here and there, and sent them trailing their crimson spirals away among remote ramparts and ribs and gorges, till as far as the eye could reach the lofty mountain fronts were webbed as it were with a tangled network of red lava streams. Away across the water the crags and domes were lit with a ruddy glare, and the firmament above was a reflected hell!

Every feature of the spectacle was repeated in the glowing mirror of the lake! Both pictures were sublime, both were beautiful; but that in the lake had a bewildering richness about it that enchanted the eye and held it with the stronger fascination.

We sat absorbed and motionless through four long hours. We never thought of supper, and never felt fatigue. But at eleven o'clock the conflagration had traveled beyond our range of vision, and the darkness stole down upon the landscape again.

Hunger asserted itself now, but there was nothing to eat. The provisions were all cooked, no doubt, but we did not go to see. We were homeless wanderers again, without any property. Our fence was gone, our house burned down; no insurance. Our pine forest was well scorched, the dead trees all burned up, and our broad acres of manzanita swept away. Our blankets were on our usual sand bed, however, and so we lay down and went to sleep. The next morning we started back to the old camp, but while out a long way from shore, so great a storm came up that we dared not try to land. So I baled out the seas we shipped, and Johnny pulled heavily through the billows till we had reached a point three or four miles beyond the camp. The storm was increasing, and it became evident that it was better to take the hazard of beaching the boat than to go down in a hundred fathoms of water; so we ran in, with tall whitecaps following, and I sat down in the stern sheets and pointed her head-on to the shore. The instant the bow struck, a wave came over the stern that washed crew and cargo ashore, and saved a deal of trouble. We shivered in the lee of a boulder all the rest of the day, and froze all the night through. In the morning the tempest had gone down, and we paddled down to the camp without any unnecessary delay. We were so starved that we ate up the rest of the brigade's provisions, and then set out to Carson to tell them about it and ask their forgiveness. It was accorded, upon payment of damages.

We made many trips to the lake after that, and had many a hairbreadth escape and bloodcurdling adventure which will never be recorded in any history.

Sierra Nevada

Climbing
Matterhorn Peak

Jack Kerouac (1922–1969) was at the center of the Beat Generation of writers that sprang up in San Francisco during the 1950s. His novel On the Road *(1957), with its energized first-person narrative and what Kerouac called "spontaneous prose," was a seminal work of that movement. His "true-story novel"* The Dharma Bums *(1958) includes the following section about a climb up Yosemite's Matterhorn Peak made by Ray Smith (Kerouac's alter ego), Henry Morley, and Japhy Ryder, a Zen-quoting free spirit modeled on the poet Gary Snyder.*

"Well here we go" said Japhy. "When I get tired of this big rucksack we'll swap."

"I'm ready now, man, come on, give it to me now, I feel like carrying something heavy. You don't realize how good I feel, man, come on." So we swapped packs and started off.

Both of us were feeling fine and were talking a blue streak, about anything, literature, the mountains, girls, Princess, the poets, Japan, our past adventures in life, and I suddenly realized it was a kind of blessing in disguise Morley had forgotten to drain the crankcase, otherwise Japhy wouldn't have got in a word edgewise all the blessed day and now I had a chance to hear his ideas. In the way he did things, hiking, he reminded me of Mike my boyhood chum who also loved to lead the way, real grave like Buck Jones, eyes to the distant horizons, like Natty Bumppo, cautioning me about snapping twigs or "It's too deep here, let's go down the creek a ways to ford it," or "There'll be mud in that low bottom, we better skirt around" and dead serious and glad. I saw all Japhy's boyhood in those eastern Oregon forests the way he went about it. He walked like he talked, from behind I could see his toes pointed slightly inward, the way mine do, instead of out, but when it came time to climb he pointed his toes out, like Chaplin, to make a kind of easier flapthwap as he trudged. We went across a kind of muddy riverbottom through dense undergrowth and a few willow trees and came out on the other side a little wet and started up the trail, which was clearly marked and named and had been recently repaired by trail crews but as we hit parts where a rock had rolled on the trail he took great precaution to throw the rock off saying "I used to work on trail crews, I can't see a trail all mettlesome like that, Smith." As we climbed the lake began to appear below us and suddenly in its clear blue pool we could see the deep holes where the lake had its springs, like black wells, and we could see schools of fish skitter.

"Oh this is like an early morning in China and I'm five years old in beginningless time!" I sang out and felt like sitting by the trail and whipping out my little notebook and writing sketches about it.

"Look over there," sang Japhy, "yellow aspens. Just put me in the mind of a haiku . . . 'Talking about the literary life—the yellow aspens.'" Walking in this country you could understand the perfect gems of haikus the Oriental poets had written, never getting drunk in the mountains or anything but just going along as fresh as children writing down what they saw without literary devices or fanciness of expression. We made up haikus as we climbed, winding up and up now on the slopes of brush.

"Rocks on the side of the cliff," I said, "why don't they tumble down?"

"Maybe that's a haiku, maybe not. It might be a little too complicated," said Japhy. "A real haiku's gotta be as simple as porridge and yet make you see the real thing, like the greatest haiku of them all probably is the one that goes 'The sparrow hops along the veranda, with wet feet,' by Shiki. You see the wet footprints like a vision in your mind and yet in those few words you also see all the rain that's been falling that day and almost smell the wet pine needles."

"Let's have another."

"I'll make up one of my own this time, let's see. 'Lake below . . . the black holes the wells make,' no that's not a haiku goddammit, you never can be too careful about haiku."

"How about making them up real fast as you go along, spontaneously?"

"Look here," he cried happily, "mountain lupine, see the delicate blue color those little flowers have. And there's some California red poppy over there. The whole meadow is just powdered with color! Up there by the way is a genuine California white pine, you never see them much any more."

"You sure know a lot about birds and trees and stuff."

"I've studied it all my life." Then also as we went on climbing we began getting more casual and making funnier sillier talk and pretty soon we got to a bend in the trail where it was suddenly gladey and dark with shade and a tremendous cataracting stream was bashing and frothing over scummy rocks and tumbling on down, and over the stream was a perfect bridge formed by a fallen snag, we got on it and lay belly-down and dunked our heads down, hair wet, and drank deep as the water splashed in our faces, like sticking your head by the jet of a dam. I lay there a good long minute enjoying the sudden coolness.

"This is like an advertisement for Rainier Ale!" yelled Japhy.

"Let's sit awhile and enjoy it."

"But you don't know how far we got to go yet!"

"Well I'm not tired!"

"Well you'll be, Tiger."

We went on, and I was immensely pleased with the way the trail had a kind of immortal look to it, in the early afternoon now, the way the side of the grassy hill seemed to be clouded with ancient gold dust and the bugs flipped over rocks and the wind sighed in shimmering dances over the hot rocks, and the way the trail would suddenly come into a cool shady part with big trees overhead, and here the light deeper. And the way the lake below us soon became a toy lake with those black well holes perfectly visible still, and the giant cloud shadows on the lake, and the tragic little road winding away where poor Morley was walking back.

"Can you see Morl down back there?"

Japhy took a long look. "I see a little cloud of dust, maybe that's him comin back already." But it seemed that I had seen the ancient afternoon of that trail, from meadow rocks and lupine posies, to sudden revisits with the roaring stream with its splashed snag bridges and undersea greennesses, there was something inexpressibly broken in my heart as though I'd lived before and walked this trail, under similar circumstances with a fellow Bodhisattva, but maybe on a more important journey. I felt like lying down by the side of the trail and remembering it all. The woods do that to you, they always look familiar, long lost, like the face of a long-dead relative, like an old dream, like a piece of forgotten song drifting across the water, most of all like golden eternities of past childhood or past manhood and all the living and the dying and the heartbreak that went on a million years ago and the clouds as they pass overhead seem to testify (by their own lonesome familiarity) to this feeling. Ecstasy, even, I felt, with flashes of sudden remembrance, and feeling sweaty and drowsy I felt like sleeping and dreaming in the grass. As we got high we got more tired and now like two true mountain climbers we weren't talking any more and didn't have to talk and were glad, in fact Japhy mentioned that, turning to me after a half-hour's silence, "This is the way I like it, when you get going there's just no need to talk, as if we were animals and just communicated by silent telepathy." So huddled in our own thoughts we tromped on, Japhy using that gazotsky trudge I mentioned, and myself finding my own true step, which was short steps slowly patiently going up the mountain at one mile an hour, so I was always thirty yards behind him and when we had any haikus now we'd yell them fore and aft. Pretty soon we got to the top of the part of the trail that was a trail no more, to the incomparable dreamy meadow, which had a beautiful pond, and after that it was boulders and nothing but boulders.

"Only sign we have now to know which way we're going, is ducks."

"What ducks?"

"See those boulders over there?"

"See those boulders over there! Why God man, I see five miles of boulders leading up to that mountain."

"See the little pile of rocks on that near boulder there by the pine? That's a duck, put up by other climbers, maybe that's one I put up myself in 'fifty-four I'm not sure. We just go from boulder to boulder from now on keeping a sharp eye for ducks then we get a general idea how to raggle along. Although of course we know which way we're going, that big cliff face up there is where our plateau is."

"Plateau? My God you mean that ain't the top of the mountain?"

"Of course not, after that we got a plateau and then scree and then more rocks and we get to a final alpine lake no biggern this pond and then comes the final climb over one thousand feet almost straight up boy to the top of the world where you'll see all California and parts of Nevada and the wind'll blow right through your pants."

"Ow . . . How long does it all take?"

"Why the only thing we can expect to make tonight is our camp up there on that plateau. I call it a plateau, it ain't that at all, it's a shelf between heights."

But the top and the end of the trail was such a beautiful spot I said: "Boy look at this . . . " A dreamy meadow, pines at one end, the pond, the clear fresh air, the afternoon clouds rushing golden . . . "Why don't we just sleep here tonight, I don't think I've ever seen a more beautiful park."

"Ah this is nowhere. It's great of course, but we might wake up tomorrow morning and find three dozen school-teachers on horseback frying bacon in our backyard. Where we're going you can bet your ass there won't be one human being, and if there is, I'll be a spotted horse's ass. Or maybe just one mountain climber, or two, but I don't expect so at this time of the year. You know the snow's about to come here any time now. If it comes tonight it's goodbye me and you."

"Well goodbye Japhy. But let's rest here and drink some water and admire the meadow." We were feeling tired and great. We spread out in the grass and rested and swapped packs and strapped them on and were rarin to go. Almost instantaneously the grass ended and the boulders started; we got up on the first one and from that point on it was just a matter of jumping from boulder to boulder, gradually climbing, climbing, five miles up a valley of boulders getting steeper and steeper with immense crags on both sides forming the walls of the valley, till near the cliff face we'd be scrambling up the boulders, it seemed.

"And what's behind that cliff face?"

"There's high grass up there, shrubbery, scattered boulders, beautiful meandering creeks that have ice in 'em even in the afternoon, spots of snow, tremendous trees, and one boulder just about as big as two of Alvah's cottages piled on top the other which leans over and makes a kind of concave cave for us to camp at, lightin a big bonfire that'll throw heat against the wall. Then after that the grass and the timber ends. That'll be at nine thousand just about."

Jumping from boulder to boulder and never falling, with a heavy pack, is easier than it sounds; you just can't fall when you get into the rhythm of the dance. I looked back down the valley sometimes and was surprised to see how high we'd come, and to see farther horizons of mountains now back there. Our beautiful trail-top park was like a little glen of the Forest of Arden. Then the climbing got steeper, the sun got redder, and pretty soon I began to see patches of snow in the shade of some rocks. We got up to where the cliff face seemed to loom over us. At one point I saw Japhy throw down his pack and danced my way up to him.

"Well this is where we'll drop our gear and climb those few hundred feet up the side of that cliff, where you see there it's shallower, and find that camp. I remember it. In fact you can sit here and rest or beat your bishop while I go rambling around there. I like to ramble by myself."

Okay. So I sat down and changed my wet socks and changed soaking undershirt for dry one and crossed my legs and rested and whistled for about a half-hour, a very pleasant occupation, and Japhy got back and said he'd found the camp. I thought it would be a little jaunt to our resting place but it took almost another hour to jump up the steep boulders, climb around some, get to the level of the cliff-face plateau, and there, on flat grass more or less, hike about two hundred yards to where a huge gray rock towered among pines. Here now the earth was a splendorous thing—snow on the ground, in melting patches in the grass, and gurgling creeks, and the huge silent rock mountains on both sides, and a wind blowing, and the smell of heather. We forded a lovely little creek, shallow as your hand, pearl pure lucid water, and got to the huge rock. . . .

At about noon we started out, leaving our big packs at the camp where nobody was likely to be till next year anyway, and went up the scree valley with just some food and first-aid kits. The valley was longer than it looked. In no time at all it was two o'clock in the afternoon and the sun was getting that later more golden look and a wind was rising and I began to think "By gosh how we ever gonna climb that mountain, tonight?"

I put it up to Japhy who said: "You're right, we'll have to hurry."

"Why don't we just forget it and go on home?"

"Aw come on Tiger, we'll make a run up that hill and then we'll go home." The valley was long and long and long. And at the top end it got very steep and I began to be a little afraid of falling down, the rocks were small and it got slippery and my ankles were in pain from yesterday's muscle strain anyway. But Morley kept walking and talking and I noticed his tremendous endurance. Japhy took his pants off so he could look just like an Indian, I mean stark naked, except for a jockstrap, and hiked almost a quarter-mile ahead of us, sometimes waiting awhile, to give us time to catch up, then went on, moving fast, wanting to climb the mountain today. Morley came second, about fifty yards ahead of me all the way. I was in no hurry. Then as it got later afternoon I went faster and decided to pass Morley and join Japhy. Now we were at about eleven thousand feet and it was cold and there was a lot of snow and to the east we could see immense snowcapped ranges and whooee levels of valleyland below them, we were already practically on top of California. At one point I had to scramble, like the others, on a narrow ledge, around a butte of rock, and it really scared me: the fall was a hundred feet, enough to break your neck, with another little ledge letting you bounce a minute preparatory to a nice goodbye one-thousand-foot drop. The wind was whipping now. Yet that whole afternoon, even more than the other, was filled with old premonitions or memories, as though I'd been there before, scrambling on these rocks, for other purposes more ancient, more serious, more simple. We finally got to the foot of Matterhorn where there was a most beautiful small lake unknown to the eyes of most men in this world, seen by only a handful of mountain-climbers, a small lake at eleven thousand some odd feet with snow on the edges of it and beautiful flowers and a beautiful meadow, an alpine meadow, flat and dreamy, upon which I immediately threw myself and took my shoes off. Japhy'd been there a half-hour when I made it, and it was cold now and his clothes were on again. Morley came up behind us smiling. We sat there looking up at the imminent steep scree slope of the final crag of Matterhorn.

"That don't look much, we can do it!" I said glad now.

"No, Ray, that's more than it looks. Do you realize that's a thousand feet more?"

"That much?"

"Unless we make a run up there, double-time, we'll never make it down again to our camp before nightfall and never make it down to the car at the lodge before tomorrow morning at, well at midnight."

"Phew."

"I'm tired," said Morley. "I don't think I'll try it."

"Well that's right," I said. "The whole purpose of mountain-climbing to me isn't just to show off you can get to the top, it's getting out to this wild country."

"Well I'm gonna go," said Japhy.

"Well if you're gonna go I'm goin with you."

"Morley?"

"I don't think I can make it. I'll wait here." And that wind was strong, too strong. I felt that as soon as we'd be a few hundred feet up the slope it might hamper our climbing.

Japhy took a small pack of peanuts and raisins and said "This'll be our gasoline, boy. You ready Ray to make a double-time run?"

"Ready. What about I say to the boys in The Place if I came all this way only to give up at the last minute?"

"It's late so let's hurry." Japhy started up walking very rapidly and then even running sometimes where the climb had to be to the right or left along ridges of scree. Scree is long landslides of rocks and sand, very difficult to scramble through, always little avalanches going on. At every few steps we took it seemed we were going higher and higher on a terrifying elevator. I gulped when I turned around to look back and see all of the state of California it would seem stretching out in three directions under huge blue skies with frightening planetary space clouds and immense vistas of distant valleys and even plateaus and for all I knew whole Nevadas out there. It was terrifying to look down and see Morley a dreaming spot by the little lake waiting for us. "Oh why didn't I stay with old Henry?" I thought. I now began to be afraid to go any higher from sheer fear of being too high. I began to be afraid of being blown away by the wind. All the nightmares I'd ever had about falling off mountains and precipitous buildings ran through my head in perfect clarity. Also with every twenty steps we took upward we both became completely exhausted.

"That's because of the high altitude Ray," said Japhy sitting beside me panting. "So have raisins and peanuts and you'll see what kick it gives you." And each time it gave us such a tremendous kick we both jumped up without a word and climbed another twenty, thirty steps. Then sat down again, panting, sweating in the cold wind, high on top of the world our noses sniffling like the noses of little boys playing late Saturday afternoon their final little games in winter. Now the wind began to howl like the wind in movies about the Shroud of Tibet. The steepness began to be too much for me; I was afraid now to look back any more; I peeked: I couldn't even make out Morley by the tiny lake.

"Hurry it up," yelled Japhy from a hundred feet ahead. "It's getting awfully late." I looked up to the peak. It was right there. I'd be there in five minutes. "Only a half-hour to go!" yelled Japhy. I didn't believe it. In five minutes of scrambling angrily upward I fell down and looked up and it was still just as far away. What I didn't like about that peak-top was that the clouds of all the world were blowing right through it like fog.

"Wouldn't see anything up there anyway," I muttered. "Oh why did I ever let myself into this?" Japhy was way ahead of me now, he'd left the peanuts and raisins with me, it was with a kind of lonely solemnity now he had decided to rush to the top if it killed him. He didn't sit down any more. Soon he was a whole football field, a hundred yards ahead of me, getting smaller. I looked back and like Lot's wife that did it. *"This is too high!"* I yelled to Japhy in a panic. He didn't hear me. I raced a few more feet up and fell exhausted on my belly, slipping back just a little. *"This is too high!"* I yelled. I was really scared. Supposing I'd start to slip back for good, these screes might start sliding any time anyway. That damn mountain got Japhy, I could see him jumping through the foggy air up ahead from rock to rock, up, up, just the flash of his foot bottoms. "How can I keep up with a maniac like that?" But with nutty desperation I followed him. Finally I came to a kind of ledge where I could sit at a level angle instead of having to cling not to slip, and I nudged my whole body inside the ledge just to hold me there tight, so the wind would not dislodge me, and I looked down and around and I had had it. *"I'm stayin here!"* I yelled to Japhy.

"Come on Smith, only another five minutes. I only got a hundred feet to go!"

"*I'm staying right here! It's too high!*"

He said nothing and went on. I saw him collapse and pant and get up and make his run again.

I nudged myself closer into the ledge and closed my eyes and thought "Oh what a life this is, why do we have to be born in the first place, and only so we can have our poor gentle flesh laid out to such impossible horrors as huge mountains and rock and empty space," and with horror I remembered the famous Zen saying, "When you get to the top of a mountain, keep climbing." The saying made my hair stand on end; it had been such cute poetry sitting on Alvah's straw mats. Now it was enough to make my heart pound and my heart bleed for being born at all. "In fact when Japhy gets to the top of that crag he *will* keep climbing, the way the wind's blowing. Well this old philosopher is staying right here," and I closed my eyes. "Besides," I thought, "rest and be kind, you don't have to prove anything." Suddenly I heard a beautiful broken yodel of strange musical and mystical intensity in the wind, and looked up, and it was Japhy standing on top of Matterhorn peak letting out his triumphant mountain-conquering Buddha Mountain Smashing song of joy. It was beautiful. It was funny, too, up here on the not-so-funny top of California and in all that rushing fog. But I had to hand it to him, the guts, the endurance, the sweat, and now the crazy human singing: whipped cream on top of ice cream. I didn't have enough strength to answer his yodel. He ran around up there and went out of sight to investigate the little flat top of some kind (he said) that ran a few feet west and then dropped sheer back down maybe as far as I care to the sawdust floors of Virginia City. It was insane. I could hear him yelling at me but I just nudged down at the small lake where Morley was lying on his back with a blade of grass in his mouth and said out loud "Now there's the karma of these three men here: Japhy Ryder gets to his triumphant mountaintop and makes it. I almost make it and have to give up and huddle in a bloody cave, but the smartest of them all is that poet's poet lyin down there with his knees crossed to the sky chewing on a flower dreaming by a gurgling *plage*, goddamit they'll never get me up here again."

Then suddenly everything was just like jazz: it happened in one insane second or so: I looked up and saw Japhy *running down the mountain* in huge twenty-foot leaps, running, leaping, landing with a great drive of his booted heels, bouncing five feet or so, running, then taking another long crazy yelling yodelaying sail down the sides of the world and in that flash I realized *it's impossible to fall off mountains you fool* and with a yodel of my own I suddenly got up and began running down the mountain after him doing exactly the same huge leaps, the same fantastic runs and jumps, and in the space of about five minutes I'd guess Japhy Ryder and I (in my sneakers, driving the heels of my sneakers right into sand, rock, boulders, I didn't care any more I was so anxious to get down out of there) came leaping and yelling like mountain goats or I'd say like Chinese lunatics of a thousand years ago, enough to raise the hair on the head of the meditating Morley by the lake, who said he looked up and saw us flying down and couldn't believe it. In fact with one of my greatest leaps and loudest screams of joy I came flying right down to the edge of the lake and dug my sneakered heels into the mud and just fell sitting there, glad. Japhy was already taking his shoes off and pouring sand and pebbles out. It was great. I took off my sneakers and poured out a couple of buckets of lava dust and said "Ah Japhy you taught me the final lesson of them all, you can't fall off a mountain."

"And that's what they mean by the saying, When you get to the top of a mountain keep climbing, Smith."

Mt. Tamalpais

A Mount for All Seasons

Harold Gilliam (b. 1918), a noted environmentalist, is a former staff writer and now frequent contributor to the San Francisco Chronicle. *In addition to hundreds of articles on environmental subjects, Gilliam has written sixteen books including* The Natural World of San Francisco *(1967) and* The San Francisco Experience *(1972), from which this essay on Marin County's cherished Mt. Tamalpais is taken.*

From Muir Woods, from Mill Valley, from almost any place around the base of Tamalpais, a trail network leads to all parts of the mountain, offering exploration and adventure, refreshment and renewal to all who can walk. In order to know this mountain of diverse moods, it is necessary to hike its trails in every season and every weather.

One August morning, for example, when San Francisco was dark beneath a heavy overcast, I drove to the mountain by way of Mill Valley and on the road above the town found myself in a thick fog. Switching on the windshield wipers, I continued slowly on the Panoramic Highway past Mountain Home, Bootjack, and Pantoll, then turned off for the road toward the summit, still fogbound. Suddenly I emerged from the mists and looked down on the roof of the layer of vapor, dazzling white in the sun. Below were big waves of fog, with shadows in the hollows. Slow volatile geysers rose from the crests of the waves to heights of one hundred feet or more and evaporated in the warm air above.

I parked near Rock Spring, where the sun was bright and warm. From the grove of big tanbark oaks next to the parking area came a crackling sound, as if some animal were walking among the dry leaves under the trees. I walked into the grove to investigate and was surprised to find that the trees were dripping copiously; the drops resounded as they hit the stiff brown tanbark leaves. For a moment I was puzzled as to why the trees were wet in the sun. Then it occurred to me that the fog had been in there all night, drenching the trees, and had burned off a few minutes before I arrived.

The theory was confirmed as I walked down the trail below the spring and noticed that the tawny grass in the meadow was still wet. The woods were aromatic with the smell of damp leaves in warm weather—the strong odor of the laurels, the special fragrance of live oaks and toyon and meadow grass, the Christmas-tree smell of the Douglas firs.

Rounding a bend, I came on a sight that brought me to a quick stop. There alongside the trail were several young Douglas firs still wet from the fog. From where I stood the sun was directly behind them, and every needle was bejeweled with drops of water that glistened in the morning light. Each drop reflected a different band of the spectrum, turning the sunlight into piercing reds and yellows, burning blues and purples. No Christmas tree was ever so brilliantly decked out as those Douglas firs with the fog jewelry on their needles.

The process of decoration had been a complicated one. Every drop of water had been lifted from the ocean by the moving masses of air, had been part of the great flowing fog bank, had been elevated two thousand feet above the ocean and hung with ten thousand others in resplendent array on these branches. All this elaborate preparation had taken place for a glittering display that would last only a few minutes, the interval between the lifting of the fog and the evaporation of the water particles. I had happened to come along at exactly the right time.

While I watched the spectacle began to disappear as the sun dried out each needle. The moisture passed invisibly into the air, seeming to give it a polished brilliance that sharpened the lines of trees and rocks and ridges in the sun.

The coming of the sunlight after the fog had produced an array of sounds almost as brilliant as the light on the leaves. Excited finches and sparrows twittered in the chaparral. Big jays cawed and chattered and whistled as they swooped among the live oaks. Woodpeckers beat out industrious rhythms on tree trunks. Yellow jackets buzzed and hummed in the chaparral, and from somewhere along a high wooded ridge came the scream of a red-tailed hawk. Underneath all the other sound there was a barely audible roar that might have been the imperceptible stirring of the leaves in the big Douglas firs on the ridge or perhaps even the far-off pounding of the surf along the oceanward foot of the mountain.

At a point where the trail led through a stretch of deep woods, the sunlight filtering through the canopy made patterns on the forest floor, illuminating the rich red browns of the dead leaves, and from the damp mossy bole of a big conifer a shaft of golden sunlight was raising a ghost of a vapor that drifted through the woods like an errant wisp of the vanished fog.

The same trail at another time or season is quite a different experience. The summertime hiker, the sunshine mountaineer, the fair-weather outdoorsman can participate in only a fraction of the beneficences this peak has to offer. He knows the mountain only in a time of quiescence, when the natural forces that created this magnificent parkland are at rest. To see the mountain in its full splendor, go there in fog or wind or rain; see the sun set and rise again; explore the high trails by the light of the stars and the woods in the full of the moon. Above all, to see the forces of creation at work, go at the climax of a winter storm, when the rain turns rivulets to torrents, the wind sets the groves and forests to waving and shaking, and the aroused energies of the mountain seem to radiate from the rocks themselves.

I took the trail down from Rock Spring during a rain one afternoon in November, listening to the music of the storm—the wind in the high branches overhead and the full range of tones of the moving waters. Over the mountain ten thousand springs were flowing copiously from the early storms; every gully was filled with a stream. Creeks that in August had been a mere trickle were now impassable torrents; in the larger canyons, cascades and cataracts and waterfalls shook the air with their thunder.

Light showers were falling as I strolled down the canyon between stands of big shiny-leaved madroños, through aromatic groves of laurels, past contorted live oaks arching over the trail. Outcrops of wet rock gleamed more brilliantly than they do in the brightest August sunshine. Every drop of water on the rock surface acted as a prism, both brightening the natural color and reflecting the light roundabout. Rocks that had a dull surface when dry now sparkled as if polished by a lapidary. Dun colors turned to orange and yellow; dull reds became rich ocher; outcrops of pale green serpentine were transformed into masses of shining emerald.

In the storm I became intimately aware of the force of the rushing water in sculpturing the mountain, in wearing away the rocks, in creating and deepening canyons, in depositing soil in the meadows and valleys. Consequently I noticed something that had not been evident to me before. About two hundred yards down the trail from Rock Spring, the canyon broadened to a grassy meadow. The stream, which above had been roaring over boulders in a white torrent, disappeared from view. I walked closer and found that the water had carved a miniature gorge with nearly vertical sides and was flowing six to eight feet below the level of the meadow. Here was an intriguing problem in geology. The walls of the gorge were not rock but rich alluvial soil that obviously had been deposited over a long period of time by slow-moving or still waters. I realized then that I was standing on the bed of an old lake or marsh.

At the lower end of this meadow the canyon bottom narrowed to about the width of the stream. Here, evidently, at some unknown time in the past, a landslide from the steep slopes above had blocked the stream, backing up the waters to form a lake. On the lake bed had been deposited the sediments I now saw being eroded away in the gorge. Probably in time the lake had been entirely filled with sediment and became a marsh or meadow. A flood breaching the landslide-dam would have caused the stream to flow swiftly again, rapidly cutting the gorge through the soft soil of the meadow.

At the foot of the old landslide a big Douglas fir, a century old or more, leaned precariously out over the stream, which was undermining the bank on which it stood. The curve of the trunk made me think that the tree had begun to lean about halfway in its lifetime, probably at the same time that the dam was breached and the stream began to deepen its bed. Another clue was that part of the gorge was thickly planted with relatively young Douglas firs, making a handsome wall of vegetation through the middle of the meadow. The firs were all about twenty-five feet high, indicating that they were of the same age. Evidently they had begun to grow here at the time when the stream had excavated the gorge down to the level of the new outlet and the cutting process was stabilized—perhaps thirty years ago. The gorge could not have been much older than that or its steep walls would have been eroded away long since. Such angularities do not last long in nature, and doubtless within a few more decades will disappear—along with most of the meadow.

Although I had hiked this same trail scores of times in fair weather, it had not occurred to me to look into the evolution of this meadow until I saw the full force of the flowing water during the storm and was acutely conscious of the forces that are continually creating and re-creating the landscape.

A totally different kind of experience with the mountain came one day in January, after a series of storms had been followed by a period of calm weather and tule fogs—the winter fogs that form in the cold inland valleys and move slowly westward toward the warmer ocean. From a high point in San Francisco I noticed a strange situation: instead of flowing outward through the Golden Gate as it would normally do at this time of year, the fog was flowing in from the ocean, as it would do in the summer. Wondering what could be the cause of this meteorological accident, I got in the car and headed for a grandstand view on Tamalpais. As the car climbed to the ridge above Mill Valley, through a gap in the hills I looked out to the bay and caught a quick glimpse that gave me a preview of the spectacle I was about to witness. Through Raccoon Strait, between Angel Island and Tiburon, a fog flood was pouring west. Climbing higher, I could see similar tongues flowing westward through the low saddles of the Tiburon Peninsula. There could be no doubt that this was a normal tule fog, forming inland and moving west. Yet at the same time the sea fog continued to blow in from the ocean through the Golden Gate. The two fog masses were on a collision course.

At Mountain Home, at the nine-hundred-foot elevation on Tamalpais, where the road leaves Throckmorton Ridge and turns west, I parked the car and continued up the ridge on foot, following the steep Throckmorton Trail. Here above the fog zone the sun beamed down warmly, but as I climbed to the upper part of the ridge I felt a breeze from the west—the advance guard of the fog moving in from the Pacific. The fog did not hang low on the water, as it would in the summertime, but was actually a deck of broken stratus clouds several hundred feet above the surface, as far west over the ocean as I could see.

This is the kind of fog-cloud that often heralds an approaching storm front. Actually, I learned later that there was at the time a storm center moving from the ocean across northern California and southern Oregon. I was standing at the extreme edge of the storm area, around which the air masses were moving, as they always do, in a counterclockwise direction, bringing the wind and fog and clouds to this area from the west. It was this foggy southern edge of the storm that was moving in over the coastal hills and about to collide with the westward-moving tule fogs around the bay. I hurried on up the ridge to witness what promised to be a major clash of the elements.

Higher up, I looked out on an extraordinary sight. The bay itself was almost completely covered with a thin white film of tule fog, as if wind-blown snow had drifted across the surface of a frozen lake. The hump-backed deck of the Richmond–San Rafael Bridge seemed to rest on the white expanse, and its foghorn moaned a bass dirge. Near the bridge, two ships appeared to be half sunken, the vapors level with their upper decks.

Suddenly I was startled by what appeared to be a silent explosion in a canyon directly below me. A big puff of white vapor forty feet high appeared from nowhere, rose, and drifted away. Then, at the head of an adjacent canyon, another smokelike puff appeared, boiled upward into a familiar mushroom shape, then disappeared. Responding to an old wartime reflex, I had an instinct to hit the dirt. In appearance the phenomenon was uncomfortably reminiscent of an artillery barrage.

Then, as similar "explosions" took place just at the heads of the canyons below, I realized what had happened. Masses of cool ocean air, moving in ahead of the fog and clouds, had reached the canyons above Muir Woods and Mill Valley, followed the canyons upward as if in a chute, cooled as they rose, and just below me had reached the point at which their moisture condensed into visible puffs of vapor.

I climbed on up beyond the area of "bombardment" to the summit of the East Peak of Tamalpais. Here a cold wind from the storm front was howling in from the west-northwest. I crouched on the lee side of the lookout station and gazed down across the bay. Along the near shore, the filmy fog covering the water had accumulated into drifts that buried the towns of San Rafael and Corte Madera and was flowing like driven smoke up through the foothill canyons. San Quentin on its point was half hidden in the vapors, and the channels of Corte Madera Slough gleamed up through the mists like sinuous tracings of light.

I had arrived at the summit just in time. The sea breeze, moving ahead of the fog and clouds it was carrying, had advanced over Mill Valley and across Richardson Bay and now met the edge of the advancing masses of tule fog along the Tiburon Peninsula. The forces from land and sea had come into contact, and the battle was suddenly joined on a front miles long. From the start there was little doubt as to which force was the stronger. The wind from the ocean had acquired too much momentum to be stopped by the low thin layer of tule fog from inland. The advance front of the tule fog was suddenly blunted and rolled over backwards like an ocean wave that hits a rocky cliff and rebounds. Everywhere along the battle front, in Raccoon Strait, in the passes through Tiburon Ridge, then out over the surface of the bay itself, the misty tide was turned as the tule fog began to retreat before the battering attack of the sea wind. The advance salients of tule fog seemed to rear back before the onslaught like the dismayed cavalry of Napoleon before the British fire at Waterloo.

The encounter between the two forces created an array of fantastic fog shapes such as I had never seen in many years of fog-watching. All along the battle line, the nebulous forms appeared and disappeared faster than I could keep track of them. Vapory castles quickly formed and vanished. Fog masses thrown back by the advancing west wind were broken up into swiftly moving spirals and parabolas. Steeples and pillars and vaulted arches came into being for a few moments, only to be destroyed by the wind.

The artillery barrage I had seen earlier on the mountain was repeated in the valleys below on a mammoth scale. A mushroom cloud loomed over San Quentin. Over the bay's edge at Corte Madera a mass of white vapor slowly rose like a column of water, spread, and spilled over at the top in a gigantic fog fountain. Then it rose even higher and changed shape until it seemed to be a towering monolith—a vaporous

Washington Monument catching the last rays of the sun before falling back into the shaded valleys below.

Out over the bay the rout was soon complete. The filmy surface fog was swept quickly backward and piled into ridges that drifted and rolled and retreated eastward, revealing the bright surface of the water. Within twenty minutes the battle was over. Thousands of people in the valleys below had been oblivious to the spectacle going on above their heads. Looking up, they could only see that it was either foggy or clearing.

By the time the sun was about to set, the bay was cleared of all but a few pockets of tule fog along the far shores, and the sea fog was moving in force across the Marin ridges. As I left the peak numb from the cold northwest wind, I could see the giant shadow of Tamalpais stretching across the bay to Carquinez and Vallejo, twenty miles away. There was still a glow of twilight on the upper slopes as I walked back down the ridge, but in the dark valleys below, the lights of the towns and villages were shining mistily through the advancing vapors from the ocean.

To innumerable people toiling in San Francisco offices, the sight of that mountain across the Golden Gate on a clear day is always a strong temptation, but in spring the attraction becomes well nigh irresistible. One bright morning in May the pile of unfinished work on my desk was reaching the point where I could not face it without a sense of panic. The mountain was shining in the spring sun, and I made the inevitable decision—or rather, some primal instinct of self-preservation made it for me. I got in the car, headed across the bridge, took the road skirting the south side of Tamalpais, parked at Pantoll, and set out at a quick pace along the Matt Davis trail around the peak's western flank.

It was one of those bright May days when the mountain seems to vibrate with life. Birds sang lustily; the grasses were refulgent green; wildflowers, after the abundant winter rains, were spread across the grassy slopes more profusely than in any previous season in memory. Still, I was unable to exorcise the compulsions of urban living. I followed the trail from the open slopes into the woods, rounded a couple of bends, and came upon a creek cascading down a ferny ravine—a perfect spot to sit on a log and watch the light on the water. But the inner time clock was not yet unwound and kept senselessly insisting that I keep moving.

Fortunately, the spell of the falling water began to overcome the corrupt influences of civilization, and I sat on the log, observing the flowing forms of the creek as it plunged down a small precipice and glissaded over a smooth boulder into a clean pool where the surface reflected dappled sunlight upward onto the leaning bole of a big maple.

The creek flowed through a natural hillside rock garden displaying a dozen shades of green—the brownish greens of a coat of mosses draped over a big boulder like velvet, the duller green of the chain fern, the pale green of the big-leafed thimbleberry, the darker greens of the laurels above, and the brilliant spring green of the new leaves on the maple, forming a back-lighted canopy over the entire garden. The sounds were hypnotic—the high-pitched purling of the cascade, the deeper note of a fall dropping into a pool, the cawing of a jay, the exuberant chatter of a sparrow, the rustling of the leaves of maple and laurel in an occasional breeze.

When I finally got up and walked down the trail, I was able to saunter rather than trot—with only fading twinges of guilt over the wasted time. Walking brought an opening in the woods; I suddenly came upon a big sloping meadow alight with color—the bright orange of the monkey flowers, the yellow of daisies, the scarlet of the trumpet flower, and the incredible blue of masses of lupine. The field of lupine seemed to change color as I watched it. Examining the plants closely, I could see the cause of this optical illusion. Each stalk of the flower carries petals of several shades, ranging from white at the tip, through pale blue, to a vibrant purple at the base. By exposing various parts of hundreds of stalks, a breeze causes the colors to change, and the white tops in the field of blue make the entire mass seem to scintillate like wind-rippled water.

I found a good spot on a grassy slope to doze in the sun, and when I opened my eyes after a few minutes I saw directly in front of me something I had failed to notice before: a perfectly formed web about eight inches in diameter, spun between three blades of grass with such engineering skill that the three stalks moved as a unit when riffled by a breeze. The web was spread like a fisherman's net to intercept whatever game might happen through that way. An iridescent-winged insect struggled haplessly in the entanglement. In the center of the web the spider waited patiently. The spider seemed to be the villain of this production, yet he was only making his living in the legitimate way nature had provided and was no more villainous, surely, than a fisherman netting his catch. As I stood up, I startled a foot-long lizard; his back was an intricate pattern of zigzagging black and yellow designs.

I wandered through groves fragrant with the spicy scent of laurels, then continued across open grassy knolls where the ocean came into view and the sweet odors of the trailside lupine were mixed with the salt smells of the sea. After a long descent through a Douglas fir grove like a big dim chamber with pillars four feet in diameter, the trail emerged onto a high rocky point with a superb panorama of the shoreline. The waves, in lines of white surf two miles long, were curving around Duxbury Reef to the beach at Stinson, where the currents have built a sand barrier across the entrance of Bolinas Lagoon. Offshore, contrasting sharply with the vast aquamarine expanse of the ocean beyond, was a long salient of brownish water that I recognized as the ebb from the Golden Gate, a current laden with silt and sand from the streams flowing into the bay and from the Sacramento and San Joaquin, the combined waters of a dozen rivers originating near California's summit peaks from Mount Shasta to Mount Whitney.

Here on this rocky promontory a thousand feet above the sea, facing the incandescent ocean, I could almost feel the geologic heaving of the earth's crust that created this spectacle. At the foot of this mountain, slicing southward into the ocean from Bolinas Lagoon and the Olema

Valley, was the San Andreas Fault. Along the colossal rift the earth's crust has moved horizontally over the eons. Here in 1906 the land on either side of the fault slid about ten feet in opposite directions in less than a second. Before long, doubtless, it will move again.

I turned back along the trail toward civilization, with its lesser dimensions of time and space. By now it seemed to me that this day on Tamalpais had been not a retreat from duty but an advance—a salutary confrontation with the real world outside the human hive.

Crossing a high ridge with a view to the south, I spotted a red-tailed hawk riding the air currents and followed him in the binoculars as he swooped against a whirling montage of sea and mountains and sky—the wave-assaulted Marin coastline to Point Bonita, the breakers pounding the cliffs at Point Lobos, the white rows of houses where San Francisco slopes slowly up from the ocean, the eucalyptus forest on Mount Davidson, and, on the far horizon, the distant peak of Loma Prieta down the Peninsula. Then the hawk seemed to top the north tower of Golden Gate Bridge and sailed upward against a backdrop of Nob Hill skyscrapers and the observatory on Mount Hamilton, seventy miles away. I lost sight of him as he disappeared against the two massive summits of Diablo.

Yosemite Valley

Trumpets of Light

Ann Zwinger (b. 1925) has written dozens of books on natural history and associated subjects. Among them are Land Above the Trees: A Guide to American Alpine Tundra *(1972) and* Run, River, Run: A Naturalist's Journey down One of the Great Rivers of the West *(1975). The following "backcountry journal" is from* Yosemite: Valley of Thunder *(1996), a book that features the photography of Kathleen Norris Cook.*

This July morning a light breeze streaks the otherwise calm surface of an alpine tarn, then dies, leaving a polished, stainless-steel skin. Yesterday my elder daughter, Susan, and I hiked eight miles into the Sierra, and twenty-five hundred feet up, into the northeast corner of the Yosemite backcountry wilderness, which brought us to this charming tarn nestled into a granite bowl at around ten thousand feet.

The sky brightens but does not heat; I enjoy earth's staging time, getting everything adjusted, ordered, before turning on the sun. By six, full sunlight stains a ridge ruddy at the far edge of the lake, reflecting in the water like warp-dyed silk. Then this July day begins with blazing trumpets of light. I've never been averse to a little glory before breakfast, and watching sunrise bestir this pond does it for me.

I suspect the real glories of Yosemite belong to the backpackers, the trudgers and trekkers, those who finish a strenuous climb and wait for their psyches to catch up, suffer a thunderstorm on an alpine fell, and most of all, let the night spirits seep into their sleep. The real glories of Yosemite belong to those who are comfortable with being uncomfortable, who know it's all right to be afraid, to be cold, wet, tired, and hungry, to be euphoric and, on occasion, ecstatic.

More than 706,000 acres, over 94 percent of the park, is managed as wilderness and can never be developed. A permit system applies to hikers and groups on horseback who plan to remain overnight, thus guaranteeing that hikers are not falling over one another or overusing one area. The park instituted a permit system because rangers counted almost five thousand campfire rings in the backcountry in 1972. The wilderness areas cope well so far with the 30 percent of the visitors who go there, perhaps because they are of a different outlook than the three million who jam into the valley and spend their time commuting between the stores at the Visitor Center and Curry Village.

Kerrick Meadow lies a little above nine thousand feet, depending on a knob here or a depression there. Laid between granite walls, the valley looks quilted in all shades of green. In this wet soil, wildflowers abound, and little apricot-colored day moths flutter up against my legs as I walk. A grasshopper with dark brown wings alights at rights angles to the sun, then ratchets off again.

Like better-known Tuolumne Meadows, Kerrick Meadow has seasonally saturated soils that maintain a water table too high for trees to grow. The meadow bears the name of James D. Kerrick, who trailed sheep here around 1880. Most of its yearly precipitation, between thirty and fifty inches, falls as snow, and the growing season seldom lasts more than nine weeks.

In the middle of Kerrick Meadow, Rancheria Creek (also probably a name used by sheepmen) flutters its way downhill on a gradual gradient. A tinsel-ribbon of water, it pauses occasionally to spread into small pools at the outside of a meander or to nibble at a bank, in no hurry to get anywhere. According to the sandy, gravelly flats alongside, its channel at high runoff sometimes widens to fifty feet. Frost heaves that make the ground expand disturb plant roots and leave bare, gravelly patches that resemble shaven spots in the lush sedge meadow that bounds the stream. These active, top layers of soil discourage plant growth and allow only the most sturdy pioneer plants, those that can withstand the thaws and freezes that unceremoniously assault their roots. These plants, like tiny daisies and lupines and bright pink pussy-paws, have many of the same adaptations as those that occupy alpine heights. They are small, close to the ground, and often densely furred with hairs.

Following the creek, Susan and I sometimes walk in a horse pack trail incised six to twelve inches below the surface. One horse concentrates more pounds per square inch and causes as much damage as twenty-five or more people. Vegetation and soil at camps where horses are tethered is impacted ten times as much as at other camps, and meadows are grazed into mud. But horse use continues because it provides easier and longer access to the backcountry.

An ominous, dark cloud to the north sits astride the valley upstream. From my perch I watch the virga, filmy veils of rain, shred down out of it. The storm crawls like a tank, filling the breadth of the canyon, scraping the granite, dragging against the ground, marching toward us with an overweening arrogance. It formed from heated air rising from the Central Valley, cooling as it rose and capturing enough moisture to form thunderheads. A grumbling muttering-in-its-beard thunder beats on the granite as if it were a tympanum, an unmistakable announcement of intent. One minute the rocks are dry, then suddenly the downpour rushes off their flanks. It rains the rest of the afternoon. It rains all night.

In the morning, watching a tent fly dry is in the same category as watching a pot boil, and the need to wait legitimizes some morning lethargy. I return to yesterday's storm-watching perch. Handfuls of moisture hang in the air, swathing everything in lingering dampness. Tiny yellow monkey flowers that would fit into a shirt button, plants maybe less than half an inch high, interweave in familial mats. The lip of each flower carries a drop of water that magnifies the red specks of its throat.

Spiny gooseberry bushes sprawl across the slope behind me, double thorns on the stems. Indians used to burn Yosemite Valley just to encourage such berry bushes to sprout, for gooseberry and other berry plants come in quicker after a burn. In more recent times, however, gooseberry and currant, shrubs of the genus *Ribes*, have been indicted as being an alternate host to white pine blister rust. Blister rust infections come in waves, usually when cool and moist conditions encourage spores to form in the gooseberry phase. For decades foresters killed gooseberries and currants to stop the spread until, in the 1960s, the rust infection was judged not to be such a threat after all. Scattered plants that escaped execution remain at higher altitudes.

While I lodgepole- and monkey-flower-watch, the sun levitates seven inches above the rock rim across the valley, and as it rises above the mists it paints sharp, clear shadows. With it comes a light breeze. I check my sleeping bag. Contrary to my pessimistic expectation of a soggy sleeping bag forever, it is dry.

Another afternoon, Susan and I hike to a higher tarn. The gravel apron around it scrunches underfoot. The water is so cold and lacking in minerals, so "pure," that no algae grow in it, no plankton, no fish.

A path crosses behind the tarn beneath its source of supply, a snowbank plastered on the scooped-out slope of granite wall a quarter mile away. Thick sedges hide threads of water that don't show up until you step into them ankle deep. At the edge of one rivulet, I spy a little half-inch tan frog with a black stripe through its eye. It hops off through skyscraper sedge—a Pacific tree frog.

After crossing the meadow, the path starts up to a divide. When it runs down again, I leave it to scramble up a bare talus slope. I intend to

go only partway to a dark rocky ridge on the horizon, but it's a Pied
Piper landscape, calling me through one more rock doorway, up one
more rise to one more interesting plant, one more different kind of
rock. I follow meekly, hypnotized, into the severe, sculptural spaces of
one of my favorite places, the alpine zone.

The dark rock outcropping is so splintered into silver-dollar pieces
that it clinks as I walk through it. The metamorphic hornfels shatters
into smaller chips than granite, contains more minerals, and is darker
and more heat absorbent than the granites, an assist to plants at cold
altitudes. The outcrop is a leftover from the metamorphics that once
completely covered the mountains. Surrounded above, below, and
alongside by pearly gray granite, the dark rock stands out as powerfully
as the clenched fist in a Rodin sculpture.

Sun shines 354 days (almost 97 percent) of the year up here, but at
the same time, it can freeze any night. Wind shaves the ground like a
straight razor. Precipitation drops to less than half an inch in July, with
August even drier. What little moisture there is comes form melting
snow.

Plants up here tend to be low cushions and mats, white phlox and
pink moss campion, tiny buckwheats and little lupines, all of which
withstand freezing and can photosynthesize at lower temperatures than
plants of lower altitude. Lupine is heavily furred, an adaptation that
lessens water loss and insulates the plant against evaporation, solar radi-
ation, and cold. Like most alpine plants, lupines are perennials. Most
annuals do not have time enough to sprout, grow, flower, and set seed in
the abbreviated growing season. Many species grow for a decade or
more before they store up enough energy to flower. Some reproduce by
vegetative means, which gives new plants a better start and an assured
source of nourishment.

Plants here take root in nearly sterile, pulverized granite, chips of
feldspar, quartz bits, and sparkly flecks of mica, with not enough organic matter in it to deserve the designation of "soil." With cold tempera-

tures and few plants, humus neither forms nor stays put on steep alpine talus slopes. Red heather, full of pink blossoms, espaliers across a rock face, preferring the acids provided by disintegrating granites. White heather nestles against a pegmatite dike full of big handsome feldspar crystals. By growing on a slight incline facing the sun, the heather receives half again more heat and light than if it grew on the flat. Creeping mats of magenta penstemons and alpine sorrel always grow along the downhill edge of rocks, capturing the runoff moisture. A dainty sandwort raises little starlike blooms with five rosy stamens hovering above five starched white petals.

Downhill, puffy patches of flake lichen tint the ground an odd and distinctive bluish-gray. Flake lichen thrives within a growing season of seven to twelve weeks and signals that this area holds snow late into the summer. Snow is more protector than growth-stopper at high altitude. On days when the wind-chill factor may drop to minus forty degrees, snow shields alpine plants from a brutal buffeting.

Upslope, narrow rivulets weep out from under a raggedy patch of snow shining like tinsel. How does a snowfield die? Rather ignominiously, I'm afraid. A beautiful expanse of pristine white snow becomes crusted with dirt and dust, its surface porous and granulated from freezing over each night, melting each day, looking like Japanese rice paper with pine needles, willow leaves, and other plant bits encased in it. These absorb enough heat to sink in a quarter inch, blackening and embedding themselves in a bezel of snow. Pink algae color teacup-sized hollows. No longer big enough to sluice a stream of icy water downhill, the snowfield drips like a dozen leaky faucets. It languishes, passing away from sun disease, a fragile Camille, a wan Traviata, a doomed Mimi, dying with operatic slowness. It goes out with neither a bang nor a whimper—just a tiny liquid tinkling, it requires the soprano of a mosquito.

As I start down, a muted clucking comes from nearby, stops, resumes. As quietly as possible, I slip out binoculars and wait. About ten feet away, close enough to see the red line above the eye, I spot a handsome male ptarmigan. About the size of a chicken, ptarmigan are an instance of Bergmann's Rule in action: creatures of cold climates tend to be larger than tropical animals, since size gives a better relationship of volume to exposed area and makes it easier to retain body heat. The bird proceeds with considerable dignity up a boulder face, snapping at flower heads, ambling up the rock to a small shady overhang. Speckled brown and white on back and wings, he blends into the dappled light under the overhang. In winter, ptarmigan turn totally white, with extravagant white pantaloons, a heavy feathering that gives extra insulation to legs and feet. Males winter above timberline, the only birds to do so in this stringent climate.

Later, after loping down a rain-greased talus slope with nothing taller in sight than I, lightning flashing and thunder banging simultaneously, a hastily donned poncho flapping, boots and pants soaked and hands stiff with cold, I finally reach a lower flat and hunker down. Just when I don't think I can get any wetter or any colder comes the hail. Stinging *petit-pois*-sized pellets insinuate themselves into every crease of my poncho, fill the puddles around my feet, and leave windrows around the rocks. What isn't already wet gets wet—soaking, irrevocably, irretrievably wet, wet from the outside and through to the other side.

At the far edge of misery a pale sun appears, not a moment too soon for this huddled mass of dripping, dirty laundry, with runny nose and squishy boots. As the last BBS of hail clear the valley, a rainbow, an incredible swatch of color, materializes against the gloomy clouds. Not your same old arch, but a rectangular banner broadcasting its blazing spectrum of color, it flutters out from under a mass of clouds in the southwest sky, undulating like northern lights.

That evening, tent pitched and trenched, clothes dry, and the comforts reestablished, I pull out the obligatory "ice-cream-and-cake-and-candle," a day-late birthday celebration for Susan: two small, slightly squashed cupcakes, one pink candle, and a packet of freeze-dried ice cream that tastes like ice cream even if it isn't cold. What's a mother for? We raise a toast of freshly filtered, very cold stream water to the pleasures of wilderness. My cup runneth over.

Waning sun, shuttered behind a pure white cloud, traces its rim with eye-blinding incandescence. Wisps of clouds radiate outward from Sawtooth Ridge like the gold rays in a baroque sculpture. Tall, dark green, narrow triangles of trees rise against a backdrop of white granite beneath a deep blue Sierran sky: unmistakably Yosemite. The sky chills to an aquamarine of limpid clarity and transparency, a cut-crystal atmosphere, before it deepens to navy blue in which stars begin to glint.

Shadows inch up the last sunlit face. With my sketchbook in my lap, I recall James D. Smillie, who published *Yellowstone to Yosemite: Early Adventures in the Mountain West* in 1872. Smillie wrote and illustrated his summer in Yosemite and with an artist's eye noted that Yosemite's granites, being so pale, are exceptionally responsive to changes in atmosphere. At sunset, he wrote that "they glow with a ruddy light, that is slowly extinguished by the upcreeping shadows of night, until the highest point flames for one moment, then dies, ashy pale, under the glory that is lifted to the sky above. Then the cold moon tips with silver those giant, sleeping forms, and by its growing light I cleared my palette, and closed the box upon my last study of the Yosemite and Sierras."

I unfold my map for the last time to check our route out tomorrow. Now its folds are worn, its edges shredded. Well used indeed. Miles calculated, elevation lines counted, meadows walked, streams crossed, heights climbed. Now, when I trace with my finger where we've been on this trip, the map lines segue into images of clumps of pines or shining tarns or mellifluous meadows. That green spot here was full of flowers and butterflies, and that blue line there was a booming waterfall, sweetened with birdsong. Those concentric ruffled circles describe the top of a dome on which I stood, those dotted blue lines the beginning of a stream that wiggled downslope.

No longer is the map two-dimensional. It is composed of height of ponderosa, breadth of valley, depth of stream, wintertime, summertime, springtime, autumntime, the vanilla smell of Jeffrey pine, the gritty feel of granite, the puckery taste of alpine sorrel, the unexpected song of a canyon wren, the senses of time, the waterfalls of the mind.

The Fourth Dimension

David Rains Wallace (b. 1945), based in Berkeley, has written nine works of natural history and two novels. One of his best books, The Klamath Knot *(1983), deals with evolution, which Wallace calls "the great myth of modern times." He explores this myth against the backdrop of the Klamath Mountains on the California-Oregon border.*

Ten years passed before I went back to the Siskiyous. During that time I walked into a number of wild places, and acquired what I thought was a fair knowledge of western mountain wilderness: of the climb from chaparral or sagebrush in the Upper Sonoran Zone; through Douglas fir, ponderosa pine, and white fir in the Transition Zone; past lodgepole pine, red fir, or Engelmann spruce in the Canadian Zone; to stunted whitebark pines and heather in the Alpine Zone. I went to a few places where there were still grizzly bear tracks as well as black bear tracks. So I didn't really expect to find much that was new when I started up the Clear Creek trail into the northern part of the high Siskiyous in June of 1979 with my down sleeping bag, gas stove, contour maps, and other sophistications. But the Siskiyous still had some things to show me.

I knew the Siskiyous are among the richest botanical areas of the

West, and I soon saw evidence of this as I followed Clear Creek upstream. Tributary ravines contained so much blossoming azalea that the forest often smelled like a roomful of fancy women, and rhododendrons were in flower on one flat bench. There were more orchids than I'd seen anywhere. California lady's slippers hung over one rivulet like tiny Japanese lanterns dipped in honey, and I found three species of coralroot, red and orange orchids that have no green leaves, lacking chlorophyll. Farther up the trail, where snow had melted recently, pink calypso orchids had just burst through the pine duff.

The forest that overshadowed these flowers was the most diverse I'd seen west of the Mississippi. Besides the Douglas fir, tan oak, madrone, golden chinquapin, and goldencup oak I had expected just east of the coastal crest, I found ponderosa pine, Jeffrey pine, sugar pine, western white pine, knobcone pine, and incense cedar. Moist ravines were full of Port Orford cedar, a lacy-foliaged tree which fluted bark like a redwood's. The diversity became confusing; it seemed I had to consult my tree field guide every few minutes.

As I climbed higher, I kept expecting this unwonted diversity to sort itself out into the usual altitudinal zones, waiting for white fir, ponderosa pine, and incense cedar to close ranks against the confusion. But it didn't happen. Douglas fir kept playing its polymorphous tricks, its foliage sometimes resembling the flattened needles of white fir, sometimes dangling like the branches of weeping spruce. I got a stiff neck looking up to see if cones hung downward, denoting Douglas fir, or stood upright, denoting white fir (or perhaps silver fir, grand fir, or noble fir, three other species found in the Klamaths).

Broad-leaved madrone and tan oak disappeared obligingly after I reached a certain altitude, but then new species appeared. I found western yew, a sturdy little tree resembling a miniature redwood, and Sadler's oak, another small tree whose serrated leaves reminded me of the chestnut oaks I'd known in the Midwest. I passed a grove of lodgepole pines, and these austere trees, which typically grow on bleak, windswept terrain, looked out of place in all the effulgent variety. The trees were sorted out somewhat according to soil conditions, but these distinctions were patchy and vague, offering cold comfort to my organizing instincts.

After two days of walking, I stood on the slopes of Preston Peak, which is 7,309 feet above sea level at its summit but seems higher as it thrusts abruptly above the forested ridges. I was surprised, on looking around at the snow-stunted trees on the glacial moraine where I stood, to find they were the same species that had accompanied me from the Klamath River: Douglas fir, ponderosa pine, incense cedar, western yew, Sadler's oak, white fir. Even goldencup oak, golden chinquapin, and bay laurel grew there at about 5,000 feet, albeit in shrubby form.

Clearly, there was something odd about the Siskiyou forest. For so many species to grow all over a mountain range simply doesn't conform to respectable western life-zone patterns. It is more like some untidy temperate deciduous forest or tropical rainforest, species promiscuously tumbled together without regard for ecological proprieties.

The high Siskiyou forest is a rare remnant of a much lusher past. Fossils of trees almost identical to those of the Siskiyous have been dug from twelve-million-year-old, Pliocene epoch sediments in what are now the deserts of Idaho and eastern Oregon. Fossils of trees not at all unlike Siskiyou species have been found in *forty*-million-year-old sediments in Alaska. In that epoch, the Eocene, a temperate forest surpassing any living today covered the northern half of this continent from coast to coast. Redwoods, pines, firs, and cedars grew with hickories, beeches, magnolias, and other hardwoods not found within a thousand miles of the Pacific Ocean today, and with ginkgoes, dawn redwoods, and other trees that don't even grow naturally in North America anymore. It is hard to imagine such a forest: it sounds like poets' descriptions of Eden. After the Eocene, though, the climate became cooler and drier; and this gradually drove the forest southward, and split it in half. Deciduous hardwoods migrated southeast, where the summer rain they needed was still available, while many conifers migrated southwest to cover the growing Rocky Mountain and Pacific Coast ranges. Ginkgoes and dawn redwoods fell by the wayside during this "long march," which has resulted in our present, relatively impoverished forests, where trees that once grew together are separated by wide prairies and plains.

There is still one area west of the Rockies, however, where rainfall and temperatures approximate the benign Eocene environment: the inner coastal ranges of southwest Oregon and northwest California, the Klamath Mountains. In the Klamaths, winters are mild enough and summers moist enough for species to grow together that elsewhere are segregated by altitude or latitude. Several species that once grew throughout the West now survive only in the Klamaths. Perched on my Siskiyou eminence, I again felt suspended over great gulfs of time. The stunted little trees and their giant relatives on the lower slopes were not a mere oddity forest where ill-assorted species came together in a meaningless jumble. They were in a sense the ancestors of all western forests, the rich gene pool from which the less varied, modern conifer forests have marched out to conquer forbidding heights from Montana to New Mexico. Looking out over the pyramidal Siskiyou ridges, I was seeing a community of trees at least forty million years old.

Later that day something hair-raising happened. There were still some patches of snow, and I had walked across one on the way to my campsite. After dinner I wandered back past that patch and found, punched deeply into each of my vibram-soled footprints, the tracks of a large bear. It probably had been foraging in Rattlesnake Meadow, heard me coming, and took the trail downhill to escape my intrusion. A simple coincidence, but it caused a sudden feeling of emptiness at the pit of my stomach, as though I were riding a fast elevator. It seemed the lesson begun ten years before was proceeding: from a realization that the world is much greater and older than normal human perception of it, to a reminder that the human is a participant as well as a perceiver in the ancient continuum of bears and forests. I was used to walking in bear tracks by this time; it was instructive to find that a bear also could walk in mine.

The Siskiyous weren't through with me. I got sick the next day for some reason, probably fatigue. I'd been living in the Midwest for three years and had grown unaccustomed to running around on mountains. It was thought-provoking to lie in the wilderness that night with the suspicion that I might have been about to have a heart attack. I had many sleepless hours to wonder why I kept going to places like the Siskiyous when so many civilized places were so much easier to get to. I'm not all *that* crazy about exercise. Wilderness areas are certainly among the most beautiful places on the planet, but I wonder if this alone is enough to explain the fascination many people feel for them, or the difficulties and real suffering they endure to reach them. I thought of Audubon, feverish and vomiting from tainted turkey meat in the trackless Ohio forest; Thoreau dragging his tuberculosis to the Minnesota frontier; Muir stumbling with frostbite across Mount Shasta's glaciers. I may have been delirious: my mind started reeling through history—tribal youths starving on mountaintops for totem visions, Taoist sages living on nettles and mushrooms in Chinese caves, Hebrew prophets eating locusts and wild honey on the Sinai peninsula, elderly Brahmins leaving comfortable estates to wander the Bengali jungle.

I wondered if my motives for going into wilderness might be more obscure, and more profound, than I had realized. While part of me was going into the mountains seeking the pleasures of exercise, self-reliance, accomplishment, and natural history, it seemed that another part was looking for things of which I had only a vague conscious awareness, as though a remote mountain or desert releases some innate human behavior, a kind of instinctive predilection for the mysterious.

So many major structures of belief have arisen at least in part from experiences in wilderness. This was to be expected with the oldest structures, such as animism and shamanism, since the entire world outside a Paleolithic camp was wilderness. But why should all the major religions of the modern world include a crucial encounter with wilderness—Moses, Jesus, and Mohammed in the desert mountains, Siddhartha in the jungle? And why should the predominant modern view of the original development of life have arisen from the five-year wilderness voyage of a Victorian amateur naturalist named Charles Darwin? There evidently is more to wilderness than meets the eye— more than water, timber, minerals, the materials of physical civilized existence. Somehow there are mental trees, streams, and rocks—psychic raw materials from which every age has cut, dammed, or quarried an invisible civilization—an imaginative world of origins and meanings— what one might call a mythology. . . .

The Klamath Mountains are an exceptionally rich storehouse of evolutionary stories, one of the rare places where past and present have not been severed as sharply as in most of North America, where glaciation, desertification, urbanization, and other ecological upheavals have been muted by a combination of rugged terrain and relatively benign climate. Klamath rocks are older than those of the California and Oregon coast ranges to the south and north or those of the Cascades in the east. They are more intricately and tortuously folded, faulted, and upthrust, forming a knot of jagged peaks and steep gorges less modified by civilization than other areas, even though they are only a day's drive from large cities. The Klamaths are not even very high as mountains go, with no peaks over ten thousand feet.

The relatively low elevation of the Klamaths, compared to the Cascades or Sierra Nevada, has caused them to be overlooked. Naturalists often say that the Klamaths are a combination of Sierra Nevada and Cascades ecosystems because the Klamaths contain species found in both other wilderness regions. This is a little like saying that a person is a combination of his brother and sister because he shares genes with both siblings. The Klamaths have a character of their own, although not perhaps as ingratiating a character as the graceful volcanic cones of the Cascades or the clean alpine country of the Sierra. There is something wizened about the Klamaths. Their canyons do not have sparkling granite walls and wide river meadows as do the U-shaped, glaciated canyons of the Sierra. Klamath canyons are preglacial, and uncompromisingly V-shaped. They've never been scoured into spaciousness by the ice flows. They seem to drop down forever, slope after forest-smothered slope, to straitened, boulder-strewn bottoms so noisy with waters and shadowed by vegetation that they may bring startling dreams and uneasy thoughts to campers.

Early explorers were stymied by these canyons. In 1828 Jedediah Smith and his party of fur trappers gave up in despair when they tried to follow the Klamath River upstream from its confluence with the Trinity River. The terrain was too rugged even for those mountain men, who had walked from Oregon to Los Angeles in search of beaver. They didn't find many beaver in Klamath Mountain rivers, which are generally too rocky and turbulent even for those ingenious rodents. The fur trappers called the Klamaths "backward," a pretty definitive judgment coming from backwoodsmen who crossed the Sierra and Cascades, not to mention the Rockies, a half-century before the railroads.

More than any other wild region I've known, the Klamaths have a venerable quality which is not synonymous with "pristine," "unspoiled," or other adjectives commonly applied to natural areas. Certainly the Klamaths are as unpolluted as any American place these days. But these adjectives imply something of the smoothness and plumpness of youth, whereas the Klamaths are marked by the wrinkles and leanness of great age. Although their peaks and high plateaus have been marked by glaciers, they are at heart preglacial mountains, with elements of flora and fauna that reach back farther into the past than any place west of the Mississippi River. The Klamaths seem so old, in fact, that I'd call them a grandparent of the Sierra and Cascades instead of a sibling.

This venerable quality is strongest in the region's National Forest wilderness areas: the Rogue River gorge and the jumbled red humps of the Kalmiopsis to the north, the jagged peaks of the high Siskiyous and Red Buttes, the huge massifs of the Marble Mountains and Salmon-Trinity Alps, the gentle but hulking summits of the Yolla Bollys to the south. (The Yolla Bollys aren't entirely within the Klamath Mountain geological province, but I include them because they're ecologically linked to the other ranges.) Wilderness in the Klamaths is still dwindling from logging and other developments, as it was when I found hiking trails so elusive in 1969, but I hope enough will eventually be protected to assure they will remain an outstanding vantage point into what I perceived during my first visit as the fourth dimension of life.

Climbing Half Dome

Daniel Duane (b. 1967) has recorded his ascents of the Northwest Face of Half Dome and the Nose route on El Capitan in his first book, Lighting Out: A Vision of California and the Mountains *(1994). He has also written about surfing in* Caught Inside: A Surfer's Year on the Pacific Coast *(1996). Duane, who earned his Ph.D. in English in 1996, lives in Santa Cruz.*

No sound disturbed the natural quarry below Half Dome. In predawn light, I smeared cream cheese on a flattened onion bagel and looked out over the whole of Yosemite Valley. A surprising view from so high above, from a place I had until now only looked up to: the right wall of the valley was an ordered row of forms: Washington, Column, the Royal Arches, Yosemite Falls, the Three Brothers, and El Capitan; the left—Glacier Point, Sentinel Rock, and the Cathedral Group. Even at five A.M. the air held midsummer heat, dried sweat and dust caked my skin from the previous night's approach, and my shoulders still ached from the load. As I ate, my own stench overpowered the blandness of the bagel. I chewed slowly and looked around at the Northwest Face—there was nothing that baffled me about the wall's beauty. So out of human scale and yet so well formed, so sculpted. A vast field of fallen boulders lay along its base, like so many sculptor's shavings from a work in progress.

Nick organized the haul bag quickly, and soon we had lifted off. Half Dome wasn't so much smaller than El Cap—twenty-six pitches by comparison to thirty-two—but somehow it seemed far more manageable, less steep, and less difficult. We climbed steadily and well on familiar gray granite, deep inside corners and cracks. Perhaps because the sun didn't strike the Northwest Face until noon, and the air remained still, the wall felt like a vast and empty indoor cathedral. We ran our rope systems, made moves well within our abilities, and were soon well off the ground. Sound took on a singular quality—even with Nick a hundred feet above, every little tap of metal on stone, every scuffle of shoe, his deep breaths and occasional remarks—each and every noise echoed alone like lonely footsteps in a huge stone hall.

At a ledge a few hundred feet up, light just breaking into the sky, I prepared for my first lead of the morning. Nick sat against the rock and looked blankly out over the high country; the haul bag was perched next to him, leaning against the wall. I dismantled the pulley system and clipped the haul line into my harness to take it up with me. Then the haul bag teetered back. Nick looked up and reached for it too late, and then it was gone. Well over a hundred pounds. We both grabbed reflexively for the rope; my hand caught it and instantly slammed back against the rock and split open. The rope burned skin off my thigh as coils flipped off the ledge. The bag had a hundred and sixty-five feet to fall before it would impact my harness. Nick and I stared at each other and waited for the inevitable. I wrapped my hands around the anchor webbing and held on.

The jolt slammed me down into the ledge, then stopped. My harness had held the fall. Nick's knuckles were raw. The bag was intact. My right hand bled down into my wrist. So close to blowing the whole climb. We looked at each other in disbelief: had he forgotten to clip it to the anchor? Had I unclipped the wrong knot? It didn't matter much, and we barely spoke of the incident; we just hauled the bag back in and went on with our work.

Hours and hours of quiet climbing in the still shade; hauling, belaying, jumaring, climbing, hauling, clipping and unclipping, reclipping and untying, backing up and reorganizing, rambling up across the tower toward the wall. Alternately lost in the sheer pleasure of motion and then drifting in the emptiness of waiting. Sitting on some little ledge high over the world and just staring. I never had many thoughts at belay ledges on long climbs. I didn't ruminate on what lay below or come to new clarity about my life. The task so absorbed me and the fatigue so calmed me that I really just looked and occasionally even just saw.

We'd exchange a few words here and there about equipment or ropes or which way the route went, but I loved the feeling that very little needed saying. We'd been climbing together for a while and knew each other well. Nick had decided that cities were crowded with psychic static; he said in a pause at a ledge that high places got him above the web of noise, especially his own. And for me Half Dome, unlike El Capitan, was charted territory. My father had been here, had climbed every inch of this rock and saw it as one of his happiest experiences.

Late in the day, at pitch eight of twenty-six, Nick led out across narrow but walkable ledges and began the Robbins Traverse, where Royal Robbins had taken the first ascent team off the tower and out onto the Northwest Face. Then, with my feet in aiders, I moved as fast as I could on ancient, strange-looking bolts—fat nails driven into spread-out sheaths. Only a few of the bolts had hangers, and even those were only partially bent pieces of aluminum. The last of the bolts was so bent out of the rock it was hard to imagine much was left inside.

In the early evening we reached our bivouac ledge at pitch eleven—a thirty-foot long, three-foot wide notch formed by a massive exfoliating flake.

"Sweet, huh?" Nick said.

After a short break, we decided to fix a line or two ahead so we could get a good start in the morning. I scrambled up to where blocks lay wedged in the opening of a chimney. Stepping across them I could hear sand and pebbles drop into the chasm. Somewhere in the darkness below, light leaked in from a crack. My pitch went well—easy aid, t.c.u.'s, fixed pieces in a beautiful white corner to the left of the chimney.

I leaned back and looked about. The crack was lined with old fixed pins; the face to either side was blank. As Nick started leading the next pitch, it became clear how tired he was—too much pro, thrashing around, stepping clumsily. At last he hung from a piece and looked back down at me with a smile.

"I'm out of here," he said.

"The whole route?" I couldn't believe my ears.

"Relax, bro. Just this pitch. Let's eat." We slid back down our skinny ropes and stumbled across blocks back to the vaguely comfortable part of the ledge. Everything came out of the bag. Feet came out of sweaty, torturous rock shoes and into clean socks. No point in so much as standing up—nowhere to walk, and everything an arm's reach away. I pulled out our dinner and started getting depressed. . . . We'd bought our food in a Berkeley health food store, and had gotten on a clean fuels kick. So we had nothing but dried this, dried that, bread, cheese, nuts, seeds—nothing that felt like a fitting meal after a hard day's work.

"Dude," Nick had his head under a rock, was reaching for something. "Check it out. Treasure!" Four full cans had been abandoned by some retreating party—blueberries, clam chowder, Spaghettios, Dinosaurs with Meatballs. Stunning good fortune—the ultimate Wall Food. I couldn't believe I hadn't thought of cans before. Nick demanded the Spaghettios, so I gladly took the Dinosaurs. The fat had congealed beautifully in the top of the can and I scooped it into my mouth with an old piton. The blueberries occupied nearly an hour as we sucked then down one by one.

A red glow rose out of the horizon and Yosemite Valley three thousand feet below softened and seemed of a piece, a valley proper. The distinct monoliths fell into a pattern of overlapping slopes and walls.

Darkness filled the valley from below as the harsh white of sun on granite faded into soft, deep grays. Lights appeared, marking Curry and Yosemite Villages. Faint car headlights crawling through the trees actually looked homey and pleasant.

I'd always though that bivies up that high should be wild, dangerous, somehow violent and disorderly. Nothing could have been farther from the truth. The wind stopped and the valley's warm air rose as a soft breeze. No valley tour busses roared, no traffic honked and smoked. No sound, no wind. Just warm air. Darkness obscured the wild exposure of our perch; it seemed a natural, even exquisite place to be.

I flaked ropes between blocks to make a bed, grinning like an idiot, almost crying with pleasure at the thought of sleep. My back, legs, arms, neck, and chest burned sore; my hands were swollen, raw, and scabbed. My extra clothing filled another spot, and the tent fly filled another. When at last I lay down I felt so heavy that rolling over and dangling in the void never occurred to me as a danger. I sank into the crevice in the rocks, comfortably lodged. But for a full hour after dark, I couldn't sleep. There was too much beauty to see, too striking and unique a view, so much precious sky. A perfect place attained by perfect means, by adequate struggle. Each time I began to fade, I wanted a last look; I whispered the whole scene out loud to myself, panting lightly as I spoke, mouthing the colors, the feeling of the warmth, the unbelievable quiet and stillness and my own attendant tiredness. I told myself the whole scene again and again to remember everything.

I opened my eyes in the middle of the night, that vast wild wall just a quiet, immobile place. The full moon, out of sight behind Half Dome, washed the sweeping granite apron of Glacier Point in cold white light. And then I realized what was before me: a moonshadow of Half Dome formed in the middle of the glow, a perfect projection of its curves on the apron. It occurred to me that these mountains always etched themselves across one another by sun and by moon, by shadow, dawn and dusk, and that for that moment on that night I lay with a blessed point of view between. Soon the shadow blurred and merged with the wider brushing of moonlight; before the moon itself rose into sight from behind the dome, I had fallen asleep.

When Nick's watch alarm beeped, the sky had iced over with light and the full moon had faded. I sat up in my sleeping bag and turned so my back was against the wall and my feet off the edge. We looked about for a while, faced once again where we were. Nick fished out our ration of bagels. I drank a whole liter of water mixed with electrolyte supplements. We were slow getting moving, but when we were both well awake, stretched and warmed, we packed the terrific mess back into the haul bag and started climbing.

I felt like a fish on a line as I thrashed up our fixed ropes in a flaring chimney. For the first lead of the day, I groveled into a miserable fissure and lost confidence—aiding behind an expanding flake at the back of another chimney. I could barely turn my head around because of my helmet. Loose rock threatened to fall and kill Nick. I asked him to lower me down to clean a piece because the rope drag was stopping my upward motion.

"You can't just haul enough up?" Nick asked. "Come on, just try to haul it. It'll take forever to lower you." I looked around, already drained, worn out, tried to pull some more rope and couldn't. I got planted on a small ledge and did a full leg-press—a foot of rope came. Another press, another foot, and then I could build the anchor and relax. The day went as smoothly as the one before, and Nick and I began to talk and yell at each other, to laugh at what an absurdity it was.

We reached our bivouac—Big Sandy Ledge—at 3:30 with a storm gathering in the high mountains. We'd just dropped our gear on the ledge and sat down when three climbers popped up and hooted with delight at the sight of the approaching clouds—without bivy gear, rain gear, or food. They'd left the car at Curry Village at 9:00 A.M. that same day and had walked eight miles and climbed seventeen pitches since: bearded, sweating, psychotic superhardmen having the time of their lives.

I admitted to one of them that I thought Nick and I might be in for a wild night on the ledge—looked like a big storm coming in; lightning flashed in the distance.

"But you'll have the greatest story to tell," he said, looking around at the sky, "and the bettys'll just be like 'give me your throbbing member.'" He was gone. Up the cracks called the zigzags. For a few hours later we could hear them yelling at each other.

With hours to kill till dark we sat on the ledge and stared, peed on different terraces, looked off into the sun for hours, watched a slow changing of the day, took turns shitting into paper bags and hurling them into space. Nick didn't even clear the ledge. Quite a mess. The storm moved overhead and deep booms and cracks sent us scampering for rain gear. Lightning charged into peaks, a black curtain of rain deluged Tenaya Canyon only a half mile away. Nick giggled with nervous anticipation, apparently hoping for the thrill. We were well anchored down, had plenty of warm clothing and rain gear, and these storms rarely lasted more than a few hours. So let us have it. Blow us off the mountain.

And then the storm pulled back, just like that, and left us with a long beautiful afternoon. Sleep was again difficult because of the beauty of the night. I watched meteors, picked out constellations, leaned over to look at the valley again and again, thinking about my dad sleeping here. We woke up late, had a slow breakfast, and mosied up the zigzags. After an hour and a half, we reached Thank God Ledge, which ran left for fifty feet. I'd seen pictures of my dad on Thank God Ledge, crawling like a lowly rat. Rather undignified. I'd bet him ten dollars I'd walk the whole thing. Nick got out the camera.

I walked right out there, no sweat. Shuffling along like a man. I could swear the ledge started narrowing a bit, but I kept walking just the same. The wall was pretty vertical above and below, and the valley floor was almost four thousand feet beneath my feet, but I just put one foot in front of the other. After ten feet or so, I turned to face the wall—spread my arms out flat against it and shuffled sideways with my cheek pressed flat—just to be safe. I mean, after all, at least I was still behaving like a biped. Five feet later, I sank right down to my knees and never looked back. The hell with it. Nick shot three frames of my retreating behind.

As we approached the summit, a few tourists looked down and waved. Under great alpine peaks—snowy pinnacles in the stratosphere —the tops of Yosemite walls feel more like endings than goals, they remind you that the great part was being on the route, not, as [my friend] Aaron [Lehrman] would say, having done it. At last I scrambled up a rather mundane series of ramps and stood on top. Hikers who'd come up the cable staircase milled about. A startled teenage girl in cutoff Levis and a bikini top looked at my haggard face and said,

"Did you just come up that way?"

Great question. God, what a good question. Thank you so much for asking that question. "Well, ah, yes. Now that you mention it, I did."

She looked at me, then off the edge.

"Rad," she said. She spun on her heels and walked away, apparently having changed the channel.

On that high mesa of exfoliating granite, overweight marmots scavenged in unattended backpacks and the twenty or thirty people sitting around spoke quietly as if in a museum. A wind blew across the summit and out into the air over the valley. Kids had their pictures taken on the diving board—a thin block that stuck straight out over the abyss. Nick lay on his belly and looked over the edge back down on the route. He yelled at me to join him, but I couldn't do it—too acute a sense of gravity.

The eight miles home were all downhill, and we ran almost the whole way, fast and stumbling, trying to make the showers before closing. Down the mist trail—steep riprapping, pounding on the knees, the fabulous torrent of Nevada Falls, and the green meadow at its base— utterly unlike the surrounding plants. Vernal Falls was a wild column of water framed by moss and ferns, and its staircase trail, absolutely paved, suggested an Inca trail. At last, into the human zoo of Curry Village for showers. After washing off the whole experience, we went to the Loft Restaurant, where a Dutch milkmaiden of a girl served us hamburgers.

"Why you guys so thirsty?" she asked. "Half Dome? The Regular Route? Oh yeah, my boyfriend and I did a one-day winter ascent. It was so great."

We slept in our clean cotton T-shirts and jeans in the back of the truck. Coffee milkshakes at ten A.M., and then back to Berkeley. A Big Wall.

THE HILLS AND VALLEYS

Salinas Valley

Into the Valley

William H. Brewer (1828–1910), as the field leader of the first California Geological Survey, headed by Josiah Dwight Whitney, traveled throughout the state during the early 1860s. His letters home were stitched together by Francis Farquhar into what would become a California classic, Up and Down California in 1860–64, *not published until 1930 — seventy years after it was written, twenty years after Brewer's death.*

Monday morning, April 29, [1861,] . . . we crossed the San Luis Pass of the Santa Lucia Mountains, a pass about 1,500 or 1,800 feet high, and entered the Santa Margarita Valley. North of the Santa Lucia chain, which trends off to the northwest and ends at Monterey, lies the valley of Salinas, a valley running northwest, widening toward its mouth, and at least a hundred and fifty miles long. The valley branches above. One branch, the west, is the Santa Margarita, into which we descended from the San Luis Pass. We followed down this valley to near its junction with the Salinas River and camped at the Atascadero Ranch, about twenty-two miles from San Luis Obispo and six from the Mission of Santa Margarita.

On passing the Santa Lucia the entire aspect of the country changed. It was as if we had passed into another land and another clime. The

Salinas Valley thus far is much less verdant than we anticipated. There are more trees but less grass. Imagine a plain ten to twenty miles wide, cut up by valleys into summits of nearly the same level, their sides rounded into gentle slopes. The soil is already dry and parched, the grass already as dry as hay, except along streams, the hills brown as a stubble field. But scattered over these hills and in these valleys are trees every few rods—great oaks, often of immense size, ten, twelve, eighteen, and more feet in circumference, but not high; their widespreading branches making heads often over a hundred feet in diameter—of the deepest green foliage—while from every branch hangs a trailing lichen, often several feet long and delicate as lace. In passing over this country, every hill and valley presents a new view of these trees—here a park, there a vista with the blue mountains ahead. I would never tire of watching some of these beautiful places of natural scenery. A few pines were seen for several miles, with a very open, airy habit, entirely unlike any pine I have ever seen before, even lighter and airier than the Italian pines common in southern France by the Mediterranean. They cast but little shade.

Camp No. 29, Jolon Ranch, on San Antonio River

I did not write last Sunday as there was an American ranch near our camp and we borrowed some magazines, rare luxuries for camp, and I read them all day. The American who has this ranch keeps fifteen or sixteen thousand sheep. He is a very gentlemanly Virginian and was very kind to us. He says that the loss of sheep by wolves, bears, and rattlesnakes is quite an item. We are in a bear region. Three men have been killed within a year near our last camp by grizzlies.

Monday we came on here, about twenty-five miles. The day was intensely hot, and as we rode over the dry roads the sun was scorching. We crossed a ridge by a horrible road and came into the valley of the San Antonio, a small branch of the Salinas, and followed up it to this point, where we are camped on its bank. We passed but one ranch and house in the twenty-five miles. In one place, two bears had followed the

road some distance the night before—their tracks were very plain in the
dust. . . .

The last two days we have been exploring the hills. Yesterday, with
Averill, I climbed some hills. Today he had to go to a store a few miles
distant for flour, so I took a long tramp of eighteen to twenty miles
alone. We got an early breakfast, and I started in the cool of the morning, with a bag of lunch, compass, canteen of water, and knife, pistol,
and hammer in belt. As one is so liable to find bears and lions here, it is
not well to be without arms. I pushed back over the hills and through
canyons about ten miles from camp to the chain of rugged mountains
west of us. I was indeed alone in the solitudes. The way led up a canyon
about four miles, with high steep hills on each side, then a ridge to be
crossed, from which I had a fine view, then down again and among gentle hills about three miles farther to the base of the mountains. Here a
stream was crossed by pulling off boots and wading, and then up a
canyon into the mountains. This last I followed as far as I considered
safe, for it was just the place for grizzlies, and I kept a sharp lookout.

Here I climbed a ridge to get a view behind. The slope was very
steep, the soil hot, no wind, and the sun like a furnace. I got the view
and information I desired. A very rugged landscape of mountains
behind, steep, rocky, black with chaparral, 3,500 to 4,000 feet high. In
front was the series of ridges I had crossed; beyond, the Salinas Valley,
with blue mountains on the distant eastern horizon. Some very peculiar
rocky pinnacles of brown rock rose like spires near me, several hundred
feet high—naked rocks. . . .

The grizzly bear is much more dreaded than I had any idea of. A
wounded grizzly is much more to be feared than even a lion; a tiger is
not more ferocious. They will kill and eat sheep, oxen, and horses, are
as swift as a horse, of immense strength, quick though clumsy, and very
tenacious of life. A man stands a slight chance if he wounds a bear, but
not mortally, and a shot must be well directed to kill. The universal
advice by everybody is to let them alone if we see them, unless we are
well prepared for battle and have experienced hunters along. They will

generally let men alone, unless attacked, so I have no serious fears of them.

Less common than bear are the California lions, a sort of panther, about the color of a lion, and size of a small tiger, but with longer body. They are very savage, and I have heard of a number of cases of their killing men. But don't be alarmed on my account—I don't court adventures with any such strangers. Deer are quite common. Formerly there were many antelope, but they are very rapidly disappearing. We have seen none yet. Rabbits and hares abound; a dozen to fifty we often see in a single day, and during winter ate many of them.

There are many birds of great beauty. One finds the representatives of various lands and climes. Not only the crow, but also the raven is found, precisely like the European bird; there are turkey-buzzards, also a large vulture something like the condor—an immense bird. Owls are very plenty, and the cries of several kinds are often heard the same night. Hawks, of various sizes and kinds and very tame, live on the numerous squirrels and gophers. I see a great variety of birds with beautiful plumage, from hummingbirds up.

But it is in reptile and insect life that this country stands preeminent. There are snakes of many species, and some of large size, generally harmless, but a few venomous. Several species of large lizards are very abundant. Salamanders and chameleons are dodging around every log and basking on every stone. Hundreds or thousands may be seen in a day, from three inches to a foot long. Some strange species are covered with horns like the horned frogs.

But insects are the most numerous. They swarm everywhere. House flies were as abundant in our tent in winter as at home in summer. Ticks and bugs get on us whenever we go in the woods. Just where we are now camped there are myriads of bugs in the ground, not poisonous, but annoying by their running over one. Last night I could scarcely sleep, and shook perhaps a hundred or two hundred out of my blankets this morning.

I shall sleep outdoors tonight—in fact, all the rest are asleep but me, and only one is in the tent. We are under some cottonwood trees, which so swarm with ladybugs that Mike yesterday counted how many he brushed off of him in an hour. They amounted to 250—but he sat still under the tree. Scorpions occur farther south and are much dreaded. The equally dreaded tarantula abounds here. It is an enormous spider, larger than a large bumblebee, and has teeth as large as a rattlesnake's. I killed one by our tent at Camp 27, and saved his teeth as a curiosity. Their holes in the ground are most ingenious.

Camp 31, Guadalupe Ranch, May 12

We left San Antonio Thursday morning, May 9, and followed up the valley a few miles, then crossed a high steep ridge over one thousand feet high, which separates the San Antonio from the Salinas, and then descended and struck down the great Salinas plain. Dry as had been the region for the last sixty or seventy miles, it was nothing to this plain.

The Salinas Valley for a hundred or more miles from the sea, up to the San Antonio hills, is a great plain ten to thirty miles wide. Great stretches are almost perfectly level, or have a very slight slope from the mountains to the river which winds through it. The ground was dry and parched and the very scanty grass was entirely dry. One saw no signs of vegetation at the first glance—that is, no green thing on the plain—so a belt of timber by the stream, from twenty to a hundred rods wide, stood out as a band of the liveliest green in this waste. The mouth of this valley opens into Monterey Bay, like a funnel, and the northwest wind from the Pacific draws up through this heated flue, with terrible force. Wherever we have found a valley opening to the northwest, we have found these winds, fierce in the afternoon. For over fifty miles we must face it on this plain. Sometimes it would nearly sweep us from our mules—it seemed as if nothing could stand its force. The air was filled with dry dust and sand, so that we could not see the hills at the sides, the fine sand stinging our faces like shot, the air as dry as if it had come from a furnace, but not so very hot—it is wonderfully parching. The poor feed and this parching wind reduced our mules in a few days as much as two weeks' hard work would. Our lips cracked and bled, our eyes were bloodshot, and skins smarting.

We stopped for lunch at a point where the mules could descend to the river. A high terrace, or bluff, skirts the present river—that is, the plain lies from 75 to 100 feet above the present river. The mules picked some scanty herbage at the base of the bluff; we took our lunch in the hot sun and piercing wind, then drove on. We pulled off from the road a mile or so at night, and stopped beneath a bluff near the river. We had slept in the open air the previous night and did so again. It runs very cold during the clear nights, yet so dry was it that no dew fell those two nights, cold as it was! The mules found some picking where you would think that a sheep or a goat would starve.

Friday we pushed on all day, facing the wind. We met a train of seven wagons, with tents and beds—a party of twenty-five or thirty persons from San Jose going to the hot springs, some on horseback. Two-thirds were ladies. A curious way for a "fashionable trip to the springs," you say, but it is the style here. They will camp there and have a grand time, I will warrant. We kept to the left bank of the river, through the Mission Soledad. Before reaching it we crossed the sandy bed of a dry creek, where the sand drifted like snow and piled up behind and among the bushes like snowbanks.

The Mission Soledad is a sorry looking place, all ruins—a single house, or at most two, are inhabited. We saw the sign up, "Soledad Store," and went in, got some crackers at twenty-five cents a pound, and went on. Quite extensive ruins surround the place, empty buildings, roofless walls of adobe, and piles of clay, once walls. It looked very desolate. I do not know where they got their water in former times, but it is dry enough now. We came on seventeen miles farther. Here we find tolerable feed and a spring of poor water, so here is a ranch.

Sorry as has been this picture, it is not overdrawn, yet all this land is occupied as "ranches" under Spanish grants. Cattle are watered at the river and feed on the plains, and scanty as is the feed, thousands are kept on this space, which must be at least four to six thousand square miles, counting way back to the Santa Lucia Mountains. The ranches do not cover all this, but cover the water, which is the same thing. We could see a house by the river every fifteen to eighteen miles, and saw frequent herds of cattle. The season is unusually dry, and the plain seems much poorer than it really is. In the spring, two months ago, it was all green, and must have been of exceeding beauty. With water this would be finer than the Rhine Valley itself; as it is, it is half desert. . . .

Yesterday I climbed the ridge southwest of camp. I ascended about 8,000 or 8,500 feet, a hard climb, and had a good view of over a hundred miles of the Salinas Valley from the Bay of Monterey to above where we last struck it, or over the extreme limits of about 130 to 150 miles, with the successive ridges beyond. Four thousand to seven thousand square miles must have been spread out before me. I have never been in a land before with so many extensive views—the wide valley, brown and dry, the green belt of timber winding through it, like a green ribbon, the mountains beyond, dried and gray at the base, and deep green with chaparral on their sides and summits, with ridge after ridge stretching away beyond in the blue distance. Then to the north, a landscape I had not seen before, with the whole Bay of Monterey in the northwest. To the west and south of me was the very rugged and forbidding chain of mountains that extends from Monterey along the coast to San Luis Obispo and there trends more easterly—the Sierra Santa Lucia.

I have found much of intense geological interest during the last two weeks. I had intended to spend at least two weeks more in this valley had we found water or feed as we expected. Not finding it, and having four weeks on our hands before the rendezvous with Professor Whitney at San Juan, I decided to push on to Monterey, which I had not intended to visit. We are now within eight or ten leagues of there—will be there in a few days. I feel now that we are indeed working north, and I long to be in San Francisco again. It is now over five months since I have attended church (Protestant), and have only had that privilege three times since I left New York.

Sunday Evening

Today has been a windier day on the plain than any other day we were on it. I am glad enough we are sheltered here in camp. Clouds of gray dust, rising to the height of five or six thousand feet, have shut out the view in the north all this afternoon, and even the hills opposite could not be seen at times, and all day they have been obscurely seen through this veil. If it is thus in May, what must it be here in July or August, as no rain will fall for at least four months yet! It was interesting yesterday, while on the peaks above, to watch the great current of air up the valley, increasing with the day until at last the valley seemed filled with gray smoke.

While speaking of the plain I forgot to mention the mirage that we had. The sun on the hot waste produced precisely the effect of water in the distance; we would see a clear lake ahead, in which would be reflected the objects on the plain. This was most marked on the dry sands near Soledad—we could see the trees at the mission mirrored in the clear surface—but it kept retreating as we advanced. The illusion was perfect. At times the atmospheric aberration would only cause objects to be distorted—wagons and cattle would appear much higher than they really were, as if seen through poor glass.

Napa Valley

The Sea Fogs

Robert Louis Stevenson (1850–1894) spent a year in California, arriving in 1879 to marry his fiancée and to improve his weak lungs. The highlight was a short honeymoon on Mount Saint Helena. That year resulted in one of the Scottish writer's most charming books, Silverado Squatters *(1883), the title referring to his visit to the abandoned Silverado Mine in Napa County.*

T he scene . . . is on a high mountain. There are, indeed, many higher; there are many of a noble outline. It is no place of pilgrimage for the summary globe-trotter; but to one who lives upon its sides, Mount Saint Helena soon becomes a center of interest. It is the Mont Blanc of one section of the Californian Coast Range, none of its near neighbors rising to one-half its altitude. It looks down on much green, intricate country. It feeds in the spring-time many splashing brooks. From its summit you must have an excellent lesson of geography: seeing, to the south, San Francisco Bay, with Tamalpais on the one hand and Mount Diablo on the other; to the west and thirty miles away, the open ocean; eastward, across the cornlands and thick tule swamps of Sacramento Valley, to where the Central Pacific Railroad begins to climb the sides of the Sierras; and northward, for what I know, the white head of Shasta looking down on Oregon. Three counties, Napa County, Lake County, and Sonoma County, march across its cliffy shoulders. Its naked peak stands nearly four thousand five hundred feet above the sea; its sides are fringed with forest; and the soil, where it is bare, glows warm with cinnabar.

Life in its shadow goes rustically forward. Bucks, and bears, and rattlesnakes, and former mining operations, are the staple of men's talk. Agriculture has only begun to mount above the valley. And though in a few years from now the whole district may be smiling with farms, passing trains shaking the mountain to the heart, many-windowed hotels lighting up the night like factories, and a prosperous city occupying the site of sleepy Calistoga; yet in the meantime, around the foot of that mountain the silence of nature reigns in a great measure unbroken, and the people of hill and valley go sauntering about their business as in the days before the flood. . . .

A change in the color of the light usually called me in the morning. By a certain hour, the long, vertical chinks in our western gable, where the boards had shrunk and separated, flashed suddenly into my eyes as stripes of dazzling blue, at once so dark and splendid that I used to marvel how the qualities could be combined. At an earlier hour, the heavens in that quarter were still quietly colored, but the shoulder of the mountain which shuts in the cañon already glowed with sunlight in a wonderful compound of gold and rose and green; and this too would kindle, although more mildly and with rainbow tints, the fissures of our crazy gable. If I were sleeping heavily, it was the bold blue that struck me awake; if more lightly, then I would come to myself in that earlier and fairier light.

One Sunday morning, about five, the first brightness called me. I rose and turned to the east, not for my devotions, but for air. The night had been very still. The little private gale that blew every evening in our cañon, for ten minutes or perhaps a quarter of an hour, had swiftly blown itself out; in the hours that followed not a sight of wind had shaken the treetops; and our barrack, for all it breaches, was less fresh that morning than of wont. But I had no sooner reached the window than I forgot all else in the sight that met my eyes, and I made but two bounds into my clothes, and down the crazy plank to the platform.

The sun was still concealed below the opposite hilltops, though it was shining already, not twenty feet above my head, on our own mountain slope. But the scene, beyond a few near features, was entirely changed. Napa Valley was gone; gone were all the lower slopes and woody foothills of the range; and in their place, not a thousand feet below me, rolled a great level ocean. It was as though I had gone to bed the night before, safe in a nook of inland mountains, and had awakened in a bay upon the coast. I had seen these inundations from below; at Calistoga I had risen and gone abroad in the early morning, coughing and sneezing, under fathoms on fathoms of grey sea-vapor, like a cloudy sky—a dull sight for the artist, and a painful experience for the invalid. But, to sit aloft one's self in the pure air and under the unclouded dome of heaven, and thus look down on the submergence of the valley, was strangely different and even delightful to the eye. Far away were hilltops like little islands. Nearer, a smokey surf beat about the foot of precipices and poured into all the coves of these rough mountains. The color of that fog ocean was a thing never to be forgotten. For an instant, among the Hebrides and just about sundown, I have seen something like it on the sea itself. But the white was not so opaline; nor was there, what surprisingly increased the effect, that breathless, crystal stillness over all. Even in its gentlest moods the salt sea travails, moaning among the weeds or lisping on the sand; but that vast fog ocean lay in a trance of silence, nor did the sweet air of the morning tremble with a sound.

As I continued to sit upon the dump, I began to observe that this sea was not so level as at first sight it appeared to be. Away in the extreme south, a little hill of fog arose against the sky above the general surface, and as it had already caught the sun, it shone on the horizon like the topsails of some giant ship. There were huge waves, stationary, as it seemed, like waves in a frozen sea; and yet, as I looked again, I was not sure but they were moving after all, with a slow and august advance. And while I was yet doubting, a promontory of the hills some four or five miles away, conspicuous by a bouquet of tall pines, was in a single instant overtaken and swallowed up. It reappeared in a little, with its pines, but this time as an islet, and only to be swallowed up once more and then for good. This set me looking nearer, and I saw that in every cove along the line of mountains the fog was being piled in higher and higher, as though by some wind that was inaudible to me. I could trace its progress, one pine tree first growing hazy and then disappearing after another; although sometimes there was none of this fore-running haze, but the whole opaque white ocean gave a start and swallowed a piece of mountain at a gulp. It was to flee these poisonous fogs that I had left the seaboard, and climbed so high among the mountains. And now, behold, here came the fog to besiege me in my chosen altitudes, and yet came so beautifully that my first thought was of welcome.

The sun had now gotten much higher, and through all the gaps of the hills it cast long bars of gold across that white ocean. An eagle, or some other very great bird of the mountain, came wheeling over the nearer pine tops and hung, poised and something sideways, as if to look abroad on that unwonted desolation, spying, perhaps with terror, for the eyries of her comrades. Then, with a long cry, she disappeared again toward Lake County and the clearer air. At length it seemed to me as if the flood were beginning to subside. The old landmarks, by whose disappearance I had measured its advance, here a crag, there a brave pine tree, now began, in the inverse order, to make their reappearance into daylight. I judged all danger of the fog was over. This was not Noah's flood; it was but a morning spring, and would now drift out seaward whence it came. So, mightily relieved, and a good deal exhilarated by the sight, I went into the house to light the fire.

I suppose it was nearly seven when I once more mounted the platform to look abroad. The fog ocean had swelled up enormously since last I saw it; and a few hundred feet below me, in the deep gap where the Toll House stands and the road runs through Lake County, it had already topped the slope, and was pouring over and down the other side like driving smoke. The wind had climbed along with it; and though I was still in calm air, I could see the trees tossing below me, and their long, strident sighing mounted to me where I stood.

Half an hour later, the fog had surmounted all the ridge on the opposite side of the gap, though a shoulder of the mountain still warded it out of our cañon. Napa Valley and its bounding hills were now utterly blotted out. The fog, sunny white in the sunshine, was pouring over into Lake County in a huge, ragged cataract, tossing treetops appearing and disappearing in the spray. The air struck with a little chill, and set me coughing. It smelt strong of the fog, like the smell of a washing-house, but with a shrewd tang of the sea salt.

Had it not been for two things—the sheltering spur which answered as a dike, and the great valley on the other side which rapidly engulfed whatever mounted—our own little platform in the canyon must have been already buried a hundred feet in salt and poisonous air. As it was, the interest of the scene entirely occupied our minds. We were set just out of the wind, and but just above the fog; we could listen to the voice of the one as to music on the stage; we could plunge our eyes down into the other, as into some flowing stream from over the parapet of a bridge; thus we looked on upon a strange, impetuous, silent, shifting exhibition of the powers of nature, and saw the familiar landscape changing from moment to moment like figures in a dream.

The imagination loves to trifle with what is not. Had this been indeed the deluge, I should have felt more strongly, but the emotion would have been similar in kind. I played with the idea, as the child flees in delighted terror from the creations of his fancy. The look of the thing helped me. And when at last I began to flee up the mountain, it was indeed partly to escape from the raw air that kept me coughing, but it was also part in play.

As I ascended the mountainside, I came once more to overlook the upper surface of the fog; but it wore a different appearance from what I had beheld at daybreak. For, first, the sun now fell on it from high overhead, and its surface shone and undulated like a great nor'land moor country, sheeted with untrodden morning snow. And next the new level must have been a thousand or fifteen hundred feet higher than the old, so that only five or six points of all the broken country below me still stood out. Napa Valley was now one with Sonoma on the west. On the hither side, only a thin scattered fringe of bluffs was unsubmerged; and through all the gaps the fog was pouring over, like an ocean, into the blue clear sunny country on the east. There it was soon lost; for it fell instantly into the bottom of the valleys, following the watershed; and the hilltops in that quarter were still clear cut upon the eastern sky.

Through the Toll House gap and over the near ridges on the other side, the deluge was immense. A spray of thin vapor was thrown high above it, arising and falling, and blown into fantastic shapes. The speed of its course was like a mountain torrent. Here and there a few treetops were discovered and then whelmed again; and for one second, the bough of a dead pine beckoned out of the spray like the arm of a drowning man. But still the imagination was dissatisfied, still the ear waited for something more. Had this indeed been water (as it seemed so, to the eye), with what a plunge of reverberating thunder would it have rolled upon its course, disemboweling mountains and deracinating pines! And yet water it was, and seawater at that—true Pacific billows, only somewhat rarefied, rolling in mid-air among the hilltops.

I climbed still higher, among the red rattling gravel and dwarf underwood of Mount Saint Helena, until I could look right down upon Silverado and admire the vapored nook in which it lay. The sunny plain of fog was several hundred feet higher; behind the protesting spur a gigantic accumulation of cottony vapor threatened, with every second, to blow over and submerge our homestead; but the vortex setting past the Toll House was too strong; and there lay our little platform, in the arms of the deluge, but still enjoying its unbroken sunshine. About eleven, however, thin spray came flying over the friendly buttress, and I began to think the fog had hunted out its Jonah after all. But it was the last effort. The wind veered while we were at dinner, and began to blow squally from the mountain summit; and by half past one, all that world of sea-fogs was utterly routed and flying here and there into the south in little rags of cloud. And instead of a lone sea-beach, we found ourselves once more inhabiting a high mountainside, with clear green country far below us, and the light smoke of Calistoga blowing in the air.

This was the great Russian campaign for that season. Now and then, in the early morning, a little white lakelet of fog would be seen far down in Napa Valley; but the heights were not again assailed, nor was the surrounding world again shut off from Silverado.

Sonoma Valley

On Sonoma Mountain

Jack London (1876–1915) was one of the first great native Californian writers, having been born in San Francisco and died at his ranch in the Valley of the Moon in Sonoma County. He wrote more than twenty books, including Call of the Wild *(1903) and* Martin Eden *(1909). In one of his more obscure novels,* Burning Daylight *(1910), he wrote splendidly of the beauty of Sonoma, where the protagonist, a wealthy financier named Daylight, seeks an escape from San Francisco.*

One weekend, feeling heavy and depressed and tired of the city and its ways, he obeyed the impulse of a whim that was later to play an important part in his life. The desire to get out of the city for a whiff of country air and for a change of scene was the cause. Yet, in himself, he made the excuse of going to Glen Ellen for the purpose of inspecting the brickyard with which Holdsworthy had gold-bricked him.

He spent the night in a little country hotel, and on Sunday morning, astride a saddle-horse rented from the Glen Ellen butcher, rode out of the village. The brickyard was close at hand on the flat beside the Sonoma Creek. The kilns were visible among the trees, when he glanced to the left and caught sight of a cluster of wooded knolls half a mile away, perched on the rolling slopes of Sonoma Mountain. The mountain, itself wooded, towered behind. The trees on the knolls seemed to beckon to him. The dry, early-summer air, shot through with sunshine, was wine to him. Unconsciously he drank it in in deep breaths. The prospect of the brickyard was uninviting. He was jaded with all things business, and the wooded knolls were calling to him. A horse was between his legs—a good horse, he decided, one that sent him back to the cayuses he had ridden during his eastern Oregon boyhood. He had been somewhat of a rider in those early days, and the champ of bit and crack of saddle-leather sounded good to him now.

Resolving to have his fun first and to look over the brickyard afterward, he rode up on the hill, prospecting for a way across country to get to the knolls. He left the country road at the first gate he came to and cantered through a hayfield. The grain was waist high on either side of the wagon road, and he sniffed the warm aroma of it with delighted nostrils. Larks flew up before him, and from everywhere came mellow notes. From the appearance of the road it was patent that it had been used for hauling clay to the now idle brickyard. Salving his conscience with the idea that this was part of the inspection, he rode on to the clay pit—a huge scar in a hillside. But he did not linger long, swinging off again to the left and leaving the road. Not a farmhouse was in sight, and the change from the city crowding was essentially satisfying. He rode now through open woods, across little flower-scattered glades, till he came upon a spring. Flat on the ground he drank deeply of the clear water, and looking about him, felt with a shock the beauty of the world. It came to him like a discovery; he had never realized it before, he concluded, and also, he had forgotten much. One could not sit in at high finance and keep track of such things. As he drank in the air, the scene, and the distant song of larks, he felt like a poker player rising from a night-long table and coming forth from the pent atmosphere to taste the freshness of the morn.

At the base of the knolls he encountered a tumble-down stake-and-rider fence. From the look of it he judged it must be forty years old at least—the work of some first pioneer who had taken up the land when the days of gold had ended. The woods were very thick here, yet fairly clear of underbrush, so that, while the blue sky was screened by the arched branches, he was able to ride beneath. He now found himself in a hook of several acres, where the oak and manzanita and madroño gave way to clusters of stately redwoods. Against the foot of a steep-sloped knoll he came upon a magnificent group of redwoods that seemed to have gathered about the tiny gurgling spring.

He halted his horse, for beside the spring uprose a wild California lily. It was a wonderful flower, growing there in the cathedral nave of lofty trees. At least eight feet in height, its stem rose straight and slender, green and bare, for two-thirds its length, and then burst into a shower of snow-white waxen bells. There were hundreds of these blossoms, all from the one stem, delicately poised and ethereally frail. Daylight had never seen anything like it. Slowly his gaze wandered from it to all that was about him. He took off his hat, with almost a vague religious feeling. This was different. No room for contempt and evil here. This was clean and fresh and beautiful—something he could respect. It was like a church. The atmosphere was one of holy calm. Here man felt the prompting of nobler things. Much of this and more was in Daylight's heart as he looked about him. But it was not a concept of his mind. He merely felt it without thinking about it at all.

On the steep incline above the spring grew tiny maidenhair ferns, while higher up were larger ferns and brakes. Great, moss-covered trunks of fallen trees lay here and there, slowly sinking back and merging into the level of the forest mould. Beyond, in a slightly clearer space, wild grape and honeysuckle swung in green riot from gnarled old oak trees. A gray Douglas squirrel crept out on a branch and watched him. From somewhere came the distant knocking of a woodpecker. This sound did not disturb the hush and awe of the place. Quiet woods' noises belonged there and made the solitude complete. The tiny bubbling ripple of the spring and the gray flash of squirrel were as yardsticks with which to measure the silence and motionless repose.

"Might be a million miles from anywhere," Daylight whispered to himself.

But ever his gaze returned to the wonderful lily beside the bubbling spring.

He tethered the horse and wandered on foot among the knolls. Their tips were crowned with century-old spruce trees, and their sides clothed with oaks and madroños and native holly. But to the perfect redwoods belonged the small but deep canyon that threaded its way among the knolls. Here he found no passage out for his horse and he returned to the lily beside the spring. On foot, tripping, stumbling, leading the animal, he forced his way up the hillside. And ever the ferns carpeted the way of his feet, ever the forest climbed with him and arched overhead, and ever the clean joy and sweetness stole in upon his senses.

On the crest he came through an amazing thicket of velvet-trunked young madroños, and emerged on an open hillside that led down into a tiny valley. The sunshine was at first dazzling in its brightness, and he paused and rested, for he was panting from the exertion. Not of old had he known shortness of breath such as this, and muscles that so easily tired at a stiff climb. A tiny stream ran down the tiny valley through a tiny meadow that was carpeted knee high with grass and blue and white nemophila. The hillside was covered with mariposa lilies and wild hyacinth, down through which his horse dropped slowly, with circum-spect feet and reluctant gait.

Crossing the stream, Daylight followed a faint cattle trail over a low, rocky hill and through a wine-wooded forest of manzanita, and emerged upon another tiny valley, down which filtered another spring-fed meadow-bordered streamlet. A jackrabbit bounded from a bush under his horse's nose, leaped the stream, and vanished up the opposite hillside of scrub oak. Daylight watched it admiringly as he rode on to the head of the meadow. Here he startled up a many-pronged buck, that seemed to soar across the meadow, and to soar over the stake-and-rider fence, and, still soaring, disappeared in a friendly copse beyond.

Daylight's delight was unbounded. It seemed to him that he had never been so happy. His old woods training was aroused, and he was keenly interested in everything—in the moss on the trees and branches; in the bunches of mistletoe hanging in the oaks; in the nest of a wood rat; in the watercress growing in the sheltered eddies of the little stream; in the butterflies drifting through the rifted sunshine and shadow; in the blue jays that flashed in splashes of gorgeous color across the forest aisles; in the tiny birds, like wrens, that hopped among the bushes and imitated certain minor quail-calls; and in the crimson-crested woodpecker that ceased its knocking and cocked its head on one side to survey him. Crossing the stream, he struck faint vestiges of a wood-road, used, evidently, a generation back, when the meadow had been cleared of its oaks. He found a hawk's nest on the lightning-shattered tipmost top of a six-foot redwood. And to complete it all, his horse stumbled upon several large broods of half-grown quail, and the air was filled with the thrum of their flight. He halted and watched the young ones "petrifying" and disappearing on the ground before his eyes, and listening to the anxious calls of the old ones hidden in the thickets.

"It sure beats country places and bungalows at Menlo Park," he communed aloud, "and if ever I get the hankering for country life, it's me for this every time."

The old wood-road led him to a clearing, where a dozen acres of grapes grew on wine-red soil. A cow path, more trees and thickets, and he dropped down a hillside to the southeast exposure. Here, poised above a big forested canyon, and looking out upon Sonoma Valley, was a small farmhouse. With its barn and outhouses it snuggled into a nook in the hillside, which protected it from west and north. It was the erosion from this hillside, he judged, that had formed the little level stretch of vegetable garden. The soil was fat and black, and there was water in plenty, for he saw several faucets running wide open.

Forgotten was the brickyard. Nobody was at home, but Daylight dismounted and ranged the vegetable garden, eating strawberries and green peas, inspecting the old adobe barn and the rusty plough and barrow, and rolling and smoking cigarettes while he watched the antics of several broods of young chickens and the mother hens. A foot trail that led down the wall of the big canyon invited him, and he proceeded to follow it. A water pipe, usually above ground, paralleled the trail, which he concluded led upstream to the bed of the creek. The wall of the canyon was several hundred feet from top to bottom, and so magnificent were the untouched trees that the place was plunged in perpetual shade. He measured with his eye spruces five and six feet in diameter and redwoods even larger. One such he passed, a twister that was at least ten or eleven feet through. The trail led straight to a small dam where was the intake for the pipe that watered the vegetable garden. Here, beside the stream, were alders and laurel trees, and he walked through fern-brakes higher than his head. Velvety moss was everywhere, out of which grew maidenhair and gold-back ferns.

Save for the dam, it was a virgin wild. No axe had invaded, and the trees died only of old age and stress of winter storm. The huge trunks of those that had fallen lay moss-covered, slowly resolving back into the soil from which they sprang. Some had lain so long that they were quite gone, though their faint outlines, level with the mould, could still be seen. Others bridged the stream, and from beneath the bulk of one monster half a dozen younger trees, overthrown and crushed by the fall, growing out along the ground, still lived and prospered, their roots bathed by the stream, their upshooting branches catching the sunlight through the gap that had been made in the forest roof.

Back at the farmhouse, Daylight mounted and rode on away from the ranch and into the wilder canyons and steeper steeps beyond. Nothing could satisfy his holiday spirit now but the ascent of Sonoma Mountain. And here on the crest, three hours afterward, he emerged, tired and sweaty, garments torn and face and hands scratched, but with sparkling eyes and an unwonted zestfulness of expression. He felt the illicit pleasure of a schoolboy playing truant. The big gambling table of San Francisco seemed very far away. But there was much more than illicit pleasure in his mood. It was as though he were going through a sort of cleansing bath. No room here for all the sordidness, meanness, and viciousness that filled the dirty pool of city existence. Without pondering in detail upon the matter at all, his sensations were of purification and uplift. Had he been asked to state how he felt, he would merely have said that he was having a good time; for he was unaware in his self-consciousness of the potent charm of nature that was percolating through his city-rotted body and brain—potent, in that he came of an abysmal past of wilderness dwellers, while he was himself coated with the thinnest rind of crowded civilization.

There were no houses in the summit of Sonoma Mountain, and, all alone under the azure California sky, he reined in on the southern edge of the peak. He saw open pasture country, intersected with wooden canyons, descending to the south and west from his feet, crease on crease and roll on roll, from lower level to lower level, to the floor of Petaluma Valley, flat as a billiard table, a cardboard affair, all patches and squares of geometrical regularity where the fat freeholds were farmed. Beyond, to the west, rose range on range of mountains cuddling purple mists of atmosphere in their valleys, and still beyond, over the last range of all, he saw the silver sheen of the Pacific. Swinging his horse, he surveyed the west and north, from Santa Rosa to Mount St. Helena, and on to the east, across Sonoma Valley, to the chaparral-covered range that shut off the view of Napa Valley. Here, partway up the eastern wall of Sonoma Valley, in range of a line intersecting the little village of Glen Ellen, he made out a scar upon a hillside. His first thought was that it was the dump of a mine tunnel, but remembering that he was not in gold-bearing country, he dismissed the scar from his mind and continued the circle of his survey to the southeast, where, across the waters of San Pablo Bay, he could see, sharp and distant, the twin peaks of Mount Diablo. To the south was Mount Tamalpais, and, yes, he was right, fifty miles away, where the draughty winds of the

Pacific blew in the Golden Gate, the smoke of San Francisco made a low-lying haze against the sky.

"I ain't seen so much country all at once in many a day," he thought aloud.

He was loath to depart, and it was not for an hour that he was able to tear himself away and take the descent of the mountain. . . .

Instead of returning to the city on Monday, Daylight rented the butcher's horse for another day and crossed the bed of the valley to the eastern hills. . . . On through the chaparral he went, following faint cattle trails and working slowly upward till he came out on the divide and gazed down into Napa Valley and back across to Sonoma Mountain.

"A sweet land," he muttered, "an almighty sweet land."

Salinas Valley

Flight

John Steinbeck (1902–1968), the Nobel Prize–winning writer best known for
The Grapes of Wrath *(1939), was born and raised in the Salinas Valley —
the "long valley" along the Salinas River in central California — where he set
much of his fiction. The following is excerpted from the short story "Flight" in
the collection* The Long Valley *(1938), about nineteen-year-old Pepé Torres,
who, after killing another man in a knife fight, flees from his farm on
Monterey's wild coast into the foothills of the Santa Lucia Mountains.*

It was the first dawn when he rode up the hill toward the little
canyon which let a trail into the mountains. Moonlight and daylight fought with each other, and the two warring qualities made it
difficult to see. Before Pepé had gone a hundred yards, the outlines of his
figure were misty; and long before he entered the canyon, he had
become a grey, indefinite shadow.

Mama stood stiffly in front of her doorstep, and on either side of her
stood Emilio and Rosy. They cast furtive glances at Mama now and
then.

When the grey shape of Pepé melted into the hillside and disappeared, Mama relaxed. She began the high, whining keen of the death
wail. "Our beautiful—our brave," she cried. "Our protector, our son is

gone." Emilio and Rosy moaned beside her. "Our beautiful—our brave, he is gone." It was the formal wail. It rose to a high piercing whine and subsided to a moan. Mama raised it three times and then she turned and went into the house and shut the door.

Emilio and Rosy stood wondering in the dawn. They heard Mama whimpering in the house. They went out to sit on the cliff above the ocean. They touched shoulders. "When did Pepé come to be a man?" Emilio said.

"Last night," said Rosy. "Last night in Monterey." The ocean clouds turned red with the sun that was behind the mountains.

"We will have no breakfast," said Emilio. "Mama will not want to cook." Rosy did not answer him. "Where is Pepé gone?" he asked.

Rosy looked around at him. She drew her knowledge from the quiet air. "He has gone on a journey. He will never come back."

"Is he dead? Do you think he is dead?"

Rosy looked back at the ocean again. A little steamer, drawing a line of smoke, sat on the edge of the horizon. "He is not dead," Rosy explained. "Not yet."

Pepé rested the big rifle across the saddle in front of him. He let the horse walk up the hill and he didn't look back. The stony slope took on a coat of short brush so that Pepé found the entrance to a trail and entered it.

When he came to the canyon opening, he swung once in his saddle and looked back, but the houses were swallowed in the misty light. Pepé jerked forward again. The high shoulder of the canyon closed in on him. His horse stretched out its neck and sighed and settled to the trail.

It was a well-worn path, dark soft leaf-mould earth strewn with broken pieces of sandstone. The trail rounded the shoulder of the canyon and dropped steeply into the bed of the stream. In the shallows the water ran smoothly, glinting in the first morning sun. Small round stones on the bottom were as brown as rust with sun moss. In the sand along the edges of the stream the tall, rich wild mint grew, while in the water itself the cress, old and tough, had gone to heavy seed. The path went into the stream and emerged on the other side. The horse sloshed into the water and stopped. Pepé dropped his bridle and let the beast drink of the running water.

Soon the canyon sides became steep and the first giant sentinel redwoods guarded the trail, great rounded trunks bearing foliage as green and lacy as ferns. Once Pepé was among the trees, the sun was lost. A perfumed and purple light lay in the pale green of the underbrush. Gooseberry bushes and blackberries and tall ferns lined the stream, and overhead the branches of the redwoods met and cut off the sky.

Pepé drank from the water bag, and he reached into the flour sack and brought out a black string of jerky. His white teeth gnawed at the string until the tough meat parted. He chewed slowly and drank occasionally from the water bag. His little eyes were slumberous and tired, but the muscles of his face were hard set. The earth of the trail was black now. It gave up a hollow sound under the walking hoofbeats.

The stream fell more sharply. Little waterfalls splashed on the stones. Five-fingered ferns hung over the water and dripped spray from their fingertips. Pepé rode half over in his saddle, dangling one leg loosely. He picked a bay leaf from a tree beside the way and put it into his mouth for a moment to flavor the dry jerky. He held the gun loosely across the pommel.

Suddenly he squared in his saddle, swung the horse from the trail, and kicked it hurriedly up behind a big redwood tree. He pulled up the reins tight against the bit to keep the horse from whinnying. His face was intent and his nostrils quivered a little.

A hollow pounding came down the trail, and a horseman rode by, a fat man with red cheeks and a white stubble beard. His horse put down its head and blubbered at the trail when it came to the place where Pepé had turned off. "Hold up!" said the man and he pulled up his horse's head.

When the last sound of the hooves died away, Pepé came back into the trail again. He did not relax in the saddle any more. He lifted the big rifle and swung the lever to throw a shell into the chamber, and then he let down the hammer to half cock.

The trail grew very steep. Now the redwood trees were smaller and their tops were dead, bitten dead where the wind reached them. The horse plodded on; the sun went slowly overhead and started down toward the afternoon.

Where the stream came out of a side canyon, the trail left it. Pepé dismounted and watered his horse and filled up his water bag. As soon as the trail had parted from the stream, the trees were gone and only the thick brittle sage and manzanita and chaparral edged the trail. And the soft black earth was gone, too, leaving only the light tan broken rock for the trail bed. Lizards scampered away into the brush as the horse rattled over the little stones.

Pepé turned in his saddle and looked back. He was in the open now: he could be seen from a distance. As he ascended the trail the country grew more rough and terrible and dry. The way wound about the bases of the great square rocks. Little grey rabbits skittered in the brush. A bird made a monotonous high creaking. Eastward the bare rock mountaintops were pale and powder dry under the dropping sun. The horse plodded up and up the trail toward a little V in the ridge which was the pass.

Pepé looked suspiciously back every minute or so, and his eyes sought the tops of the ridges ahead. Once, on a white barren spur, he saw a black figure for a moment, but he looked quickly away, for it was one of the dark watchers. No one knew who the watchers were, nor where they lived, but it was better to ignore them and never to show interest in them. They did not bother one who stayed on the trail and minded his own business.

The air was parched and full of light dust blown by the breeze from the eroding mountains. Pepé drank sparingly from his bag and corked it tightly and hung it on the horn again. The trail moved up the dry shale hillside, avoiding rocks, dropping under clefts, climbing in and out of old water scars. When he arrived at the little pass he stopped and looked back for a long time. No dark watchers were to be seen now. The trail behind was empty. Only the high tops of the redwoods indicated where the stream flowed.

Pepé rode on through the pass. His little eyes were nearly closed with weariness, but his face was stern, relentless, and manly. The high mountain wind coasted sighing through the pass and whistled on the edges of the big blocks of broken granite. In the air, a red-tailed hawk sailed over close to the ridge and screamed angrily. Pepé went slowly through the broken jagged pass and looked down on the other side.

The trail dropped quickly, staggering among broken rock. At the bottom of the slope there was a dark crease, thick with brush, and on the other side of the crease a little flat, in which a grove of oak trees grew. A scar of green grass cut across the flat. And behind the flat another mountain rose, desolate with dead rocks and starving little black bushes. Pepé drank from the bag again, for the air was so dry that it encrusted his nostrils and burned his lips. He put the horse down the way, starting little stones that rolled off into the brush. The sun was gone behind the westward mountain now, but still it glowed brilliantly on the oaks and on the grassy flat. The rocks and the hillsides still sent up waves of the heat they had gathered from the day's sun.

Pepé looked up to the top of the next dry withered ridge. He saw a dark form against the sky, a man's figure standing on top of a rock, and he glanced away quickly, not to appear curious. When a moment later he looked up again, the figure was gone.

Downward the trail was quickly covered. Sometimes the horse floundered for footing, sometimes set his feet and slid a little way. They came at last to the bottom where the dark chaparral was higher than Pepé's head. He held up his rifle on one side and his arm on the other to shield his face from the sharp brittle fingers of the brush.

Up and out of the crease he rode, and up a little cliff. The grassy flat was before him, and the round comfortable oaks. For a moment he studied the trail down which he had come, but there was no movement and no sound from it. Finally he rode out over the flat, to the green streak, and at the upper end of the damp he found a little spring welling out of the earth and dropping into a dug basin before it seeped out over the flat.

Pepé filled his bag first, and then he let the thirsty horse drink out of the pool. He led the horse to the clump of oaks, and in the middle of the grove, fairly protected from sight on all sides, he took off the saddle and the bridle and laid them on the ground. The horse stretched his jaws sideways and yawned. Pepé knotted the lead rope about the horse's neck and tied him to a sapling among the oaks, where he could graze in a fairly large circle.

When the horse was gnawing hungrily at the dry grass, Pepé went to the saddle and took a black string of jerky from the sack and strolled to a oak tree on the edge of the grove, from under which he could watch the trail. He sat down in the crisp dry oak leaves and automatically felt for his big black knife to cut the jerky, but he had no knife. He leaned back on his elbow and gnawed at the tough strong meat. His face was blank, but it was a man's face.

The bright evening light washed the eastern ridge, but the valley was darkening. Doves flew down from the hills to the spring, and the quail came running out of the brush and joined them, calling clearly to one another.

Out of the corner of his eye Pepé saw a shadow grow out of the bushy crease. He turned his head slowly. A big spotted wildcat was creeping toward the spring, belly to the ground, moving like thought.

Pepé cocked his rifle and edged the muzzle slowly around. Then he looked apprehensively up the trail and dropped the hammer again. From the ground beside him he picked an oak twig and threw it toward the spring. The quail flew up with a roar and the doves whistled away. The big cat stood up for a long moment; he looked at Pepé with cold yellow eyes, and then fearlessly walked back into the gulch.

The dusk gathered quickly in the deep valley. Pepé muttered his prayers, put his head down on his arm, and went instantly to sleep.

The moon came up and filled the valley with cold blue light, and the wind swept rustling down from the peaks. The owls worked up and down the slopes looking for rabbits. Down in the brush of the gulch a coyote gabbled. The oak trees whispered softly in the night breeze.

Pepé started up, listening. His horse had whinnied. The moon was just slipping behind the western ridge, leaving the valley in darkness behind it. Pepé sat tensely gripping his rifle. From far up the trail he heard an answering whinny and the crash of shod hooves on the broken rock. He jumped to his feet, ran to his horse, and led it under the trees. He threw on the saddle and cinched it tight for the steep trail, caught the unwilling head and forced the bit into the mouth. He felt the saddle to make sure the water bag and the sack of jerky were there. Then he mounted and turned up the hill.

It was velvet dark. The horse found the entrance to the trail where it left the flat and started up, stumbling and slipping on the rocks. Pepé's hand rose up to his head. His hat was gone. He had left it under the oak tree.

The horse had struggled far up the trail when the first change of dawn came into the air, a steel greyness as light mixed thoroughly with dark. Gradually the sharp snaggled edge of the ridge stood out above them, rotten granite tortured and eaten by the winds of time. Pepé had dropped his reins on the horn, leaving direction to the horse. The brush grabbed at his legs in the dark until one knee of his jeans was ripped.

Gradually the light flowed down over the ridge. The starved brush and rocks stood out in the half light, strange and lonely in high perspective. Then there came warmth into the light. Pepé drew up and looked back, but he could see nothing in the darker valley below. The sky turned blue over the coming sun. In the waste of the mountainside, the poor dry brush grew only three feet high. Here and there, big outcroppings of unrotted granite stood up like mouldering houses. Pepé relaxed a little. He drank from his water bag and bit off a piece of jerky. A single eagle flew over, high in the light.

Without warning Pepé's horse screamed and fell on its side. He was almost down before the rifle crash echoed up from the valley. From a hole behind the struggling shoulder, a stream of bright crimson blood pumped and stopped and pumped and stopped. The hooves threshed on the ground. Pepé lay half stunned beside the horse. He looked slowly down the hill. A piece of sage clipped off beside his head and another crash echoed from side to side of the canyon. Pepé flung himself frantically behind a bush.

He crawled up the hill on his knees and one hand. His right hand held the rifle up off the ground and pushed it ahead of him. He moved with the instinctive care of an animal. Rapidly he wormed his way toward one of the big outcroppings of granite on the hill above him. Where the brush was high he doubled up and ran, but where the cover was slight he wriggled forward on his stomach, pushing the rifle ahead of him. In the last little distance there was no cover at all. Pepé poised and then he darted across the space and flashed around the corner of the rock.

He leaned panting against the stone. When his breath came easier he moved behind the big rock until he came to a narrow split that offered a thin section of vision down the hill. Pepé lay on his stomach and pushed the rifle barrel through the slit and waited.

The sun reddened the western ridges now. Already the buzzards were settling down toward the place where the horse lay. A small brown bird scratched in the dead sage leaves directly in front of the rifle muzzle. The coasting eagle flew back toward the rising sun.

Pepé saw a little movement in the brush far below. His grip tightened on the gun. A little brown doe stepped daintily out on the trail and crossed it and disappeared into the brush again. For a long time Pepé waited. Far below he could see the little flat and the oak trees and the slash of green. Suddenly his eyes flashed back at the trail again. A quarter of a mile down there had been a quick movement in the chaparral. The rifle swung over. The front sight nestled in the V of the rear sight. Pepé studied for a moment and then raised the rear sight a notch. The little movement in the brush came again. The sight settled on it. Pepé squeezed the trigger. The explosion crashed down the mountain and up the other side, and came rattling back. The whole side of the slope grew still. No more movement. And then a white streak cut into the granite of the slit and a bullet whined away and a crash sounded up from below. Pepé felt a sharp pain in his right hand. A sliver of granite was sticking out from between his first and second knuckles and the point protruded from his palm. Carefully he pulled out the sliver of stone. The wound bled evenly and gently. No vein nor artery was cut.

Pepé looked into a little dusty cave in the rock and gathered a handful of spider web, and he pressed the mass into the cut, plastering the soft web into the blood. The flow stopped almost at once.

The rifle was on the ground. Pepé picked it up, levered a new shell into the chamber. And then he slid into the brush on his stomach. Far to the right he crawled, and then up the hill, moving slowly and carefully, crawling to cover and resting and then crawling again.

In the mountains the sun is high in its arc before it penetrates the gorges. The hot face looked over the hill and brought instant heat with it. The white light beat on the rocks and reflected from them and rose up quivering from the earth again, and the rocks and bushes seemed to quiver behind the air.

Pepé crawled in the general direction of the ridge peak, zigzagging for cover. The deep cut between his knuckles began to throb. He crawled close to a rattlesnake before he saw it, and when it raised its dry head and made a soft beginning whirr, he backed up and took another way. The quick grey lizards flashed in front of him, raising a tiny line of dust. He found another mass of spider web and pressed it against his throbbing hand.

Pepé was pushing the rifle with his left hand now. Little drops of sweat ran to the ends of his coarse black hair and rolled down his cheeks. His lips and tongue were growing thick and heavy. His lips writhed to draw saliva into his mouth. His little dark eyes were uneasy and suspicious. Once when a grey lizard passed in front of him on the parched ground and turned its head sideways he crushed it flat with a stone.

When the sun slid past noon he had not gone a mile. He crawled exhaustedly a last hundred yards to a patch of high sharp manzanita, crawled desperately, and when the patch was reached he wriggled in among the tough gnarly trunks and dropped his head on his left arm. There was little shade in the meager brush, but there was cover and safety. Pepé went to sleep as he lay and the sun beat on his back. A few little birds hopped close to him and peered and hopped away. Pepé squirmed in his sleep and he raised and dropped his wounded hand again and again.

The sun went down behind the peaks and the cool evening came, and then the dark. A coyote yelled from the hillside. Pepé started awake and looked about with misty eyes. His hand was swollen and heavy; a little thread of pain ran up the inside of his arm and settled in a pocket in his armpit. He peered about and then stood up, for the mountains were black and the moon had not yet risen. Pepé stood up in the dark. The coat of his father pressed on his arm. His tongue was swollen until it nearly filled his mouth. He wriggled out of the coat and dropped it in the brush, and then he struggled up the hill, falling over rocks and tearing his way through the brush. The rifle knocked against stones as he went. Little dry avalanches of gravel and shattered stone went whispering down the hill behind him.

After a while the old moon came up and showed the jagged ridgetop ahead of him. By moonlight Pepé traveled more easily. He bent forward so that his throbbing arm hung away from his body. The journey uphill was made in dashes and rests, a frantic rush up a few yards and then a rest. The wind coasted down the slope rattling the dry stems of the bushes.

The moon was at meridian when Pepé came at last to the sharp backbone of the ridgetop. On the last hundred yards of the rise no soil had clung under the wearing winds. The way was on solid rock. He clambered to the top and looked down on the other side. There was a draw like the last below him, misty with moonlight, brushed with dry struggling sage and chaparral. On the other side the hill rose up sharply and at the top the jagged rotten teeth of the mountain showed against the sky. At the bottom of the cut the brush was thick and dark.

Pepé stumbled down the hill. His throat was almost closed with thirst. At first he tried to run, but immediately he fell and rolled. After that he went more carefully. The moon was just disappearing behind the mountains when he came to the bottom. He crawled into the heavy brush feeling with his fingers for water. There was no water in the bed of the stream, only damp earth. Pepé laid his gun down and scooped up a handful of mud and put it in his mouth, and then he spluttered and scraped the earth from this tongue with his fingers, for the mud drew at his mouth like a poultice. He dug a hole in the stream bed with his fingers, dug a little basin to catch water; but before it was very deep his head fell forward on the damp ground and he slept.

The dawn came and the heat of the day fell on the earth, and still Pepé slept. Late in the afternoon his head jerked up. He looked slowly around. His eyes were slits of wariness. Twenty feet away in the heavy brush a big tawny mountain lion stood looking at him. Its long thick tail waved gracefully, its ears were erect with interest, now laid back dangerously. The lion squatted down on its stomach and watched him.

Pepé looked at the hole he had dug in the earth. A half inch of muddy water had collected in the bottom. He tore the sleeve from his hurt arm, with his teeth ripped out a little square, soaked it in the water, and put it in his mouth. Over and over he filled the cloth and sucked it.

Still the lion sat and watched him. The evening came down, but there was no movement on the hills. No birds visited the dry bottom of the cut. Pepé looked occasionally at the lion. The eyes of the yellow beast drooped as though he were about to sleep. He yawned and his long thin red tongue curled out. Suddenly his head jerked around and his nostrils quivered. His big tail lashed. He stood up and slunk like a tawny shadow into the thick brush.

A moment later Pepé heard the sound, the faint far crash of horses' hooves on gravel. And he heard something else, a high whining yelp of a dog.

Pepé took his rifle in his left hand and he glided into the brush almost as quietly as the lion had. In the darkening evening he crouched up the hill toward the next ridge. Only when the dark came did he stand up. His energy was short. Once it was dark he fell over the rocks and slipped to his knees on the steep slope, but he moved on and on up the hill, climbing and scrabbling over the broken hillside.

When he was far up toward the top, he lay down and slept for a little while. The withered moon, shining on his face, awakened him. He stood up and moved up the hill. Fifty yards away he stopped and turned back, for he had forgotten his rifle. He walked heavily down and poked about in the brush, but he could not find his gun. At last he lay down to rest. The pocket of pain in his armpit had grown more sharp. His arm seemed to swell out and fall with every heartbeat. There was no position lying down where the heavy arm did not press against his armpit.

With the effort of a hurt beast, Pepé got up and moved again toward the top of the ridge. He held his swollen arm away from his body with his left hand. Up the steep hill he dragged himself, a few steps and a rest, and a few more steps. At last he was nearing the top. The moon showed the uneven sharp back of it against the sky.

Pepé's brain spun in a big spiral up and away from him. He slumped to the ground and lay still. The rock ridgetop was only a hundred feet above him.

The moon moved over the sky. Pepé half turned on his back. His tongue tried to make words, but only a thick hissing came from between his lips.

When the dawn came. Pepé pulled himself up. His eyes were sane again. He drew his great puffed arm in front of him and looked at the angry wound. The black line ran up from his wrist to his armpit. Automatically he reached in his pocket for the big black knife, but it was not there. His eyes searched the ground. He picked up a sharp blade of stone and scraped at the wound, sawed at the proud flesh and then squeezed the green juice out in big drops. Instantly he threw back his head and whined like a dog. His whole right side shuddered at the pain, but the pain cleared his head.

In the grey light he struggled up the last slope to the ridge and crawled over and lay down behind a line of rocks. Below him lay a deep canyon exactly like the last, waterless and desolate. There was no flat, no oak trees, not even heavy brush in the bottom of it, And on the other side a sharp ridge stood up, thinly brushed with starving sage, littered with broken granite. Strewn over the hill there were giant outcroppings, and on the top the granite teeth stood out against the sky.

The new day was light now. The flame of the sun came over the ridge and fell on Pepé where he lay on the ground. His coarse black hair was littered with twigs and bits of spider web. His eyes had retreated back into his head. Between his lips the tip of his black tongue showed.

He sat up and dragged his great arm into his lap and nursed it, rocking his body and moaning in his throat. He threw back his head and looked up into the pale sky. A big black bird circled nearly out of sight, and far to the left another was sailing near.

He lifted his head to listen, for a familiar sound had come to him from the valley he had climbed out of; it was the crying yelp of hounds, excited and feverish, on a trail.

Pepé bowed his head quickly. He tried to speak rapid words but only a thick hiss came from his lips. He drew a shaky cross on his breast with this left hand. It was a long struggle to get to his feet. He crawled slowly and mechanically to the top of a big rock on the ridge peak. Once there, he arose slowly, swaying to his feet, and stood erect. Far below he could see the dark brush where he had slept. He braced his feet and stood there, black against the morning sky.

There came a ripping sound at his feet. A piece of stone flew up and a bullet droned off into the next gorge. The hollow crash echoed up from below. Pepé looked down for a moment and then pulled himself straight again.

His body jarred back. His left hand fluttered helplessly toward his breast. The second crash sounded from below. Pepé swung forward and toppled from the rock. His body struck and rolled over and over, starting a little avalanche. And when at last he stopped against a bush, the avalanche slid slowly down and covered up his head.

Spirits of the Valley

Mary Frances Kennedy Fisher (1908–1992) was raised in Whittier, California. She later lived in France for extended periods, and spent the last twenty years of her life in a house built for her in a vineyard in Glen Ellen, California. Acclaimed in particular for her writing on culinary subjects, she is admired for her fine prose styling. Her more than twenty books include The Art of Eating *(1954),* Among Friends *(1971), and* Stay Me, Oh Comfort Me: Journals and Stories, 1933–1941 *(1993), which includes a recollection of her years near Hemet, written in 1984, of which the following is an excerpt.*

Some people believe that it is a fortunate thing if a person can live in a real valley instead of on flat open land, and they may well be right. For some sixteen years, from 1940 on, I lived most of the time on ninety acres of worthless land southeast of the little town of Hemet in southern California, and they were fine magical ones, important in the shaping of many people besides me, perhaps because Hemet Valley was a true one in every sense. At its far eastern end rose the high mountains that separated coastal land from desert, and our little town lay almost as near their base as Palm Spring did on their other side. Mount San Jacinto loomed on the north; to the south, high rocky hills rolled toward the Mexican border, and westward the valley opened gently, as any proper valley should, toward broad coastal flats and the far Pacific Ocean.

My husband, Dillwyn Parrish, and I bought our land for almost nothing: it was haunted, for one thing, and completely untillable. And we lived there intensely until he died three years later, according to medical schedule, of Buerger's disease. Then I stayed on, through another marriage and two little daughters, who spent their first years there with me after I divorced their father. When the oldest was going on six, we moved to my family ranch near Whittier to live with Father after Mother died. I worked half-time on his newspaper and ran the household, and as often as possible (weekends, vacations) we went back to Hemet to the little ranch house in the wild rocky hills.

It became clear that I could not raise two growing females there alone, where I had decided to remain. Now and then I found someone to repair storm damage and so on, but finally it seemed wise to sell the place. I felt thankful for everything I had learned there, and when I said it was no longer mine, I withdrew forever from it, even though ashes of my love and my mother may still blow from under some of its great rocks. I know the wind still sings over the Rim of the World and always will.

Tim (my husband was always called that by people who loved him, which meant everyone) named our ranch Bareacres, after a character in *Vanity Fair* who had several marriageable daughters and countless acres of barren land. He managed to sell the land, bought a string of pearls and a husband for each girl, and he and Lady Bareacres lived penniless but happy ever after, as I remember.

Certainly our land was bare! It rose in rough steep hills, with one deep canyon that split it down from the Rim of the World, its horizon, to the wide dead riverbed that was its northern boundary. A thin little road track went up from the valley floor, past our house and on up past the trickle of our only spring, to a deserted old ranch on the Rim of the World. There was a big sturdy redwood tank at the spring and a hand-ful of stubby cottonwoods, and down nearer our house in the canyon, dry except for an occasional mud puddle from the underground trickle, stood a few tall eucalyptus trees. The rest of the place was covered with great harsh boulders, some of them bigger than a house. On the flat top of an enormous rock above the spring, two oblong tubs had been chipped out centuries ago, and we were told that sick Indians were brought there to lie in the hot sun while soothing water was poured over them, water that we found was heavy with lithium.

In front of the house, which stood about a thousand feet up off the wide dry riverbed that separated us from Hemet Valley, the land was steep but with fewer big rocks, almost like a meadow, covered with sage and mesquite and low cactus. Across the riverbed, northward, between us and Mount San Jacinto, lay the flat valley land, rich with apricot orchards. It was neatly laid out with roads and little houses here and there, but we could see only a general kind of lush carpet, flowery in spring, then green, and then winter-silver. Hemet was westward, invisible.

Our narrow dirt road went straight across the riverbed and up to the valley floor to meet Crest Drive, which curved the whole length of the valley. Directly opposite us, a small grove of eucalyptus trees grew down the slope where Fredrika van Benschoten had a little orange orchard along Crest, and in that grove the Squawman, who had left his land for us to find, had a correct Navaho house built for his bride. It was of adobe, one room and wide closet and a corner hearth, and it was so heavily plastered that there were no hard corners or lines but a softness to everything under the thick whitewash, as if it were a robe to be worn, firm and protecting but with no part of it to cut or hurt or rub against. The floor was of dark crude tile. The beams across the low ceiling were slender eucalyptus trunks. There was a kind of kitchen in the closet whose wall came up only to eye height, and Freda had piped cold water to a small sink. There was no toilet, and since the Squawman had not made an outhouse, I decided the grove was answer enough.

I spent much time in the squaw house, mostly after Tim died. I wrote a couple of books there. I never slept there, strange to say, but would go down from Bareacres in the mornings. I always took a thermos of broth or a cool drink, and about 11:00 I'd go out and look up across the riverbed and see my home there, sometimes with my two little girls waving from the west terrace, with a neighbor to watch them until I got back. The trees Tim and I had planted back of the house and down into the canyon were thriving: sycamores, eucalyptus, tough cottonwoods.

When Tim and I bought the place, with a veteran's bonus of $2,000 plus $225 we borrowed (we were dead broke after his illness made us leave Switzerland in 1938 when World War II got under way), it was flatly undesirable, even according to the realtor who showed it to us. It had been owned by a shady fellow said to be a degraded government Indian trader, an army officer, whose Navaho woman followed him to Hemet Valley. He bought what we called Bareacres twenty years later, but she, of course, did not live there, so her relatives unwillingly came from New Mexico and built her a decent house across the riverbed from Freda's grove.

Because of strict caste laws, the Navaho was not only called a lost member of her own tribe but could not have anything to do with the local Indians, the Sobodans, who were beneath her social level. It must have been very lonely for her. The Squawman, as he was always scorn-fully called, had a lot or some or a few valuable Indian artifacts, depending on who was talking about him to us, and most of them were gone when his body was found in the house and a clean bullet hole showed in the south window. Perhaps it was robbery? Navaho are good shots, we were told. The little house in Freda's grove was empty, with not even a blanket or cup left. Nobody knew "anything." Up on the hill across the dead riverbed the air blew through the unlocked door of the Squawman's house. Everything in it was stolen, gradually and without real harm . . . no vandalism, no ugly dirt, no mischievous fires. It was haunted, for sure.

It looked empty and welcoming when Tim and I first saw it in the kind January sunlight, and we stepped into it past the bullet hole as if it had been waiting. We rented an airy little house near Moreno, toward Riverside, and came every day over the Jack Rabbit Trail around the base of the mountain with two old carpenters Tim found. We shifted a few walls around and screened the long front porch that was held up by six trunks of cedar trees that Indians had brought from Mexico, it was said, for the Squawman. . . .

[Our friend] Arnold knew more about native desert plants than anyone I ever heard of, and while he was the caretaker up at the Ramona Bowl it was a kind of secret paradise for botanists and crackpot gardeners who came to watch him plant the unplantables and whom he in turn watched like a hawk, because they almost always tried to steal some of his cuttings. It was a game they all played, and Arnold reported every sneaky trick, every artful dodge, of this unending tournament of trickery among the famous people who came to watch him. He turned weeds into jewels, for sure.

After Tim died, Arnold buried the little tin box of clinkers [Tim's ashes] under an enormous hanging rock. I said, "Let's go up to the Rim of the World and let the winds catch them," but he said, "Nope," and simply walked off. I knew it was all right, and went back to Bareacres and waited, and when he came back, we had a good nip of whiskey. . . .

That is the way Bareacres is, of course. I am told that the fine pure air that first drew us there, half mountain and half desert, is now foul with smog and that the rich carpet of fruit trees we looked down on is solid with RVs and trailer parks. One block on Main Street is now in the *Guinness Book of World Records*, or maybe it is *Ripley's Believe It or Not:* something like 182 banks and savings-and-loan offices on that sleepy little stretch of sidewalk! And there are almost a hundred doctors, most of them connected with "convalescent homes" of varying status and opulence. And Crest Drive is lined with million-dollar villas, with the subdivision where Bareacres was (a "ninety-acre hell of red-hot rocks and rattlesnakes," as one New Yorker described it to us after a lost weekend there) the most snobbish and stylish area between Palm Springs and Los Angeles.

That is the way it is, I say, and I do not grieve or even care, any more than I did when Arnold went up the hill with the little box. I have taken and been given more than can ever be known that is heartwarming and fulfilling forever from that piece of wild haunted untillable land we named Bareacres for a time. No doubt roads have been cut into it and rocks have been blasted away, but I know that the contours cannot change much in a few hundred years in that country. And meanwhile the ghosts are there, even of the sick sad Indians who went to lie in the magic lithium waters of the spring, and even of the poor Squawman with a bullet in his heart, and of my own mother who loved the place . . . they are all there to cleanse and watch over it. They, and many more of us, keep an eye on things so that time itself can stay largely unheeded, as anyone will know who spends more than a few minutes in country like Bareacres.

There are many pockets of comfort and healing on this planet, and I have touched a few of them, but only once have I been able to stay as long and learn and be told as much as there on the southeast edge of Hemet Valley.

A Reflection
on White Geese

*Barry Lopez (b. 1945) grew up in the San Fernando Valley in southern
California and lives today in the Cascade Mountains of Oregon. The author of
such important works of natural history as* Arctic Dreams *(1986), which won
the National Book Award, and* Of Wolves and Men *(1978), he has been
called one of "the leading contemporary spokesman for an ethical revaluation of
our ecological behavior." "A Reflection of White Geese" appeared originally as
a magazine piece with photographs by Frans Lanting, and was republished in*
Crossing Open Ground *(1988).*

I slow the car, downshifting from fourth to third, with the melan-
cholic notes of Bach's sixth cello suite in my ears—a recording of
Casals from 1936—and turn east, away from a volcanic ridge of
black basalt. On this cool California evening, the land in the marshy
valley beyond is submerged in gray light, while the far hills are yet
touched by a sunset glow. To the south, out the window, Venus glistens,
a white diamond at the horizon's dark lapis edge. A few feet to my left
is lake water—skittish mallards and coots bolt from the cover of bulrushes and pound the air furiously to put distance between us. I am cha-

grined, and slow down. I have been driving like this for hours—slowed by snow in the mountains behind me, listening to the cello suites—driving hard to get here before sunset.

I shut the tape off. In the waning light I can clearly see marsh hawks swooping over oat and barley fields to the south. Last hunts of the day. The eastern sky is beginning to blush, a rose afterglow. I roll the window down. The car fills with the sounds of birds—the nasalized complaints of several hundred mallards, pintails, and canvasbacks, the slap-water whirr of their halfhearted takeoffs. But underneath this sound something else is expanding, distant French horns and kettledrums.

Up ahead, on the narrow dirt causeway, I spot Frans's car. He is here for the same reason I am. I pull up quietly and he emerges from his front seat, which he has made into a kind of photographic blind. We hug and exchange quiet words of greeting, and then turn to look at the white birds. Behind us the dark waters of Tule Lake, rippled by a faint wind, stretch off north, broken only by occasional islands of hardstem bulrush. Before us, working methodically through a field of two-row barley, the uninterrupted inquiry of their high-pitched voices lifting the night, are twenty-five thousand snow geese come down from the Siberian and Canadian Arctic. Grazing, but alert and wary in this last light.

Frans motions wordlessly to his left; I scan that far eastern edge of Tule Lake with field glasses. One hundred thousand lesser snow geese and Ross's geese float quietly on riffles, a white crease between the dark water and the darkening hills.

The staging of white geese at Tule Lake in northern California in November is one of the most imposing—and dependable—wildlife spectacles in the world. At first one thinks of it only as a phenomenon of numbers—it's been possible in recent years to see as many as three hundred thousand geese here at one time. What a visitor finds as startling, however, is the great synchronicity of their movements: long skeins of white unfurl brilliantly against blue skies and dark cumulonimbus thunderheads, birds riding the towering wash of winds. They rise from the water or fall from the sky with balletic grace, with a booming noise like rattled sheets of corrugated tin, with a furious and unmitigated energy. It is the *life* of them that takes such hold of you.

I have spent enough time with large predators to know the human predilection to overlook authority and mystery in the lives of small, gregarious animals like the goose, but its qualities are finally as subtle, its way of making a living as admirable and attractive, as the grizzly bear's.

Geese are traditional, one could even say conservative, animals. They tend to stick to the same nesting grounds and wintering areas, to the same migration routes, year after year. Males and females have identical plumage. They usually mate for life, and both sexes care for the young. In all these ways, as well as in being more at ease on land, geese differ from ducks. They differ from swans in having proportionately longer legs and shorter necks. In size they fall somewhere between the two. A mature male lesser snow goose (*Chen caerulescens*), for example, might weigh six pounds, measure thirty inches from bill to tail, and have a wingspan of three feet. A mature female would be slightly smaller and lighter by perhaps half a pound.

Taxonomists divide the geese of the Northern Hemisphere into two groups, "gray" and "black," according to the color of their bills, feet, and legs. Among black geese like Canada geese and brandt they're dark. Snow geese, with rose-pink feet and legs and pink bills, are grouped with the gray geese, among whom these appendages are often brightly colored. Snow geese also commonly have rust-speckled faces, from feeding in iron-rich soils.

Before it was changed in 1971, the snow goose's scientific name, *Chen hyperborea*, reflected its high-arctic breeding heritage. The greater snow goose (*C. c. atlantica*)—a larger but far less numerous race of snow goose—breeds in northwestern Greenland and on adjacent Ellesmere, Devon, and Axel Heiburg islands. The lesser snow goose breeds slightly farther south, on Baffin and Southampton islands, the east coast of Hudson Bay, and on Banks Island to the west and Wrangel Island in

Siberia. (Many people are attracted to the snow goose precisely because of its association with these little-known regions.)

There are two color phases, finally, of the lesser snow goose, blue and white. The combined population of about 1.5 million, the largest of any goose in the world, is divided into an eastern, mostly blue-phase population that winters in Texas and Louisiana, and a western, white-phase population that winters in California. (It is the latter birds that pass through Tule Lake.)

The great numbers of these highly gregarious birds can be misleading. First, we were not certain until quite recently where snow geese were nesting, or how large their breeding colonies were. The scope of the problem is suggested by the experience of a Canadian biologist, Angus Gavin. In 1941 he stumbled on what he thought was a small breeding colony of lesser snow geese, on the delta of the McConnell River on the east coast of Hudson Bay—14,000 birds. In 1961 there were still only about 35,000 birds there. But a 1968 survey showed 100,000 birds, and in 1973 there were 520,000. Second, populations of arctic-breeding species like the snow goose are subject to extreme annual fluctuations, a boom-and-bust cycle tied to the unpredictable weather patterns typical of arctic ecosystems. After a series of prolonged winters, for example, when persistent spring snow cover kept birds from nesting, the Wrangel Island population of snow geese fell from 400,000 birds in 1965 to fewer than 50,000 in 1975. (By the summer of 1981 it was back up to 170,000.)

The numbers in which we see them on their wintering grounds are large enough to be comforting—it is hard at first to imagine what would threaten such flocks. Snow geese, however, face a variety of problems. The most serious is a striking loss of winter habitat. In 1900 western snow geese had more than 6,200 square miles of winter habitat available to them on California's Sacramento and San Joaquin rivers. Today, ninety percent of this has been absorbed by agricultural, industrial, and urban expansion. This means ninety percent of the land in central California that snow geese once depended on for food and shelter is gone. Hunters in California kill about twenty percent of the population each year and leave another four to five percent crippled to die of starvation and injuries. (An additional two to three percent dies each year of lead poisoning, from ingesting spent shot.) An unknown number are also killed by high-tension wires. In the future, geese will likely face a significant threat on their arctic breeding grounds from oil and gas exploration.

The birds also suffer from the same kinds of diseases, traumatic accidents, and natural disasters that threaten all organisms. Females, for example, fiercely devoted to the potential in their egg clutches, may choose to die of exposure on their nests rather than abandon them in an unseasonable storm.

In the light of all this, it is ironic that the one place on earth a person might see these geese in numbers large enough to cover half the sky is, itself, a potential threat to their existence.

The land now called Tule Lake National Wildlife Refuge lies in a volcanic basin, part of which was once an extensive 2,700-square-mile marshland. In 1905 the federal government began draining the area to create irrigated croplands. Marshland habitat and bird populations shrank. By 1981 only fifty-six square miles of wetland, two percent of the original area, was left for waterfowl. In spite of this reduction, the area, incredibly, remains an ideal spot for migratory waterfowl. On nearly any given day in the fall a visitor to the Klamath Basin might see more than a million birds—mallards, gadwalls, pintails, lesser scaups, goldeneyes, cinnamon teals, northern shovelers, redheads, canvasbacks, ruddy ducks; plus western and cackling Canada geese, white-fronted geese, Ross's geese, lesser snow geese, and whistling swans. (More than 250 species of birds have been seen on or near the refuge, and more than 170 nest here.)

The safety of these populations is in the hands of a resident federal manager and his staff, who must effectively balance the birds' livelihood with the demands of local farmers, who use Tule Lake's water to irrigate adjacent fields of malt barley and winter potatoes, and waterfowl hunters, some of whom come from hundreds of miles away. And there is another problem. Although the Klamath Basin is the greatest concentration point for migratory waterfowl in North America, caring well for birds here is no guarantee they will fare well elsewhere along the flyway. And a geographic concentration like this merely increases the chance of catastrophe if epidemic disease should strike.

The first time I visited Tule Lake I arrived early on a fall afternoon. When I asked where the snow geese were congregated I was directed to an area called the English Channel, several miles out on the refuge road. I sat there for three hours, studying the birds' landings and takeoffs, how they behaved toward each other on the water, how they shot the skies overhead. I tried to unravel and to parse the dazzling synchronicity of their movements. I am always struck anew in these moments, in observing such detail, by the way in which an animal slowly reveals itself.

Before the sun went down, I drove off to see more of the snow goose's landscape, what other animals there might be on the refuge, how the land changed at a distance from the water. I found the serpentine great blue heron, vivacious and melodious flocks of red-winged blackbirds, and that small, fierce hunter, the kestrel. Muskrats bolted across the road. At the southern end of the refuge, where cattails and bulrushes give way to rabbit brush and sage on a volcanic plain, I came upon mule deer, three does and four fawns standing still and tense in a meandering fog.

I found a room that evening in the small town of Tulelake. There'd not been, that I could recall, a moment of silence all day from these most loquacious of geese. I wondered if they were mum in the middle of the night, how quiet they were at dawn. I set the alarm for 3 A.M.

The streets of Tulelake are desolate at that hour. In that odd stillness —the stillness of moonlit horses standing asleep in fields—I drove out into the countryside, toward the refuge. It was a ride long enough to hear the first two movements of Beethoven's Fifth Symphony. I drove in a light rain, past white farmhouses framed by ornamental birches and weeping willows. In the 1860s this land was taken by force from the Modoc Indians; in the 1940s the government built a Japanese internment camp here. At this hour, however, nearly every landscape has a pervasive innocence. I passed the refuge headquarters—low shiplapped buildings, white against a dark ridge of basalt, facing a road lined with Russian olives. I drove past stout, slowly dying willows of undetermined age, trees that mark the old shore line of Tule Lake, where it was before the reclamation project began.

The music is low, barely audible, but the enthusiasm in some of the strong passages reminds me of geese. I turn the tape off and drive a narrow, cratered road out into the refuge, feeling the car slipping sideways in the mud. Past rafts of sleeping ducks. The first geese I see surge past just overhead like white butterflies, brushing the penumbral dimness above the car's headlights. I open the window and feel the sudden assault of their voices, the dunning power of their wings hammering the air, a rush of cold wind and rain through the window. In a moment I am outside, standing in the roar. I find a comfortable, protected place in the bulrushes and wait in my parka until dawn, listening.

Their collective voice, like the cries of athletic young men at a distance, is unabated. In the darkness it is nearly all there is of them, but for an occasional and eerie passage overhead. I try to listen closely: a barking of high-voiced dogs, like terriers, the squealing of shoats. By an accident of harmonics the din rises and falls like the cheering of a crowd in a vast stadium. Whoops and shouts; startled voices of outrage, of shock.

These are not the only voices. Cackling geese pass over in the dark, their cries more tentative. Coyotes yip. Nearby some creature screeches, perhaps a mouse in the talons of a great horned owl, whose skipping hoots I have heard earlier.

A gibbous moon shines occasionally through a wind-driven overcast. Toward dawn the geese's voices fall off suddenly for a few moments.

The silence seems primordial. The black sky in the east now shows blood red through scalloped shelves of cloud. It broadens into an orange flare that fades to rose and finally to the grays of dawn. The voices begin again.

I drive back into Tulelake and eat breakfast amid a throng of hunters crowding the tables of a small cafe, steaming the windows with their raucous conversation.

Bob Fields, the refuge manager, has agreed to take me on a tour in the afternoon. I decide to spend the morning at the refuge headquarters, reading scientific reports and speaking with biologist Ed O'Neill about the early history of Tule Lake.

O'Neill talks first about the sine qua non, a suitable expanse of water. In the American West the ownership of surface water confers the kind of political and economic power that comes elsewhere with oil wells and banks. Water is a commodity; it is expensive to maintain and its owners seek to invest the limited supply profitably. A hunting club that keeps private marshland for geese and ducks, for example, will do so only as long as they feel their hunting success warrants it. If the season is shortened or the bag limit reduced by the state—the most common ways to conserve dwindling waterfowl populations—they might find hunting no longer satisfying and sell the marsh to farmers, who will turn it into cropland. Real estate speculators and other landowners with substantial surface-water rights rarely give the birds that depend on their lands a second thought when they're preparing to sell. As O'Neill puts it, "You can't outweigh a stack of silver dollars with a duck."

The plight of western waterfowl is made clearer by an anomaly. In the eastern United States, a natural abundance of water and the closure of many tracts of private land to hunting provide birds with a strong measure of protection. In the West, bird populations are much larger, but water is scarcer and refuge lands, because they are largely public, remain open to hunting.

By carefully adjusting the length of the hunting season and the bag limits each year, and by planting food for the birds, refuge managers try to maintain large bird populations, in part to keep private hunting clubs along the flyway enthusiastic about continuing to provide additional habitat for the birds. Without the help of private individuals, including conservation groups that own wetlands, the federal and state refuge systems simply cannot provide for the birds. . . .

Some birds, the snow geese among them, have adapted to shortages of food and land. Deprived of the rootstocks of bulrushes and marsh grasses, snow geese in the West have switched to gleaning agricultural wastes and cropping winter wheat, a practice that has spread to the Midwest, where snow geese now feed increasingly on rice and corn. A second adjustment snow geese have made is to linger on their fall migrations and to winter over farther north. That way fewer birds end up for a shorter period of time on traditional wintering grounds, where food is scarcer each year.

As we spoke, O'Neill kept glancing out the window. He told me about having seen as many as three hundred thousand white geese there in years past. With the loss of habitat and birds spreading out now to winter along the flyway, such aggregations, he says, may never be seen again. He points out, too, looking dismayed and vaguely bitter, that these huge flocks have not been conserved for the viewer who does not hunt, for the tourist who comes to Tule Lake to see something he has only dreamed of.

We preserve them, principally, to hunt them.

In broad daylight I was able to confirm something I'd read about the constant, loud din of their voices: relatively few birds are actually vocalizing at any one time, perhaps only one in thirty. Biologists speculate that snow geese recognize each other's voices and that family units of three or four maintain contact in these vast aggregations by calling out to one another. What sounds like mindless chaos to the human ear, then, may actually be a complex pattern of solicitous cries, discretely distinguished by snow geese.

Another sound that is easier to decipher in daylight is the rising squall that signals they are leaving the water. It's like the sustained hammering of a waterfall or a wind booming in the full crowns of large trees.

One wonders, watching the geese fly off in flocks of a hundred or a thousand, if they would be quite so arresting without their stunning whiteness. When they fly with the sun behind them, the opaque white of their bodies, the white of water-polished seashells, is set off against grayer whites in their tail feathers and in their translucent, black-tipped wings. Up close these are the dense, impeccable whites of an arctic fox. Against the grays and blues of a storm-laden sky, the whiteness has a surreal glow, a brilliance without shadow.

I remember watching a large flock rise one morning from a plowed field about a mile distant. I had been watching clouds, the soft, buoyant, wind-blown edges of immaculate cumulus. The birds rose against much darker clouds to the east. There was something vaguely ominous in this apparition, as if the earth had opened and poured them forth, like a wind, a blizzard, which unfurled across the horizon above the dark soil, becoming wider and higher in the sky than my field of vision could encompass, great swirling currents of birds in a rattling of wings, one fluid recurved sweep of ten thousand passing through the open spaces in another, counterflying flock, while beyond them lattice after lattice passed like sliding walls, until in the whole sky you lost your depth of field and felt as though you were looking up from the floor of the ocean through shoals of fish.

At rest on the water the geese drank and slept and bathed and preened. They reminded me in their ablutions of the field notes of a Hudson Bay trader, George Barnston. He wrote of watching flocks of snow geese gathering on James Bay in 1862, in preparation for their annual two-thousand-mile, nonstop thirty-two-hour flight to the Louisiana coast. They finally left off feeding, he wrote, to smooth and dress their feathers with oil, like athletes, biding their time for a north wind. When it came they were gone, hundreds of thousands of them, leaving a coast once "widely resonant with their petulant and incessant calls" suddenly as "silent as the grave—a deserted, barren, and frozen shore."

Barnston was struck by the way snow geese do things together. No other waterfowl are as gregarious, certainly no other large bird flies as skillfully in such tight aggregations. This quality—the individual act beautifully integrated within the larger movement of the flock—is provocative. One afternoon I studied individual birds for hours as they landed and took off. I never once saw a bird on the water move over to accommodate a bird that was landing nor a bird ever disturbed by another taking off, no matter how tightly they were bunched. In no flight overhead did I see two birds so much as brush wing tips. Certainly they must; but for the most part they are flawlessly adroit. A flock settles gently on the water like whiffling leaves; birds explode vertically with compact and furious wing beats and then stretch out full length, airborne, rank on rank, as if the whole flock had been cleanly wedged from the surface of the water. Several thousand bank smoothly against a head wind, as precisely as though they were feathers in the wing of a single bird.

It was while I sat immersed in these details that Bob Fields walked up. After a long skyward stare he said, "I've been here for seven years. I never get tired of watching them."

We left in his small truck to drive the narrow causeways of Tule Lake and the five adjacent federal refuges. Fields joined the U.S. Fish and Wildlife Service in 1958, at the age of twenty-two. His background is in range biology and plant ecology as well as waterfowl management. Before he came to Tule Lake in 1974, to manage the Klamath Basin refuges, he worked on the National Bison Range in Montana and on the Charles Sheldon Antelope Range in Nevada.

In 1973 a group of visitors who would profoundly affect Fields arrived at Tule Lake. They were Eskimos, from the Yukon-Kuskokwim delta of Alaska. They had come to see how the geese populations, which they depend on for food, were being managed. In the few days they were together, Fields came to understand that the Eskimos were appalled by the waste they saw at Tule Lake, by the number of birds hunters left crippled and unretrieved, and were surprised that hunters took only the breast meat and threw the rest of the bird away. On the other hand, the aggregations of geese they saw were so extensive they believed someone was fooling them—surely, they thought, so many birds could never be found in one place.

The experience with the Eskimos—Fields traveled north to see the Yukon-Kuskokwim country, and the Eskimos returned to Tule Lake in 1977—focused his career as had no other event. In discussions with the Eskimos he found himself talking with a kind of hunter he rarely encountered anymore—humble men with a respect for the birds and a sense of responsibility toward them. That the Eskimos were dumbstruck at the number of birds led him to more sobering thoughts: if he failed here as a refuge manager, his failure would run the length of the continent.

In the years following, Fields gained a reputation as a man who cared passionately for the health and welfare of waterfowl populations. He tailored, with the help of assistant refuge manager Homer McCollum, a model hunting program at Tule Lake, but he is candid in expressing his distaste for a type of hunter he still meets too frequently—belligerent, careless people for whom hunting is simply violent recreation; people who trench and rut the refuge's roads in oversize four-wheel-drive vehicles, who are ignorant of hunting laws or who delight in breaking them as part of a "game" they play with refuge personnel.

At one point in our afternoon drive, Fields and I were watching a flock of geese feeding in a field of oats and barley on the eastern edge of the refuge. We watched in silence for a long time. I said something about the way birds can calm you, how the graceful way they define the sky can draw irritation right of you. He looked over at me and smiled and nodded. A while later, still watching the birds, he said, "I have known all along there was more to it than managing the birds so they could be killed by some macho hunter." It was the Eskimos who gave him a sense of how a hunter should behave, and their awe that rekindled his own desire to see the birds preserved.

As we drove back across the refuge, Fields spoke about the changes that had occurred in the Klamath Basin since the federal reclamation project began in 1905. Most of the native grasses—blue bench wheat grass, Great Basin wild rye—are gone. A visitor notices foreign plants in their place, like cheatgrass. And introduced species like the ring-necked pheasant and the muskrat, which bores holes in the refuge dikes and disrupts the pattern of drainage. And the intrusion of high-tension power lines, which endanger the birds and which Fields has no budget to bury. And the presence of huge pumps that circulate water from Tule Lake to farmers in the valley, back and forth, back and forth, before pumping it west to Lower Klamath Refuge.

It is over these evolving, occasionally uneasy relationships between recent immigrants and the original inhabitants that Fields keeps watch. I say goodbye to him at his office, to the world of bird poacher, lead poisoning, and politically powerful hunting and agricultural lobbies he deals with every day. When I shake his hand I find myself wanting to thank him for the depth with which he cares for the birds, and for the intelligence that allows him to disparage not hunting itself but the lethal acts of irresponsibility and thoughtless people.

I still have a few hours before I meet Frans for dinner. I decide to drive out to the east of the refuge, to a low escarpment which bears the carvings of Indians who lived in this valley before white men arrived. I pass by open fields where horses and beef cattle graze and cowbirds flock after seeds. Red-tailed hawks are perched on telephone poles, watching for field rodents. A light rain has turned to snow.

The brooding face of the escarpment has a prehistoric quality. It is secured behind a chain link fence topped with barbed wire, but the evidence of vandals who have broken past it to knock off souvenir petroglyphs is everywhere. The castings of barn owls, nesting in stone pockets above, are spread over the ground. I open some of them to see what the owls have been eating. Meadow voles. Deer mice.

The valley before me has darkened. I know somewhere out there, too far away to see now, long scarves of snow geese are riding and banking against these rising winds, and that they are aware of the snow. In a few weeks Tule Lake will be frozen and they will be gone. I turn back to the wall of petroglyphs. The carvings relate, apparently, to the movement of animals through this land hundreds of years ago. The people who made them made their clothing and shelters, even their cooking containers, from the lake's tule reeds. When the first white man arrived—Peter Ogden, in 1826—he found them wearing blankets of duck and goose feathers. In the years since, the complex interrelationships of the Modoc with this land, largely unrecorded to begin with, have disappeared. The land itself has been turned to agriculture, with a portion set aside for certain species of birds that have passed through this valley for no one knows how many centuries. The hunters have become farmers, the farmers landowners. Their sons have gone to the cities and become businessmen, and the sons of these men have returned with guns, to take advantage of the old urge, to hunt. But more than a few come back with a poor knowledge of the birds, the land, the reason for killing. It is by now a familiar story, for which birds pay with their lives.

The old argument, that geese must be killed for their own good, to manage the size of their populations, founders on two points. Snow goose populations rise and fall precipitously because of their arctic breeding pattern. No group of hunters can "fine-tune" such a basic element of their ecology. Second, the artificial control of their numbers only augments efforts to continue draining wetlands.

We must search in our way of life, I think, for substantially more here than economic expansion and continued good hunting. We need to look for a set of relationships similar to the ones Fields admired among the Eskimos. We grasp what is beautiful in a flight of snow geese rising against an overcast sky as easily as we grasp the beauty in a cello suite; and intuit, I believe, that if we allow these things to be destroyed or degraded for economic or frivolous reasons we will become deeply and strangely impoverished.

I had seen little of my friend Frans in three days. At dinner he said he wanted to tell me of the Oostvaardersplassen in Holland. It has become a major stopover for waterfowl in northern Europe, a marsh that didn't even exist ten years ago. Birds hardly anyone has seen in Holland since the time of Napoleon are there now. Peregrine falcons, snowy egrets, and European sea eagles have returned.

I drive away from the escarpment holding tenaciously to this image of reparation.

In Condor Country

David Darlington (b. 1951) is a freelance writer based in Berkeley, California, who has published widely on natural history. His book In Condor Country *(1987) traces the efforts made to save the California condor from extinction.*

It is early in the morning and we are near the top of a mountain. Along the shoulders of the road, hunters appear and disappear; their fluorescent orange hats and coats take shape and then diminish in the fog, the visual equivalent of clanging buoys. Visibility perhaps extends to one hundred feet. Rain and wind have drawn a maze of channels on the windshield of the pickup, although it is September—officially too early for rain in California. Nevertheless, water falling from the sky is beating a steady snare-drum roll on the camper top. I sit under it in the back, bouncing on the tire wells with Eben [McMillan]; we face each other across a chilly atmosphere that makes faint clouds of our breath.

The truck is climbing a badly rutted dirt road toward the summit. Granite extrusions and Ponderosa pines pass within a foot of the windows. Eben stares out at them as he rocks from side to side, gripping the edges of his ridged steel seat. He wears a bent gray felt cowboy hat and a navy blue windbreaker. In the early light his eyes seem as cold as the air; when Eben takes his glasses off and isn't squinting in the sun, his eyes reveal their true color, which is the color of ice.

On top of the mountain, seven cars sit facing a billboard in a full-bore gale. Rain comes in horizontally up here; we get out of the truck, and I have to pull my hat low on my head to prevent it from flying away. Just downhill, a park ranger is pulling a gigantic pump hose toward an outhouse from a light green truck. Thoroughly soaked, he smiles up at us. The pines around him are white bark and Jeffrey; lightning has transformed the trunk of one into an upside-down U, but the tree is still living.

The billboard says:

The California condor, a rare and endangered species fully protected by state law, can be seen from this point. Adult birds may
be identified by their large size, black color with orange head, and
by the triangular white patch on the underside of each wing. The
condor has an average wing-spread of nine feet, the longest of any
North American land bird. Riding favorable air currents, it can soar
and glide for more than one hour at a time in steady flight. From
June through October one or more condors may usually be seen
soaring in the vicinity of this observation site. Help protect and
preserve this vanishing species.

Los Padres National Forest
U.S. Department of Agriculture

On clear days, the view from this spot encompasses great vistas of brown cliffs, blue ridges bordering the Cuyama River, and the multi-colored patchwork of farms in the San Joaquin Valley. Today the view is about what you'd get from inside an oxygen tent. Nevertheless, Eben insists on walking the narrow trail to the lookout to make sure that no one from our proposed party is out there looking for condors. "They'd have to be crazy to be out there," he allows, "but birders are crazy."

The path to the lookout is covered with asphalt and lined with granite rocks. No one—not even a birder—is out there. We return to the parking lot, and Eben confers with several of the people sitting in the cars. Satisfied that we've found everyone we're going to find, he climbs back into the truck, but this time we ride in front, with heat and other humans, back down the mountain to a wide place in the road, which Eben has designated a meeting spot.

The mountain is Mount Pinos—at nine thousand feet, the highest peak in the Tehachapis. If you look at the major mountain ranges of California on a map, they form a kind of horseshoe: the open end of the shoe is in the north; the eastern prong is the Sierra Nevada; the Coast Ranges constitute the wing to the west. The southern segment of the shoe—the part you might grip if you aimed to pitch all these mountains toward a stake somewhere in, say, the USSR—is made up of the Transverse Ranges (including the Tehachapis), which run east-west sixty miles north of the Los Angeles basin. To some ways of thinking, these mountains are the true barrier between northern and southern California: dry, rugged country of sandstone and chaparral where time-worn cliffs loom like parapets in a Pleistocene animals' Alamo—the last refuge of the California condor.

Once a year Eben leads a condor watch for the National Audubon Society's Golden Gate chapter (one that has broken with the organization's leadership and rejected captive breeding). The traditional site for the event is Mount Pinos and the traditional time is late September—calving season on the cattle ranches in the foothills of the Tehachapis. Many of the calves are stillborn, and about one cow in ten will fail to survive the ordeal of childbirth; the result on enormous grazing tracts like the Hudson, Snedden, and San Emidio ranches (especially when combined with the effects of the first week of deer hunting season) is a landscape littered with carcasses and afterbirth—and, as a consequence, condors. . . .

It was a gray, dank day that made the barren brown early-autumn landscape seem oppressive—even emptier than usual. As we traveled through it, the normal complement of natural phenomena was performed by the local fauna. A golden eagle tearing at a squirrel carcass on the side of the road allowed the car to come unusually close, then took off and flew alongside us, its huge wings flapping just feet from the car. "This time of year you see things like that," Eben said. "The mammals go underground and the migrating eagles get pretty hungry." Farther on, an enormous fuzzy spot was crossing the road—a tarantula, as it turned out. Eben: "They claim that the ones we see are more than twenty years old. They're looking for a female and that's why they're out traveling. This is a high-mortality time of year for them. The pepsis wasp is a leavening factor on spider populations. They call it the tarantula hawk—it paralyzes the tarantula, then lays its eggs on it. The larvae tunnel inside and develop there. There are hundreds of different kinds of pepsis wasp, and each one uses a different spider."

The highway lost its straightness now, bending into big curves as it climbed through humped yellow hills of increasing steepness. I noted the onset of the dizzy euphoria that accompanies entry into foothills. To the west, the craggy ridges of the Caliente Mountains seemed to be stacked on top of one another, receding into the distance under a low, dark gray sky that matched the color of the road.

We pass by our campground at Valle Vista. A couple of miles farther is the Los Padres National Forest sign, surrounded now by cars and people. The cars are laden with equipment; cameras, lenses, tripods, telescopes. One license plate says BIRDIN. . . .

Eben's entrance into the scene as usual stimulates a minor stir. He is the eccentric old man, the colorful sage, the back country guru. His effect on this group of amateur naturalists is that of a magnet on iron filings. As people greet him he grins amiably, shaking various right hands with his left. One man says, "This is my fourth trip down here and I haven't seen a condor yet."

Eben says "Well, you'll see one today."

"You heard him," the man tells the others.

The view from this lookout offers a roadside panorama of condor country, a powerful dose of the immensity of America. Steep red and white cliffs descend from both right and left to frame a section of dull brown foothills, gentle in comparison with the cliffs. There are distant dirt roads and cattle trails traversing the tops of open ridges, and immense brown sandstone rocks in the middle of the landscape. Beyond these hills stretches the San Joaquin Valley, a flat quilt of green and brown squares—those that are irrigated and those that are plowed. Away to the northwest the hills go white, or almost pink, like tortured flesh—the southern end of the Temblors, a forbidding no man's land that appears to be suffocating in some sort of haze. To the southeast, the Tehachapis are faintly blue on the horizon when they're visible at all; the fitful storm clouds come and go, obscuring sections of the entire picture, occasionally reducing our field of vision to the bare brown hillsides immediately before us. . . .

Noon. Eric [Caine, a birder,] announces, "There's a pair of condor at five o'clock. They're circling. They're gonna get up above the horizon in about thirty seconds." He looks at his watch, then back at the black dots in the distance. "They just hit. Took 'em eighteen seconds."

"Where are you talking about?"

"In the flat beyond Lone Tree there's a red and white tower. Not the Purina one, though. Above it there's a line of white clouds superimposed on the gray. The birds are just to the right of it."

"Oh, yeah!"

"Oh, they're huge!"

"Those are condor," Eric says. "Two adults."

"I just lost them over Brush Mountain."

Eric says, "They'll be back, and they might be close." . . .

Four P.M. The air is filled with a gusty drizzle. Someone says, "There's something big above Lone Tree. It's being chased by two smaller birds."

"Condor!" cries Eben. "Flex-glide!"

"What I'm seeing ain't in a flex-glide," says Eric.

"Well," says Eben, "I can't see so good."

"Condor," confirms Eric, studying the speck. "Coming our way."

The bird is cruising in leisurely loops, like a toy boat circling in an eddy. When it enters the foreground below us, still too distant for its white wingpatches to be visible, it turns, banks, and rises. Now it does go into the flex-glide, dipping its wings and suddenly soaring behind the ridge to our left. Having tired of the social scene, I climb the clay embankment on the other side of the road, slip through the barbed-wire fence, and set off in the direction where the condor disappeared.

The warm wind is blowing now; the rain has stopped. I tie my coat around my waist and ascend a hill of oak and foxtail. Beyond the ridge that borders the road is a broad brown and yellow valley with gigantic outcroppings of pockmarked rocks. The surrounding hillsides are bare, eroded; but on the higher hills the bush takes over—green manzanita, chaparral. Behind these foothills four ridges recede, becoming bluer as they grow more distant. There are flat banks of fog in the far valleys and stacks of gray clouds on the horizon. A black dot rises from the ridgeline; I raise my glasses and it leaps into close-up: the condor, its white patches clearly visible against the black, widespread wings.

The bird banks and rises in lazy circles, another smaller raptor behind it, and I realize for the umpteenth time how regal raptors are on their rounds; it has to do with how little effort they seem to expend, how steady their bearing is, how unchallenged their place in the sky. As advertised, this particular condor is steady to the point of an aeronautic appearance; it looks like a glider or Piper Cub with wings supported by solid struts. Nevertheless, the fingerlike pinion feathers seem to express an attitude of relatedness; they're spread the way your fingers would be if you were shooing something away from you—an air of utter independence.

After a lengthy period of circling, the bird comes to earth on the valley floor, a few hundred yards from a cluster of farm buildings. I watch through the binoculars for a while, but the condor doesn't move, so I keep on hiking. There are lots of brightly colored wildflowers in the barren-looking landscape—purple asters with yellow centers, scarlet buglers being visited by iridescent hummingbirds. I find the big brown rocks in the valley to be filled with caves, and I crawl inside one to get out of the rain—which has, not surprisingly, resumed. Eventually, though, opting for view, I climb the exterior of the cliff in a fine misting shower. When I get to the tip, I look up and am startled to see the condor above me.

The bird seems to be scrutinizing me (I remember Ken Brower's line: "When man and condor meet today, it is with a glance of mutual appraisal, each to see whether the other is yet extinct"). What, I wonder, do you say when you're finally face-to-face with an absolute—the biggest bird in North America, the embodiment of all endangered species, a messenger from the living to the dead. I don't say anything; I stand in the rain with upturned face, a lone earthling rooted to a rock, regarding the hovering form of extinction. This condor is an anomaly, I know; a living incarnation of mortality. Spinning high in the air above me, framed against storm clouds, with warm sheets of water blowing between us, it seems a specter. It occurs to me that this spooky creature has on a hell of a Halloween costume: a skeleton suit and a jack-o'-lantern head, a vivid uniform for a vulture. The decoration alone would set it apart from any other bird, and the temptation to assign it symbolic status is irresistible. But as I watch it, the condor doesn't strike me as a symbol of extinction so much as a totem for North America itself. It's because of the coloring, somehow—red, white, and black is a morbid heraldry for a once-promising continent, a land that's been dying since 1492, a place that harbors the exotics of the earth and in doing so drives its native inhabitants into oblivion.

In spite of this, the condor does not appear gloomy; it seems polite, tolerant, curious. After a moment, having witnessed enough of me and my perambulations, it dips its wings and glides away. I glass it in profile and see the naked head extended, held slightly lower than the rest of the horizontal body in the sulky demeanor of vultures. It disappears in the direction of the lookout, and soon I hear distant, excited voices wafting across the sodden landscape: "Hey!" "Hey!" then a second of silence and, finally, cheers and clapping.

For those of us raised far away from wilderness—in places populated solely by domesticated animals, with untamed ones glimpsed only in books or on television—there's something miraculous about seeing them in the wild. The first time I saw a bear in the woods, I couldn't believe there was something so big that nobody owned, fed, or kept on a leash. The self-sustaining ability of nature seems a marvel, though it's literally the oldest thing in the world. Similarly, seeing the condor here where it "belongs" is simultaneously remarkable and mundane. I was actually surprised by how natural it seemed; there were no trumpets, no soundtrack music, no caustic debate, no fee of admission. The condor seemed unaware of its celebrity or of the controversy that surrounds it. It was just a big black and white bird flying around in a quiet canyon. To be sure, its size and bearing distinguish it from any other animal you might imagine; but, for me, the most extraordinary thing about the condor was the fact that it was free.

San Joaquin Valley

Winter's Fog

David Mas Masumoto (b. 1954) is a third-generation Japanese-American peach and grape farmer, a freelance writer, and a farm activist. After graduating from the University of California at Berkeley in 1976 he earned a master's degree in community development from UC Davis. This selection is from his 1995 "chronicle of four seasons on my family farm," Epitaph for a Peach.

On cold winter nights I step out into our porch to check the thermometer. It has not changed much all day, ranging between a cold in the low thirties to a high in the mid-forties with a damp, biting fog blanketing the valley farmlands. From my porch I hear the tap-tap-tap of dewdrops trickling down the barren branches, falling and landing on the damp leaves below. I can feel the cold on my cheeks and the warmth of our home's wood stove still within my sweater.

Beyond me the vines and peach trees change seasons too. I think of the past year and the decisions I would have altered, modifications I can plan for in the coming season. Yet no matter what new course I may choose, a natural rhythm remains. I know the vines and trees will still be pruned soon, as they have been for generations.

The fog continues to roll in. Where it's heading I do not know. It passes in front of the porch like a shifting cloud. If I stare at it long enough, it seems that I start to move instead. I imagine our farmhouse cutting through the gray mist like a lost ship, my porch transformed into the bridge. I lean against the rail and peer into the drifting fog as my vessel heads into the night.

I sail on, the thermometer the only instrument on board. I like watching the gradual temperature changes, the measurement of a cold front moving in or the dramatic drop in readings with the loss of sunlight. Several years ago an arctic blast moved into the valley like a silent wolf. For days it hunted, freezing oranges and killing trees. I monitored its progress on my thermometer, recording historic low temperatures— dropping below twenty and never rising above freezing even in sunshine. Farmers could do little except watch. We only had our thermometers to help us verify what we already knew.

But a thermometer enables me to see the wild. The arctic wolf of that winter came alive in the dropping mercury. During the summer a different creature ventures into our valley—the searing heat that stays above one hundred degrees into the evening hours. My senses feel the extremes and my thermometer enables me to process the impression like a series of snapshots. The wild is seen.

A naturalist may disagree, claiming that agriculture tames the wild and farmers manipulate their world to disable the beast of nature. Judging by my last year trying to save a peach, though, I'd say that gives us farmers too much credit. On a farm, much more is out of control than is in control. I fool myself when I call myself master of my farm. My thermometer reveals my impotence, for I cannot even consistently predict a day's highs or lows.

The fog carries a deep, penetrating cold with it. It doesn't take long before I'm chilled to the bone, especially when I'm in the fields, walking in the damp grass. Once my boots and pants get wet, I have only hours before my legs grow numb. At night, while standing on my porch deck, I feel the fog invade my clothes, infiltrating the layers, announcing itself with my involuntary shiver.

I return inside, where I can watch the fog sail past our large windows. We have few curtains in our house, most of our windows are bare. From the inside I can see the panorama of the farm. I am exposed to the wild nature beyond the glass. I've spent hours in front of the windows, watching storms march in from the west and wind blow rain and hail onto the porch. I can witness the sun rise and set on the mountains that ring the valley, study the ripples of August heat rising from the earth, and feel the glass warm against my skin.

The exchange is reciprocal, especially during the winter. The cold easily permeates the interiors, chilling the house and forcing me to wear sweaters even inside. The intrusion is welcomed though, the season a natural cadence I feel within, a natural clock I respond to.

The change of season connects me with the surrounding wild, a wild I work within. I grow crops from the earth and have discovered that the best soil is also wild. This past year I have learned that productivity is little more than managed chaos, wildness the source of fertility.

In the fog I can hear the voices of farmers before me. Once I believed their old stubborn ways had no place in the progressive world of modern farming. But now they sing of traditions that have a place in my winter season more than ever.

Two wind socks flutter in the shifting fog. In Japanese, the wind is called *kami*, with an honorific *sama* often added. Wind is respected and revered, *kamisama* becomes a spirit that's alive. I can see that spirit in a wind sock, the energy captured for a moment in a dance of colors, then released as the tail flaps and waves.

Even in winter there is life on the farm. I feel something sacred, a meaning added to my work and my peaches and grapes. I feel connected with the universe. The world of nature and human nature are my teachers, showing and not telling me the secrets of the wild and sacred. From my porch deck I sail into a new world. Discoveries loom in the fog, opportunities inhabit this wilderness. It is a sacred place for myself and my family because I can call this farm home.

Altadena foothills

A Vanishing Land

Hildegarde Flanner (1899–1987), poet, playwright, and essayist, was also an early environmentalist. She moved to southern California soon after graduating from the University of California at Berkeley in 1923. The following is taken from A Vanishing Land, *a booklet written in the 1950s that came out of her experience of having lived thirty-six years in one suburban garden in the foothills of Altadena. "From there," she wrote, "I was closely aware of what was going on in the valley and the coastal plain below. We were within reach of the smog and often affected by it." In 1962 she moved to Napa Valley.*

When I first came to live in southern California, around 1925, I was looked upon as a foreigner from Indiana, so much was the lack of nativity formerly noticed by born Californians. I had not been here long before I saw how desirable it would have been, in a country whose character was equally strange and absorbing to me, to be bred and born in the grain of mountain, desert, palm, and semi-tropic. My family came here for the same comfortable and aesthetic reason that has always turned midland and prairie Americans toward the coast. We came to live in a choice landscape in a choice climate. As a child in Indiana I had known the northern forests, where summer evenings brought the enchantment of fireflies and the cold unrolling song of the whippoorwill, and where the squally lakes held quiet shallows for slender rushes and my light canoe. Yet the Middle West had never offered the satisfactions we found here in southern California, where it is difficult to locate a dull view and where the weather is so easygoing and bohemian as to make the exotic out-of-doors a free and informal conservatory for daily living. To own a small piece of earth endowed with fine scenery in an amiable climate, this was what we came for and what, before long, we obtained. Since that time I have lived in the same garden in the foothills above the city of Pasadena. Eleven miles away the tall city hall of Los Angeles is visible on a clear day.

Western sensitivities, like western mockingbirds, are sometimes given to intoxicated utterance, and rather like the mockingbirds, to a certain defensiveness also, as if such extravagance anticipated a rebuke. When it comes to writing about the western earth, this makes for a sort of self-consciousness, a sense of being watched; or is it only that we are watching ourselves be cautious? Yet if we have anything here that could be called a tradition, it lies simply in appreciation of the earth, an appreciation that is perhaps captive but neither hysterical nor insincere. The person to whom a modest and genuine identity with the scene is important must wait for that relationship to overtake him, for he will never discover it by pursuit. Romantic enthusiasm comes quickly, but insight into the unexpected delicacies and extremities of the dry western earth, a taste for its arid cryptic literalness, and the excitement of its antiquity where the massive inner centuries have left their tracks in view, such familiarity comes only with living close enough to the earth and long enough, and under the touch of its very physical and poetic spirit of place. The attachment which has made the westerner seem naive or very regional is not so hard to tolerate if it is recollected that to live here is in a way a challenge, at least for those who stop to think of it. As a nation with the habit of going west, more and more of us have reached the last barrier. It is a fascinating barrier of mountain, desert, and ocean, and it is also psychological because it is unfamiliar and final. Our material and gainful energies can soon be at ease, but our minds turn in more slowly, inquisitive though they may be to create. Of the influence we encounter we make not one but many images of the earth, and gradually through that possessiveness we learn to be at home.

Now after years of living with the western earth I believe that I have learned some of its native truths, not profound, it may be, but possibly better than profound, the kind that accumulate personal human meanings, which relate one to environment. For instance, it is of the nature of things here that sunlight seems to be absorbed by what it shines on and to last over in a contained state so that objects then are bright from inside out with a long-deposited glow, an old mineral light that is like no other reflection in other climates as it falls into the eye and slips into the mind. It is an ordinary phenomenon of matter, light, color, and drought, and one notes it as fact, not as fantasy, not because there is any desire to be mystified. Explained or unexplained, it gives ocular pleasure. Also it soon comes to one here that, because of some desert discipline nature has known, ethereal things may be strong and enduring, like the frosty-white flowers of the yucca in whose reality we feel no difference of degree compared with the harsh hot boulders the plant grows among. And when I burn eucalyptus in my fireplace (a tree, like myself, not indigenous but long since deeply settled), the smell of the smoke is not merely a woody pungence to my sense, it carries an image of life. And when a bird sings at night in my own garden, garrulous and exaggerated though he may be, his meaning is plain and simple, for it is about this land I have come to love, and its spirit. Yet love alone is not all. If assurance of identity has overtaken me through the years, it comes lately with disturbed concern and in company with the amazements, the losses, and the pressures of progress and change. Today I can see with melancholy that time and too many other things have passed this way since I came to live above the valley near the foot of the mountains. Most difficult to accept, even the earth itself is altered. That which overtakes me now, threatens to become a memory. Southern California, as I have known it, is a vanishing land. . . .

The first aggressive dream of California, that of the Spanish centuries, was a tough, hard-hitting dream mingled of avarice, valor, and fable. That dream has by now had a good many lives, always including something of "where life is better." It has taken on new burdens and new boasts and is full of the commotion of success. Southern California, always alluring in its character of hope, so typical of the West and the frontier, has, until recently, had more to offer to vacationers than to workers. Now, in this small area between the mountains and the ocean, the Californian dream has built, in a few thickly crowded years, a concentration of industry valued annually at five billion dollars, including the nation's third largest concentration of petroleum processing, while the dream rides to work and to pleasure in one of the world's largest mobs of automobiles, on a network of recently built and already antiquated freeways.

To these very considerable realities, and because of them, something else had been added to our land, our lives, and our times, something that baffles and evades final definition yet is itself unpleasantly actual. Let me describe, as I fondly observe it, the scene over which this enigma has thrown a shadow.

The mountains that stand across the northern side of the Los Angeles basin are not among the most spectacular in the state. They lack the huge loft of the Sierra Nevada, they do not have the fossil-like, handsome satanic look of antiquity seen on the slopes of the Panamint, they do not glow with all the hyacinth and magenta that burn the San Jacinto in the desert evening, nor do they take cloud shadows with the ghostly elegance of the lifeless hills at the head of the Coachella Valley. Yet choose a good morning to see them from the edge of the mesa looking up the Arroyo Seco, on the land first settled by the founders of the city of Pasadena, and you will see why people have been glad to live where the abrupt and sheltering range of the San Gabriel Mountains could be seen. Locally we call them the Sierra Madre, and beneath their close, tough, and dwarfish forest of dark chaparral the long sweep of their variable undershape is clearly visible. They are noble enough, but not beyond the scale of human feelings. The psalmist who said "From whence cometh my help" was not looking at an Alp. The ocean and ages out of which they rose have perished, but our mountains are with us, with cold sweet water in their granite veins. They show their inner structure, as western mountains do, in pale, delineating streaks and angles of clear rocky strength which leave their mounting and descending pyramidal patterns in the mind. Between the scenic semicircle of this range on the north and the Pacific on the south are Los Angeles and its attendant cities lying in a large landscape of idyllic forms in hill and valley well colored with winter's greens or the dark yellows of summer.

There are sometimes mornings that are clear, still, and soft. From the foothills above Pasadena I can see for sixty miles or more, at least as far as a Mt. Santiago in Orange County, at whose foot years ago Madam Modjeska, the renowned Polish actress, made an Arcadian home in a grove of oaks. Closer at hand the hills of El Monte and La Puente stand, and the San Jose hills below Covina, and on the coast the Long Beach headlands, and out in the Pacific show the two heights of Catalina Island. Much nearer through the vast lens of the morning I can see a part of the complex aesthetic detail of the San Gabriel Valley. Cities, scenery, boulevards, and trees make a design of such textural charm as to suggest the quality of a Hokusai print, an intimate distance of green precisions in which a host of hills are floating and made darkly distinct with froth of dissolving mist at their feet. Clustered buildings appear in spots of colored emphasis, and thousands of palms and deodars add vertical and verdant steeples. All this delights the eye, the mind, the heart, with romantic geometries and the pride of home. But not for long. Gradually all those remarkable harmonies and differences of texture fade and flatten, while a horizon of spectral murk advances and takes the valley from below and to the east, flows up arroyos, climbs the foothills, surrounds and fills my own garden, and goes on west along the mountains, obscuring them from sight behind a mobile, drifting wall. Although I live less than a mile from the mountains, they are repeatedly lost to view, and the scene I knew for years in clean bright air can most often now be observed only as a dim copy of the original. . . .

It is asking too much of the vigorous present to be plaintive over what it destroys. Yet is not for plaintive reasons that memory fits together the fragments scattered in the velocity of progress. If there are things too good to lose, then in some way the pleasures of possessing them must be protected. As conservation, memory is only a frail force, but fanatic. No least little pearly grit of desirable recollection escapes it. And so it is I happen to recall the patch of modest nievitas. They were growing in the brief grass of the season where a side road led from the highway toward the foothills. It started to rain and the odor of rain on earth rose in the air. Nievitas are very small flowers noticeable only because they grow companionably in fresh white crowds. On that day as the rain came on, slowly at first and scattered, the large drops here and there pecked at a flower spike which quickly began to bob and nod. As the rain increased, the show of spattered pecking and the bobbing flowers took on a faster pace and all through the colony was that continual ripple of nodding and straightening flowers. It was a diminutive spectacle and the little nievitas are over-dainty on their thin hirsute stems, yet they are flowers too fine to forget, for they provided for me this gently animated scene. On that corner of the crossroad something has now been built, a place to eat or buy gas or sell real estate, it could not matter which. No roots of any kind will grow there again. I have a true concern to keep this fragile recollection of an ephemeral thing very clear. In the shelter of memory, as long as these words may last, those small white flowers, bending in the spring rain and rising, are safe in a vanishing land.

I cannot say as I look back when or quite how it was that the mountain above my home with its tenacious chaparral and lean granite ceased to be the remote profile of the unknown and became the familiar form below which a human life has taken what shape it has, touched in many ways by the life in the mountain above. It was the angry whine of the puma heard one evening from the distance, or the thrash of storm wind as it came savagely down, or the way the naked stones stop the full moon as it floats up, or the gleaming of a flock of pure white pigeons flying into the blue mountain, or over the years a hundred other things, that gave uncanny intimations and certainties beyond bare stone and altitude, until finally the hard light in the high rocks glowed more warmly, as if words had been spoken and a meaning given. And once on a green afternoon of winter I followed the trail in Rubio or Las Flores Canyon and found proof that a mountain is not a towering monument of solitude and time but a small and perfect gift for a moment of exquisite pleasure. On the moist bank and close to see were ferns no broader than a squirrel's foot, and tiny pointed flowers and fruits of moss on little slopes of velvet, and in a frail fungus goblet one diamond, one drop of brilliant rain, a deep drink for Oberon of the mountains. The spell cast by the sylvan weathers that made this pretty thing lay on my mind as I went home, and lies there still.

A dull haze now comes between me and the mountain. The great form that had been so explicit is often dim or not seen at all. A continuity is broken, a symbol is threatened, and the thought of home itself is altered and confused.

It was something so different from the present that one remembers, only to find that the telling evaporates in the busy realism of our day. Yet the difference is real also, and memory tries to assess it with no illusions and no elegiac foolishness, wanting only to keep faith with the fragrant groves and with a valley whose light was beneficent and clear, so clear that the least stem of filaree or pannicle of wild oat was set apart from the rest in thin flake of truth like the mica that drops from a stone. And that long summer view of dry brown Californian earth stretching in peace under native oak and sycamore—it is sad to love this landscape as much as we still do, since love like that will now be always thinking of the end.

It is not too strange that our occasional bright days are haunted days, haunted not by the past but by the future, and the future begins to feel as finished and fatalistic as the past. On these uncommon days when the weather itself seems intuitive, the future is physically visible. I can see it from the loud freeway as my car carries me to an elevation. There

below me lies my valley. Everything is terribly clear, sharp, and veridi-
cal, big things are plain and portentous, little things plain as old bright
bones, all seen as it must be, quickly, but seen for miles, and everything
splitting intensely into a million of itself in precise excess of infatuated
destiny. Revelation, prophecy, history, change, and progress, what dazed
and dim figures they are, moving confounded among their works in a
vanishing land.

Los Altos Hills

Remnants

> We are a remnant people in a remnant country. We
> have used up the possibilities inherent in the youth of
> our nation; the new start in a new place with new vision
> and new hope. . . . We have come, or are coming fast,
> to the end of what we were given.
>
> *Wendell Berry*

*Wallace Stegner (1909–1993) was long identified with Stanford University,
where he taught for many years and where a writing fellowship bears his
name. His award-winning fiction, essays, biographies, and histories display his
love and concern for the West, both that which has vanished and that of the
present. In 1983 he collaborated with nature photographer Eliot Porter on*
American Places, *where "Remnants" first appeared.*

Nearly every morning a coyote works the pasture beyond our
yard fence. He comes up out of the woods that fill the little
canyon to the south—woods out of sight from our windows,
under the roll of the hill—and quarters the field, hunting under the
unpastured grass now matted by the rains. He is as pointed as an arrow;
his plume, carried straight out behind his lean shape, feathers him for
swift accuracy. His nose is long and sharp, his ears are alert, his head is

always turning while nose, ears, and eyes appraise some tenuous signal. His sonar is tuned to the slightest stir of a mouse among the grass roots, a gopher turning in its sleep underground, a cricket uncrossing its legs. Every so often he points, stiffens, lifts one trembling front paw, quivers, flattens, and pounces. His paws hold down whatever he has caught, his nose probes under them. Generally there is nothing there, and he goes back to his restless search. Occasionally, he digs, never very hopefully or very long. And even while digging, even while preparing to pounce, he is never for more than a second or two unaware of our house a hundred feet away. He gives us long stares, with his head turned from whatever a moment ago preoccupied him. He watches us to see if we have moved.

Perhaps he sees our shapes beyond the glass; perhaps he sees no more than the morning reflected there. Perhaps he hears faint murmurs of the "Today Show" or "Good Morning America" or the "CBS Morning News" that we take with our breakfast coffee. Over the years we have watched many things out these bedroom windows—pygmy nuthatches at the bird feeder, quail pecking in coveys among the grass, deer standing on their hind legs to browse the pyracantha berries, a redtailed hawk sitting in a pasture oak getting warm enough to fly. But the coyotes are new. We have seen them only in the last year or two. Perhaps they have been driven in from the Pacific side of the Coast Range by drouth or some drastic shutting off of a food supply.

Whatever brought them, whether they came as refugees or, like most of us, in search of better economic opportunities, they are now here in numbers. On nights of big moons they hunt through the woods and pastures and close up to the houses scattered through the hills. When one catches something, or wishes he could catch something, or grows furious that he has not caught something, his yell goes up and is answered from a half dozen different directions. That chilling bloodcry makes my wife shiver and recall stories about Siberian wolves. It also starts every dog within two miles to asserting his territory. Dobermans, police dogs, Airedales, bull terriers, basset hounds, beagles, short-haired pointers, Labradors, St. Bernards, Kerry blues, mutts big and small all declare their solidarity of domestic protectiveness and unease when they hear the wild summons from out under the moon.

Watching this morning coyote scrounge for mice and crickets in the pasture, bold at the very doors of the suburbs, I am reminded of a story Robert Frost used to tell about meeting on a train a young man who, questioned about what he did for a living, admitted that he was an exterminator. "Ha!" said the poet, interested. "Tell me. What can you exterminate?" The exterminator grew embarrassed. "Confidentially," he said, "nothing."

Wouldn't it be nice to think so! This coyote, a member of a species that has been shot, trapped, poisoned, and chased with dogs for as long as his kind and the human kind have known one another, would seem to corroborate the exterminator's pessimism. He survives; there is a modus vivendi. Nobody is setting out poison, I hear no shooting among the hills. The professors, electronics executives, and engineers from Silicon Valley who live around here don't keep sheep or chickens. An old enemy has come to seem harmless, even attractive. We point him out to visitors, who are charmed. We crowd to the windows to watch him pounce on the matted grass. We cock our ears to his yelling in the moonlight, and smile, glad he is out there, and making it.

The coyote is to native American folklore what the fox was to the fabulists of the Old World. Trickster, demigod, he is very smart and never careless, bold but not brash. If he had an escutcheon, his motto would be *Non timeo sed caveo*. Like the wolf, he has a family and pack life that comforts and assists him in a hard world, but he can get along without it when he needs to. He is fast, shifty, good at running, good at hiding out, nocturnal when he has to be, diurnal when he chooses. Like the buzzard, he can eat anything. Content with small blessings—a lamb here, a chicken there—he will make do on mice and crickets when better is not available. And he seems to know that he is safer here among the engineers and executives in their thickening subdivisions than he used to be over on the other side of the range, where ranchers carry rifles in the racks of their pickups and the Fish and Game people, when not prevented by environmentalist outrage, drop from airplanes pieces of meat laced with 1080. The coyote finds our suburb a peach bowl, and has happily adapted himself.

But he is a special case, and in the end even he may prove to be not exempt from the consequences of sharing the earth with *Homo sapiens.* Many other local species, including some that the coyote was evolved to prey on, are already fading as my breath fades on our windowpane. In the thirty-two years we have lived in this house in these Coast Range foothills we have watched it happen. Helped it happen.

The marriage of people to a place may be close and considerate, and it may be hardly more than sanctioned rape. It may arise from choice, chance, or necessity, like human marriages. In practice, arranged marriages work out about as often as romantic elopements—a good thing, too, for not many of us can choose the place we live in. We can love a well-lived-in place even when it is essentially unlovable. I have seen a black girl, brought to a Vermont lake for the summer, grieve for the hot days in Harlem when a hydrant would be opened. If a place is a real place, shaped by human living, and not a thing created on a speculator's drawing board and stamped on a landscape like a USDA stamp on a side of beef, it will interact with the people who live in it, and they with it. The trouble is that places work on people very slowly, but people work on places with the single-minded ruthlessness of a beaver at a cottonwood tree. Occasionally they make the desert blossom as the rose, as the Mormons are fond of saying. As often, they simply make deserts.

Europeans and their American descendants did not set out to live with this continent, learn its rules and its moods, love, honor, and obey it. They set out to "tame" or "conquer" or "break" the wilderness. They imposed their old habits on the new land, they "improved," as in homesteads, they "developed," as in towns. They replaced, destroyed, and polluted, they bent the earth and all its native forms of life to the satisfaction of their own needs. The process was dramatized in North and

South America, and later in Australia, but it is not peculiarly American or Australian. I have read that in Sicily, that island which was a kind of dry run for the American melting pot, colonized by Greeks, Carthaginians, and Romans, invaded by Visigoths, Normans, and God knows who else, there is not now a single tree or shrub of the varieties that clothed the island in the sixth century B.C. People have come close to altering the whole biotic community, animals and plants alike. And though blood oranges and olives may be an improvement on some things that used to grow there, what once grew there is lost forever and its importance simply cannot be determined now.

Changes will occur whether we intend them or not. We cannot leave one footprint in a new country, pass through it with horses or mules, careen our *Golden Hind* on its empty beach, without bringing in our luggage or our pockets, in our infested hair or clothes, in our garbage, in the dung of our animals and the sputum of our sick and the very dirt under our fingernails, things which were not there before, and whose compatibility with the native flora and fauna is utterly unknown. That is why the patriot who tucked an American flag into a moon capsule could have spoiled everything for the exobiologists eager to determine whether any life existed on the moon. Here on earth, the conservationists who created our national wilderness system knew from the beginning that by this date, wilderness in America is an approximation only. There is no such thing as a true, pure, unmodified wilderness in the entire world. The Greenland glaciers are layered with particulate pollution, Antarctic penguins have DDT in their livers. A wind blowing across Seattle or Portland carries the taint of man in the Montana backwoods.

As naturally as ants herd aphids, we encourage the plants that feed or pleasure us, and extirpate those that don't. We cut forests, impound rivers, plow grasslands, seal millions of acres under sterile concrete, pump out fossil water, change climates to some degree. Planted crops go wild, wild crops are sprayed or crowded out, and changed plant communities encourage the ascendancy or the elimination of animal species. In mining our habitat, we destroy the habitat of whole biotic communities. We commit multiple genocide, we create population explosions. Ecology, a science hardly two generations old, has begun to teach us something about cause and consequence: that is the earth speaking, trying to state its case for survival. But experience might have taught us much sooner.

My family were homesteaders in southern Saskatchewan during World War I. In every acre we could plow, we planted wheat. One consequence, unforeseen and not understood, was that the gophers—"flickertails," Richardson's spermophiles—throve incontinently. They came from miles of bald prairie to feast on our wheat, and stayed to dig burrows and raise families. For their convenience we had dammed a coulee and created a waterhole. Lovely. A land of milk and honey.

I spent my summers trying to exterminate them. They multiplied faster than my traps, poisons, .22, and buckets for drowning them out could reduce them. By replacing buffalo grass with wheat we had touched off a population explosion beyond our containing. The creatures that preyed on gophers—the weasels, ferrets, badgers, hawks, coyotes, shrikes, and gopher snakes—multiplied too, though more slowly, and I killed them too, though in smaller numbers, not knowing they were my allies. Nothing availed. Everything gained on us. Then came a dry cycle, the wheat failed three summers in succession, and we were driven out. The drouth that defeated us also defeated the legions of creatures we had baited into life by tampering with their environment. Once we were gone, the prairie should have settled back into something like its natural populations in their natural balances, except. Except that we plowed up two hundred acres of buffalo grass, and had imported Russian thistle—tumbleweed—with our seed wheat. For a season or two, some wheat would volunteer in the fallow fields. Then the tumbleweed would take over, and begin to roll. We homesteaded a semiarid steppe and left it nearly a desert.

Not deliberately. We simply didn't know what we were doing. People in new environments seldom do. Their only compulsion is to impose themselves and their needs, their old habits and old crops, upon the new earth. They don't look to see what the new earth is doing naturally; they don't listen to its voice.

Ours was short-grass prairie. Historically the tall-grass variety east of the 100th meridian did better. It is changed, but it is no desert; there is probably no more fertile farmland in the world. Nevertheless, much was lost. As white settlement advanced from the Mississippi to the Missouri and beyond, prairie flowers did not grow older hour by hour. They got plowed up and grazed off. Where once big bluestem and switchgrass and Indian grass grew as high as a horse, and flowers snagged in the stirrups of a rider, we have made cities, towns, shopping centers, parking lots, feed lots, highways, and fields of corn, sorghum, and soybeans. The old species are gone or only precariously hanging on. As Aldo Leopold discovered, almost the only places where the native plants could sustain and reproduce themselves were the fenced rights of way of railroads, protected from both plows and grazing animals. Those accidental preserves are now beyond price, precious to biologists trying to reconstruct the vanishing prairie biota, and more precious to all of us than we may realize.

Obviously not all human tinkering is thoughtless, nor is all of it destructive. People coming to a new world take back the new plants and animals that native peoples have domesticated. American potatoes, tomatoes, maize, turkeys, and tobacco literally revolutionized the eating and living habits of the world, and vastly increased its carrying capacity of *Homo sapiens.* A wave of green revolution rushed eastward from our shores from the sixteenth century on. Before too long, Englishmen were smoking, and were eating a bird they called a turkey, and the Italian cuisine was being enlarged by tomatoes and the maize that Italians still call *gran turco,* apparently under the impression that it came from the Near East. By the eighteenth century there were representations of corn leaves in Chinese art.

But there was a reverse process, too. Settlers brought in seeds and cuttings and some of them had the messianic enthusiasm of Johnny

Appleseed. Read in the letters between Thomas Jefferson and John Bartram the eagerness with which intelligent people experimented with Old World plants in the New World. So far as I know, neither Jefferson nor Bartram introduced any killing pests into America, but their sort of experimentation conducted indiscriminately elsewhere has produced a history of ecological trauma, an elaborate industry of biological study and control, and the beginnings of a public concern that is sometimes sentimental but is indispensable.

Cause begets consequences, in nature as in logic. We understand that in its cruder manifestations—kill off the hawks and coyotes and you will be swamped periodically by rodents—but the subtler relationships, the web of small tensions and accommodations and standoffs that make for ecological health, we have hardly begun to appreciate.

How could the Spaniards have known (and what would they have cared, being hot for the riches of Cíbola?) that the horses they brought to the New World would find some parts of it horse heaven, and that the multiplying get of escaped studs and mares would transform the life of whole nations of Indians, and hence of the whites who fought them? How could they possibly have foreseen that after the conquest was over and the Indians crushed, the merest remnants of the wild horse herds would become a cause of contention among western ranchers who want to make dog food of them, animal lovers determined to save them, and federal land managers uncertain which course to follow?

Why didn't Captain James Cook stop to think, before he released goats in the Hawaiian Islands, that goats are very destructive and very adaptable, and that the islands contained no predators to hold them in check? Why couldn't he have predicted that the goats would defy efforts to control them, and two centuries after their release would still be peeking at tourists around the crags of Waimea Canyon?

Could the prospectors who turned burros loose in the Grand Canyon country have known that burros are as durable and tenacious as goats, and as destructive of their range? Would they have done anything if they had realized that one day the feral burros would threaten the existence of the desert bighorn and the desert range itself? And how should we respond to the tender-hearted and tender-minded people who block the National Park Service and the Bureau of Land Management from applying the only management tactic—shooting a lot of burros—that will have any effect?

Cause and consequences occur in many combinations. It is one kind of mistake to shoot all the millions of passenger pigeons, or cut down all the sandalwood trees in Hawaii to provide incense for Chinese joss houses. It is another to import European chestnuts or Dutch elms, each carrying its endemic disease, into a continent whose native chestnuts and elms have no resistance to those diseases. Florida must find a way to deal with the water hyacinths it planted in an ill-advised hour. Virginia must somehow clear its woods of the engulfing Japanese honeysuckle that it first brought in to stabilize railroad embankments. Hawaii, a group of islands almost as much altered by exotics as Sicily, finds itself at war with plants such as lantana, a garden flower elsewhere, a weed in the islands; and with animals like the mongoose, imported to prey on rats, which has become as much a nuisance as the rats themselves.

Considerations such as these are the ABC's of our growing environmental consciousness. We are a weed species, and wherever we go we crowd out natives and carry with us domesticated species that may become weeds in the new environment. What we destroy we often do not intend to harm. What we import, we import with the best intentions. But I find myself wondering, as I watch this coyote who has survived all our direct attacks on him and our indirect attacks on his habitat, why we should have had to repeat so much dreary history on the San Francisco Peninsula in the years since World War II, why we seem to have learned so little since Segesta and Agrigento were metropolises twenty-five hundred years ago.

When we moved into them, the Peninsula foothills back of Stanford University seemed to us as untouched as New South Wales must have seemed to Captain Cook. Actually they were far from virginal. White men have been here for two hundred years, and as a consequence the pastures are a mixture of native plants and of runaways from hayfields and ranch yards. Some—shooting stars, poppies, lupines, blue-eyed grass, tarweed—are surely natives. Others—wild oats, filaree, ryegrass, burclover—are just as surely Europeans naturalized. I don't know whether needlegrass, screwgrass, foxtail grass, and yellow star thistle are natives or not. They ought to be, else why are their seeds armored to withstand a climate that is rainless seven months of the year, and so cunningly equipped to attach themselves to any fur, sock, or trouser cuff that happens by? In cursing these plants for what they do to my dog's feet, ears, and tear ducts, I may be cursing intrusive weeds, but more likely I am objecting to species that have more right here than I do. If I don't like what grows here, why did I move in? Why do I stay? And in trying to eradicate them I am being both human and futile, for they are at least as indestructible as the coyote.

The woods are more native than the pastures, for trees and shrubs must survive not simply a season, but cycles of seasons, and not many exotics have the genes to make it without human help. These live oaks, blue oaks, white oaks, buckeyes, and bay laurels, with their understory of toyon and poison oak, gooseberry and blackberry and elderberry, maidenhair and lady fern, must have grown in pretty much these proportions, in these same creek bottoms and on these same north-facing slopes, since the Ohlone Indians used to gather acorns here; but I never see "wild plums" blooming in the ravines without suspecting that the rootstock of hill apricot orchards has gone wild and adapted itself.

As for the wildlife that we found—the foxes, raccoons, opossums, skunks, wood rats, jackrabbits, cottontails, gophers, moles, voles, field mice, lizards and skunks and newts and toads and tree frogs, gopher snakes and rattlesnakes and king snakes and ring-necked snakes, hawks and owls and buzzards and quail and the layered populations of songbirds, both winterers and summer dwellers—it must have been much the same, perhaps with a few mountain lions, bears, and eagles, when this land was a Spanish grant. And bobcats. There had to be bobcats where there were so many gophers and mice and quail, and I know there are still bobcats because I have seen their pug tracks around a spring. But I have never seen a bobcat in the flesh in all the years we have lived here. That puts the bobcat in a special class, more durable than most of the nocturnals and small predators, perhaps as durable as the coyote.

In any case, changes that had taken place before our coming did not trouble us, and had not seriously damaged the hills. We accepted our surroundings as if they had just been smoothed and rounded and peopled by the hand of God, and we tried to keep them as we found them. Nevertheless, we disturbed them a great deal, occasionally for good, sometimes neutrally, often for ill.

We disturbed them simply because we were *Homo fabricans.* We built structures, we brought water to a dry hilltop, we planted exotic trees, shrubs, flowers, fruits, and vegetables, we brought in our domesticated animals and birds. And everything we established, even our garbage cans and our compost heap, sent out urgent messages to impoverished species that were barely holding their own in the pastures and ravines. Because we were one of only three or four houses in a wide area, we had the impact of pioneers.

Some of our installations were gestures of friendship: bird feeders and sugar-water suppers. But our inadvertent invitations were accepted as eagerly as our deliberate ones. A dozen species could have sued us for creating attractive nuisances. From every direction things converged on our island of artificial green. We brought on population explosions of several kinds, and then had to deal with them or submit to them.

Sometimes the consequences of our invasion pleased us. The linnets and Bewick's wrens that found nesting places in our carport were welcome, and we were troubled only when our car desolated a nest. The golden-crowned sparrows that roosted by dozens in the *Eucalyptus globulus* with which I screened the watertank were even more welcome, for through the winter and spring they sweetened the air with their tremulous, plaintive, three-note call. Ditto for the mockingbirds that made our pyracantha hedge their own. Ditto for the deer that came to dine on pyracantha berries, crabapples, roses, and anything else they found. Having to choose between a garden and the deer, we would have chosen the deer, though we might have forgotten that if we had not grown the garden the deer would not be there. Because of the open pasture next to us, we did not drive away the meadowlarks, or haven't yet.

We did not much mind the raccoons, foxes, opossums, and skunks that were enticed by our garbage cans and our little clutch of bantam hens. I grumbled, but not excessively when the coons tipped over garbage cans and pried off the lids and left me with a lot of wilted lettuce, coffee grounds, and bloody butcher paper to clean up. As for the bantams, they could look after themselves; they were not the soft touch that other hens would have been. They could fly like pheasants, they roosted high in the oaks. They laid their eggs in hidden places. Any coon or possum or fox that got a meal off them deserved it. One by one they disappeared, but meanwhile we had these bandit coons looking in our windows at night, and sometimes, sitting in my study, I could watch a pair of foxes come up onto my deck and groom themselves, apparently unable to see or smell me where I sat, six feet away, behind the glass. Once or twice a skunk gave it to the dog cold turkey, but that was a permanent harm neither to the dog nor to us. In fact, it taught each of our dogs in turn how to behave himself, and not to rush out all bravado and teeth when something stirred in the yard.

And the frogs. Where do frogs come from on a dry hill a mile from any spring or creek, in a climate where for half the year it simply cannot rain? Nevertheless, the week we built a fishpond, they were there, and homesteaded it happily, and filled it with their slimy eggs that turned in spring to pollywogs. Every night, in season, they conducted love concerts that could drown out conversations even inside the house. Stamp on the patio bricks and they fell silent so suddenly, from such a crescendo of noise, that the stillness rang like quinine in the ears, the sort of silence I have heard nowhere else except in the middle of the Amazon jungle.

Even a peacock moved in on us—arrived one morning by air, discovered the dog's dish with some leftover kibbles in it, and stayed. He stayed for three years, roosting ceremonially in the live oaks and making hopeless, fantastic, love to the cat, and on spring nights drowning out even the frogs with his piercing call for a peahen.

Country living, the Peaceable Kingdom. But that was only one side of it. Being human, we found some forms of life more attractive than others. We believed in weeds and pests, and they found us like fulfilled prophecy.

Gophers, not the Richardson's spermophiles of my boyhood but a surlier, more underground race, tunneled in from the dry pastures to enjoy our tomatoes and tulip bulbs and gnaw on the sweet rootlets of our cherry trees. Snakes followed them. We did not mind the gopher snakes and king snakes, in fact were glad to have them, as well as the tiny ring-necked snakes that lived under damp patches of leaves and fed on angleworms. But rattlesnakes dozing on our doormat made my wife nervous, and so we applied the human remedy, the remedy my family had found in Saskatchewan for any unwanted life. We killed them, as we killed gophers when we could catch them, and mice when they got too thick, and wood rats when they nested in the storage cupboards. In this we had the enthusiastic cooperation of our Siamese cat, an efficient killer but indiscriminate. He not only kept the mice and gophers on their toes, he decimated the lizards, got his share of linnets and sparrows and wrens, salvaged the cedar waxwings and robins that got drunk on fermented berries and tried to fly through the plate glass, and brought in, on special occasions, such rarer game as squirrels, and once a jackrabbit bigger than he was. All this in spite of our canned cat food and our precautions, our shuttings-in and our bells.

As with mammals, so with insects. We did not like to spray, for that meant undoing friend and foe alike. So we had ants, and with the ants, aphids. We had whiteflies and mealybugs and red spiders and thrips. We had leaf miners and twig borers and oak-leaf caterpillars. And especially we had earwigs and sowbugs. It is not a pleasure to a husbandman to find his strawberries infested with sowbugs. They eat their way into a succulent berry like hyenas into the body of a dead elephant. As for earwigs, they make lace of citrus leaves, and one spring they found the clematis vine over the entrance such a beautiful place to breed in that when I shook the vine I was showered with hundreds of crawling, pincered, vicious little bodies. Shuddering, I cut off the vine at the ground, dragged its infested tangle into the driveway, threw gasoline on it, and set it afire. Then I went downtown and bought snail, earwig, and sowbug poisons. Having played Tempter, I found that I had to play God in self-defense.

We have not been alone. There have been other gods before us and after us. In our first years here, though we had neighbors within a comfortable half mile, we could see not a single light at night except stars and moon and the glow on the sky above the valley conurbia. There was a great healing in that darkness that is not present now. Now we look out on constellations of lights, nebulae spiraling up hillside roads called Way and Lane and Drive. We see white dwarfs, but few black holes. The security lights of some neighbors burn into our windows all night long—perhaps to scare away the coyotes. Many yards are surrounded by chain-link fences to keep the deer out. On Saturday nights our walls and ears pound with the hard rock blasting from decks where the young are holding parties. The weeds, of whom we were among the first, have closed in.

And the life forms that we tempted, enjoyed, struggled against, loved? Alas.

It has been years since I had to go out into the moonlight, drawn by the barking of the dog, and rescue from carport or lumber pile an opossum that, lifted upon to a safe oak limb, plays possum for a while and then creeps away. I am not philosophical about cleaning up garbage spilled by a neighbor's dalmatian, as I was when the coons used to spill it. It is years since I heard that muscular rush into the dark as the dog charged and the coon fled. No foxes have groomed themselves in the light beyond my study window for a decade, and we would have thought the foxes gone for good if we had not seen, just the other day, a survivor out in the coyote's pasture hunting ground, walking as it were in the coyote's tracks and pouncing on the same mice or insects. If I thought installing bantam hens would bring them back in force, I would call on some henhouse tomorrow.

Nowadays, few skunks come by to drink out of our fishpond and teach our dog manners. The bloom of enveloping scent now rarely spreads and lingers in our bedroom when one walks around the house. There has not been a rattlesnake on our doormat for a decade and a half, and even gopher and king snakes are getting so scarce that when I see one in the road I get out and carry it off into the grass where it will not get run over. Sometimes I bring one home and make it welcome on our turf, but so far as I can see, none has stayed. Either neighbors kill them, or they find that the neighborhood cats have so thinned out the gophers and mice that there is nothing here to live on. It is a rare spring, nowadays, when even a single gopher kicks out his piles of dirt, making his underground beeline toward our garden.

The trees are tougher, and the native species may survive all our efforts to replace them with exotics. Development has brought water mains into the hills, and except in drouth years such as 1976 and 1977, there is plenty of Sierra water for the nursery plants and trees that new householders instantly set out. For a while, at least, this semi-desert may blossom as the rose. On the other hand, what one sees around old homesteads is likely to be native, reinforced by the Monterey pines, eucalyptus, pepper trees, and oleanders that have adapted to this climate; and that may be what surrounds us all a generation from now. The genes that were evolved for these hills have a way of asserting themselves whenever a fifty-year freeze or hundred-year drouth teaches local gardeners humility. Clear away the corpses of the exotics, and you find in the duff underneath them the sturdy oak seedlings, the sprays of poison oak, the insistent coyote-brush.

But also—and this should have been just as predictable—nursery escapees with the toughness to survive. Around the place where I once had a flowering peach (I cut it down because I couldn't control the peach-leafcurl) there is a stubborn patch of lippia that each season spreads a foot or two in every direction before the summer drouth slows it down. Around the basin of my new lime tree is a patch of crabgrass that I know will be even more stubborn. Both those patches came from the same nursery, an inadvertent bonus. Like the wild oats and the bur-clover, they may be part of tomorrow's pasture. If the pasture is there.

There is no reason to expect it will be. The town's policies are friendly to subdividers. In suburbs such as this, people with a tenderness for the earth seldom get elected to town councils or appointed to planning commissions. Their sentiments are seen as interfering with profits and growth. The towns are run by people who see land as a commodity. James Fenimore Cooper once described this tendency as the defeat of Principle by Interest. Whatever it is, I observe with foreboding that every individual who has held and left the post of town manager in our suburb has left it to become a developer.

So the pasture is likely to go, and with it will go much that has made our thirty years here a long delight, a continual course in earth-keeping. All around it the bulldozers are at work tearing up the hills for new houses—twelve here, thirty-one there, fifteen across the gully. That may be the reason why we see coyotes where we never used to see them, and why the one fox we have seen in years was in that same field. There may literally be no other place for them, or for the deer that in these winter months herd up in bunches of eighteen or twenty and come and go through our yard, sliding through our sagging barbed wire fences as smoothly as swallows hit a hole in a barn. What we see out of our bedroom windows may be only the remnants, deceptively numerous because concentrated in this one patch of open space.

There are, thank God, other centers—Stanford's Jasper Ridge preserve, Palo Alto's Foothill Park, various parcels held as open space by the Mid-Peninsula Regional Park District—where the wild things can keep a foothold. But all of those places are close to developed areas, all are near roads, and the creatures which live in them are regularly exposed to their greatest natural enemy, the automobile. And here is another observation that sours my ruminations: we have lived on our country road for thirty-two years. In that time, though I have seen hundreds of animals crossing the road, I never hit one. Yet the road is rarely without its flattened carcass, skunk or opossum or raccoon or snake. If I can miss these things, driving the road several times a day every day of the week, why can't other drivers? I have to assume that they try not to miss but to hit them, that they are like some trigger-happy neighbors we have had through the years—the policeman who sat on his patio in pajamas on Sunday mornings and popped off quail and towhees with a .38 revolver, the Texas lady who kept a loaded .22 in her kitchen and blazed away out the door at anything passing through.

We live among the remnants. Feral housecats, as efficient at hunting as the foxes, opossums, and raccoons, and more efficient at breeding—and constantly replenished by hit-and-run owners who drop them off in the country and drive away—have almost cleaned out the gophers, and I suppose the mice as well. That means that most of the animals who depend on that food supply couldn't make a living now even if we restocked the area with them. Even if there were enough food, the other hazards would be fatal. The last pair of great horned owls went several years ago, both of them apparently indirect victims of the poisoned carrots that some neighbor put out for the gophers. Both came to die in our yard. As one of them squatted in the patio, panting with open beak in the full sun, I passed my hand across above him to cut off the sun from his blinded eyes, and watched the slit of pupil widen instantly in the shadow, a miraculously controlled lens shutter, before the fierce yellow eyes went out. It wasn't quite what Aldo Leopold saw as the green fire went out of the eyes of a dying wolf, but it carried something like the same message, and it shook me.

Remnants. The pair of red-tails that we have known for a long long time still nest in the eucalyptus at the south edge of the pasture, but I don't expect, ever again, to be sitting in the patio talking to a visitor and see one of them come over at thirty feet, struggling with a four-foot gopher snake and very close to crashing. The visitor, a New York editor, accused me of staging that episode to plug California living. If I could stage it now, I probably would, knowing that the snake is in danger of starving to death anyhow, or of having his head crushed by somebody who can't see that he wears no rattles on his tail.

THE DESERT

Desert Walking

John Daniel (b. 1948) was a student of Wallace Stegner at Stanford, where Daniel later taught for a number of years. A widely published poet, he has also written nature essays infused with a poetic consciousness, such as this recollection of a desert ramble published in The Trail Home: Nature, Imagination, and the American West *(1992).* Looking Back: A Son's Memoir *was published in 1996. Daniel lives with his wife in the foothills of Oregon's Coast Range.*

My friend John, whom I've known since childhood, entered a Vedic monastic order after college and spent ten years as a renunciate monk in southern California, cut off from his former life and the outside world. In those years he studied rigorously and meditated four to five hours a day. When he decided to emerge from isolation, he bought a four-wheel-drive pickup and started traveling to desert places in California and Arizona. He camped and hiked, usually alone, for days and sometimes weeks at a time. It was in the desert that he felt closest to the mystery of being. The created universe, as I understand his belief, is in reality a vibration, a single tone struck in the beginning from Spirit. Alone in the quiet of stone and sand, my friend listens for the sound of all that is.

John and I argue when we see each other. We have never hiked together in the desert, possibly never will—there's a good chance we would drive each other crazy. But I listen to him. There's much in his religion that seems strange to me, but I respect his search, I respect his discipline, and I understand him when he talks about the desert. I too keep going there. Something in its silences keeps calling me. I see a little farther there. Religion is from *religare*, to tie back. Walking freely in desert emptiness, I learn a little more of what it is that I am tied to.

The lowering sun was still much too hot, my neck and arms already burned, I wondered why I had driven eight hundred miles for this. I had done a lot of backpacking, but all in mountains, the Sierra Nevada and Oregon Cascades, among lakes and flowery high meadows, in conifer woods as comfortable as old clothes. This was different. This was glaring knife-edged boulders strewn down barren slopes, clumps of wizened and eaten prickly pear, a scattering of stunted pines. This was the rank green scummy pool by which I'd dropped my pack, miserably heavy with five gallons of city water, and now sat panting in disgust, waiting for the sun to dive behind the Panamint crest.

The beautiful is a dangerous idea. Once inside it, it's hard to see out. I knew the High Sierra was beautiful, with its tumbling runnels and glacial brilliance and green expanses—but this oven of a desert gorge? This stark prison I had worked so hard to enter, scattering lizards, chucking rocks at the braying goomered burro who'd stood in my way? It was like spending years reading Wordsworth, page after lovely page, and suddenly hitting William Carlos Williams. Is this *poetry?* These fractured lines, these bare *things?* Unadorned in the rhetoric of green?

But the place was working on me, of course, even as I sat there. Even in my sunburned weariness I felt its freshness. By sundown I was admiring how pinyon roots jam right in rock crevices, how their stiff limbs creak in a rise of wind. The land's red and yellow mineral streaking glowed in the last light. Death Valley cooled in pale haze below me.

Two frogs started to chirp at dusk—they liked this place just fine, and kept telling me. A cool wash of moonlight, the stones radiant with hoarded warmth, a little wind at work, And next morning, as I hiked on, the canyon took me in. Narrowing, it played a slow winding rhythm between sheer walls, each turn a gateway to the unknown. I climbed dry waterfalls, clattered across loose gravel, slogged through sand, and kept on walking, winding in and out of light and shadow, breeze and stillness, following the scent of sun-warm stone and the bright piping of a bird I never saw.

Driving Highway 140 southeast from the Warner Mountains in Oregon, you pass from pine forest down into Deep Creek Canyon, where the slopes are studded with the squat green flame-shapes of junipers. The canyon dumps you out into open basin and range, a few trees fringing the higher ground. They grow sparser as you drive on, deeper into the Great Basin, until topping out on Doherty Rim you see a wind-beaten clump on the left, and way off to the right there's a single flat-crowned juniper—the final tree.

Somehow, by bird or rat or stormwind, a seed arrived in the right place at the right time. In a crevice among lichen-crusted scabrocks, possibly shaded by a clump of sage, it found just enough moisture for just enough time to elaborate its roots and begin to rise, imperceptibly through the seasons, alone in a high dryland sea. Beyond that tree, except for the planted poplars of an occasional ranch, it's nothing but small sage and rabbit-brush, crumbling crops of volcanic rock, nothing but the long contours of the open land, all the many miles to the Pine Forest Mountains of Nevada.

Desert presents itself in particularities. Thirty miles across wavering flats, Shiprock stands in stillness. A coyote lopes along a ridge and disappears. Deep in a canyon, one cottonwood flares yellow against pink stone. A silvery luminescence next to my foot takes shape as *frog* on gray limestone. Above me on a ledge, one clump of cactus has unfurled its papery burgundy flowers. A raven croaks—part of me waits all day to hear it again. The parched hillside I've been climbing reveals a small band of aspens huddled in a crease of land where a clear spring rises.

The eye moves from point to point, thing to particular thing, great and small. The mind can take its time, surrounding what it wonders at without distraction, and each object takes on heightened life. Maybe that's why my own life feels brightened in the desert. I too am here, a singularity myself, as improbably rightful as the one juniper, the clear spring, the sundown glow that flares the canyon walls and dies away.

As I walk up a canyon, I move toward source and seeing. Each twisting turn, each dry chute I climb opens the way a little farther. When the canyon forks, I hesitate. I have to choose one way. On steep sections my hands and feet work in concert—I have purpose. I am focused ahead, I ascend as if toward an astonishing secret at the canyon's origin. If I'm allowed to climb far and high enough, the walls that have been confining me may lower themselves. The sky broadens, surrounding me slowly, openness on my shoulders. I see the canyon that led me here winding away below. I see parts of neighboring canyons, spires of stone, buttes and mesas, blue mountains ranging away on the world's curve. The secret may be the rock I'm sitting on. Or it may be out there somewhere, in the complication of the carved land.

As I walk down a canyon, the tendency of the entire land collects me. I was alone on the dry flat where I started, but as little walls channel the sandy wash, company appears. Bunchgrass may be the first. A single flower shouts blue. The sand is damp, and after a while water is trickling beside me, sloshing around my boots, and the walls have shouldered higher. Willows trail their limbs in the current. Cottonwoods tremble in a breeze I can't feel. Swallows chatter overhead, where the blue sky has been squeezed thin by stone expanses only the sun can climb. Along their base, other humans left markings long ago. Like me. Like the grasses and the willows, the swallows and the cottonwoods, they followed the voice of steady changefulness, the fluent voice that says, *I am the one who sings through stone. I called you here. I know the way.*

Brown boulders the size of houses choke the mouth of a side canyon, jagged-edged, lighter colored where they split away, not long ago, from the upper walls. A forty-foot spire has sheared from the wall and dropped straight down, implanting itself among the riverbank cotton-woods whose contortions bear witness to brutal floods. Titanic violence composes this serenity I come for. These monolithic walls are splitting, sliding, crumbling to sand. The canyon is scouring deeper. I miss a lot, visiting for a dot of time, a week, a human life.

Any wilderness speaks silently of time, but time is nowhere clearer than in desert canyons. Descending millions of years through solid sand dunes, red mud mires, the rippled bottoms of ancient seas, here I walk in time, dwarfed by the mute magnitude of eons. Here, along with other newcomers—wren, cottonwood, lizard—I am swallowed in the long story of Earth. I walk in a stillness like no other, and though I don't hear what John hears, the sound of all that is, I feel it close. I imagine walking deeper than I can, down to the black stone that cooled from fiery tor-rents when the planet's face was red and flowing. And I dream deeper still, of entering the original fire itself, where if I lost myself I might for just one instant grasp the puzzle of being, my mind in its last speck of time might ride the leaping arc from nothingness to solid worlds.

The answers to the biggest questions are hard to come by, even in the desert. Bruce, my frequent hiking partner, is a molecular biologist. He studies the minute workings of life, and he tells me it's very much a mystery how life became alive. It's simply unknown to the bright minds and prodigious equipment of science how nucleic acids began to repli-cate themselves, how the translation of RNA into proteins evolved, and how these baffling developments came to be incorporated within a cell membrane. Once you have the cell, says Bruce, it's not too hard—

though it took another two billion years—to get to the elaboration of complex life forms. Once you have the cell.

The startling fact is that a rock-and-water planet came to life. Nothing is more apparent, and nothing is less understood. Unlike many of his colleagues, Bruce doesn't scorn this idea that life may have originated from spores that arrived in meteors. Given how little is known, he says, no plausible theory can be dismissed. He will entertain any explanation with the bounds of nature, any explanation short of God. Bruce is a scientist. He doesn't care much for religion.

"But what if God is nothing outside nature," I'm arguing tonight. "What if God is in nature, is nature, and evolution is God's way of being born?"

"Why do you have to call it God?" he says. "Listen. Matter is so subtle and so incredibly complex it doesn't *need* to be dressed up with divinity."

I can't refute that. I'm not sure I want to refute it. We look at the fire, drinking our brandy, and after a while I wander off to my sleeping bag. Staring at the brink of cliff straight overhead, silhouetted against stars, I'm unsettled. *Nothing, something. No-life, life.* We're looking at the same thing, neither of us can explain it, and we make different leaps of faith. Being is so extraordinary I can only call it divine. We see contrariwise and we see the same. What we see, we love.

The bumpy shadows on the cliff brink are bothering me. I'm worried that one of the less subtle acts of matter might flatten me in the night, and so I drag my sleeping bag farther under the overhang, a little closer to the fire, a little closer to where Bruce is sleeping. Tomorrow we'll talk more. We'll walk on up the canyon, and we'll both keep our eyes open.

This heat is *palpable*, it's pressing solid, almost seems to hold me upright as I lurch and stumble with my load. I'm not hot, I'm *wired*. I'm dancing with the bees around pink cactus blooms, the stones a bright dry river passing under. Somewhere along this big bajada there's a canyon mouth, there's cool rock shade, there's a place to drop this water tank I've packed for miles—a water tank myself, of course, a pouch of ancient sea traipsing on two legs through a hundred twelve degrees of blessed sun. Is this what evolution had in mind when that lungfish flopped out on the shore? Am I the avant-garde, the pioneer? I'm a fool, I'm way outside my depth. I'm stumbling like a drunkard here where stones and cactus, everything but bees holds still in heat, I'm crazy with bright clarity—those peaks across the valley close enough to touch, to drink, to swallow whole and keep on walking, as this lit vastness swallows me.

First it was soft hail beads, falling thickly, bouncing off the red sandstone, sliding down the angled slabs, jumping on the ground as if alive. Then papery flakes, with wind, thinning now to fine sugar specks. The silent storm fills the wash, gray and blind and steadily sifting down.

The snow terraces itself on ledges, sticks in delicate scallops on steeper surface. The busy pines and junipers are forested with it. Yuccas gather it in, each of them holding a loose ball, their straight yellow spines sticking through. Each tree and shrub, alive and dead, gracefully accepts the snow. I hear it ticking on the rocks. Water drips from the overhang. My fire flutters.

Waiting out a snowstorm under a dripping ledge is not what I expected. I had hoped to be miles farther by now, miles closer to the canyons I came to see. But the canyons will be there tomorrow. They'll be there for a long time. A destination sets you in motion, but once you're moving here, what's important is where you are. That's what I keep forgetting out there among cars and books and jobs. I forget this presentness. I need this slowing down—to open outward, to be still, to gather in what comes as the yuccas gather their globes of snow.

After breakfast Bruce and I eat a few mushrooms and set out to explore the little canyon where we've camped. It's a hot morning. The stream collects in several deep tanks, clear and green, and Bruce can't resist.

Scientists need to relax. They lead intense lives, one eye screwed to the microscope, the other scanning for the next grant—and hoping for a glimpse of the wild Nobel. I leave him splashing, a goofy grin on his face, and continue upcanyon.

A fly drones under a tree. Ambling along, I'm clothed in the heat of the day. Nothing changes really. Rocks don't turn to jelly, visions don't boil from the sky. Mind emerges from its usual cave, infusing the body, and with all our senses you remember—*yes, this is how it is.* The tree, the droning fly, everything is only more itself. Climbing the slope of bitterbrush, I smooth my hands along the canyon wall, press my cheek to its coolness, inhale its ancient smell.

From the earth will I cry unto thee, when my heart is overwhelmed: lead me to the rock that is higher than I. It's more than I can comprehend, almost more than my heart can bear, this beauty we are born to. All this earth, and we alive in it, to walk here, to touch this solid truth. . . . *Being is its own answer . . .*

On up the canyon, hiking with a boy's happiness, I'm thinking about the sixties. We were kids in a new car, revving the engine, driving way too fast. But what we glimpsed was real, the realest thing we'd ever seen. I remember me and John standing in the light rain with blankets on our shoulders, shivering half the night in a field as we tried to speak our sense of sacredness, how near it was. How near. He followed the glimpse to a monastery and out again. I followed into the world and into words. We both followed to the desert, and we're still following.

Bruce catches up, refreshed and laughing. He's been watching me, amused at how my head's been rotating angle to angle as I've walked, as if I were some yellow-capped root. Ridiculous, I tell him. I've been immersed in important thoughts, oblivious to outward things. His vision must be affected.

We stop for a small lunch, walk again, and after a few turns of canyon we arrive where we didn't know we were heading. We're standing in a pool looking up a tall waterslide cut so deeply into stone it forms a chamber, a cool grotto crossed above our heads by a slanting arch. The smooth sculpted walls rise past the arch to a crack of blue sky far above, and the green shimmer of the water we have stirred fills the chamber—wavering sheens of light alive on our bodies, our faces, around and above us, intermingling on the surfaces of stone.

I follow a necessity older than my conscious choice, older than my life or any life, a way worked out through ages between the tendencies of rain and rock. Where the walls lift high, I cannot leave. My freedom is to follow, my confinement my opportunity. In the light or sun, I move forward in my human way. I walk a while in the open hold of land. Wind and water, the beautiful blind carving—none of it for me, yet there's room. I'm walking, and the way is clear.

I used to hope for a monumental discovery in the desert. Around each canyon bend, above each dry waterfall, up the shadowy passage of a side canyon, I longed for something I had never seen—an undisturbed Indian village, the eyes of a cougar, a visible spirit. What I really longed for was a vision, a flash of knowing in whose light I would understand my life and death, and all the hieroglyphic forms of nature.

I've walked some desert miles now, and I'm beginning to think that vision is not a sudden kind of thing. Maybe it's a progress, a slow gathering of small seeings. Maybe it has to be. Walking a canyon sometimes I'll stop, vowing to look up so intensely at a certain thing—a purple flower, a sandstone spire—that its entire being will come clear to me. I stare, but my mind grows weary. The flower's language is untranslatable. I could stare until I fell to bones at the base of that rock tower, and still its sheer, water-stained surface would thwart me. Maybe, as the greatest friend and lover of these canyons insisted, its meaning *is* its surface. It stands in its peculiar form, unlike any other spire in the desert, in the universe, a monument to nothing but itself.

And so I walk again. The canyon keeps on going, and ordinary wonders mark its way. A cactus grows in a dead juniper. A small dinosaur rests on a rock. Rippling water goes orange in the late sun. The canyon keeps on winding, part shadow and part sun, revealing itself before me as it closes behind. What I see I touch with my awareness, the only light I have, and enough. I walk. And a good place to end my walk is the impassable overhang that finally blocks my way, to lie curled in its cool shade with the few ferns that live there, listening to a slow drip of water. The way I came, the way I will return, is waiting when I'm ready. And winding on above me is the canyon I will never climb, winding deep among the bluffs and spires, winding on through distant ranges, through the wilderness of scattered stars.

Here, where I come to get away from people, there are people who come with me. They travel the canyons too, their faces drifting in and out of my awareness—my wife, my mother and my brother, Bruce the scientist, John with this gray head listening, all my closest friends. As my mind quiets here, I see them lit with a certain still clarity, and I sense that all of us are living a forgotten story, acting perfectly ourselves, as perfectly as the stones are stones, as perfectly as the water flows. The story is close around me here, and it's never closer than in fall, when the cottonwoods turn yellow-gold against the red rock walls.

The story those trees tell is the same story sunset tells, the glad and fearful story, the story I'm alive to learn. Sunset tells it grander—you can see how vast and old it is, how other stories all form part of it, all end in that rich light. But you can't touch the sunset. You can't stand next to it or lean against it. With their trunks and limbs, their leaves that stir in the least of winds, cottonwoods bring the story down from sky and place it here, close to us, in ground.

There are graceful ones that rise in a few gentle curves of trunk. There are those with two trunks, or three, or four. There are trees that circle upon themselves in corkscrew loops. There are bowed and twist-ed trees, trees that wander along the ground like blind beggars, trees that dive down into sand and lift upward again. And there is one tree I've seen that grows sideways out of a silt shelf and arches back above the shelf to bury its broken crown at the bottom of the canyon wall. Its crumbling bark exposes cracked and riddled grain, and for part of its contorted length the tree is split clear open, filled with stones and dead leaves caught from the crushing floods. Along its great body it still raises a few living limbs, small trees themselves, flagged with the bright leaves of its kind.

If we didn't hide our histories inside us, we'd see our own lives as we see the trees. We'd see how some of us rise true and easily, how some are bent or split from their beginnings. We'd see where we were chafed or broken, where love failed or never was, where love returned. We'd see where troubles beset us, how we bent and twisted beneath their weight, how we've grown as we've been able to grow and never have stopped growing, branching form the single source, how in our bodies' heaviness we touch the air and tremble—how each of us, in one peculiar unlikely way, rises in the light.

Death Valley

Edward Abbey (1927–1989) was both a novelist and a nature writer whose work brought into bold relief the conflict between civilization and nature, whether in his anarchic novel The Monkey Wrench Gang *(1975) or his classic testament to the Sonoran Desert,* Desert Solitaire *(1968). This essay is from* The Journey Home *(1977).*

Summertime

From Daylight Pass at 4,317 feet we descend through Boundary Canyon and Hell's Gate into the inferno at sea level and below. Below, below . . . beneath a sea, not of brine, but of heat, of shimmering simmering waves of light and a wind as hot and fierce as a dragon's breath.

The glare is stunning. Yet also exciting, even exhilarating—a world of light. The air seems not clear like glass but colored, a transparent, tinted medium, golden toward the sun, smoke-blue in the shadows. The colors come, it appears, not simply from the background, but are actually present in the air itself—a vigintillion microscopic particles of dust reflecting the sky, the sand, the iron hills.

On a day in June at ten o'clock in the morning the thermometer reads 114 degrees. Later in the day it will become hotter. But with humidity close to zero such heat is not immediately unpleasant or even uncomfortable. Like the dazzling air, the heat is at first somehow intoxicating—one feels that grace and euphoria that come with just the right ration of Old Grandad, with the perfect allowance of music. Sunlight is magic. Later will come. . . . Yes, out of the car and standing hatless under the sun, you begin to feel the menace in this arid atmosphere, the malignancy within that silent hurricane of fire.

We consider the dunes, the sea of sand. Around the edges of the dunes grow clumps of arrowweed tall as corn shocks, scattered creosote shrubs bleached out and still, a few shaggy mesquite trees. These plants can hardly be said to have conquered the valley, but they have in some way made a truce—or found a point of equilibrium in a ferocious, inaudible struggle between life and entropy. A bitter war indeed: The creosote bush secretes a poison in its roots that kills any other plant, even its own offspring, attempting to secure a place too near; in this way the individual creosote preserves a perimeter of open space and a monopoly of local moisture sufficient for survival.

We drive on to the gas station and store at Stovepipe Wells, where a few humans huddle inside beneath the blast of a cold-air blower. Like other mammals of the valley, the human inhabitants can endure its summer only by burrowing deep or by constructing an artificial environment —not adaptation but insulation, insularity.

Sipping cold drinks, we watch through the window a number of desert sparrows crawl in and out of the grills on the front of the parked automobiles. The birds are eating tourists—bugs and butterflies encountered elsewhere and smashed, baked, annealed to the car radiators. Like the bears of Yellowstone, the Indians of Arizona, and roadside businessmen everywhere, these birds have learned to make a good thing off passing trade. Certainly they provide a useful service; it's a long hot climb out of here in any direction, and a clean radiator is essential.

The Indians of Death Valley were cleverest of all. When summer came they left, went up into the mountains, and stayed there until it was reasonable to return—an idea too subtle in its simplicity for the white man of today to grasp. But we too are Indians—gypsies anyhow—and won't be back until September.

Furnace Creek, September 17. Again the alarming descent. It seemed much too hot in the barren hills a mile above this awful sinkhole, this graben (for Death Valley is not, properly understood, a valley at all), this collapsed and superheated trench of mud, salt, gravel, and sand. Much too hot—but we felt obliged to come back once more.

A hard place to love, Death Valley. An ugly place, bitter as alkali and rough, harsh, unyielding as iron. Here they separate the desert rats from the mice, the hard-rock prospectors from the mere rock hounds.

Cactus for example. There is none at all on the floor of the valley. Too dry or too brackish or maybe too hot. Only up on the alluvial fans and the side canyons a thousand feet above sea level do we find the first stunted and scrubby specimens of cholla and prickly pear and the pink-thorned cottontop—poor relation of the barrel cactus.

At first glance, speeding by car through this valley that is not a valley, one might think there was scarcely any plant life at all. Between oases you will be impressed chiefly by the vast salt beds and the immense alluvial fans of gravel that look as hostile to life as the fabled seas of the moon.

And yet there is life out there, life of a sparse but varied sort—salt grass and pickleweed on the flats, far-spaced clumps of creosote, salt-bush, desert holly brittlebush, and prickly poppy on the fans. Not much of anything, but a little of each. And in the area as a whole, including the surrounding mountains up to the eleven-thousand-foot summit of Telescope Peak, the botanists count a total of nine hundred to a thousand different species, ranging from microscopic forms of algae in the salt pools to limber pine and the ancient bristlecone pine on the peaks.

But the first impression remains a just one. Despite variety, most of the surface of Death Valley is dead. Dead, dead, deathly—a land of jagged salt pillars, crackling and tortured crusts of mud, sunburnt gravel bars the color of rust, rocks and boulders of metallic blue naked even of lichen. Death Valley is Gravel Gulch.

Telescope Peak, October 22. To escape the heat for a while, we spend the weekend up in the Panamints. (Summer still baking the world down below, far below, where swirls of mud, salt, and salt-laden streams lie motionless under a lake of heat, glowing in lovely and poisonous shades of auburn, saffron, crimson, sulfurous yellow, dust-tinged tones of white on white.)

Surely this is the most sterile of North American deserts. No matter how high we climb it seems impossible to leave behind the influence of aridity and anti-life. At 7,000 feet in this latitude we should be entering a forest of yellow pine, with grassy meadows and freshwater brooks. We are farther north than Santa Fe or Flagstaff. Instead there are only the endless barren hills, conventional in form, covered in little but shattered stone. A dull monotonous terrain, dun-colored, supporting a few types of shrubs and small, scattered junipers.

From 7,000 to 9,000 feet we pass through a belt of more junipers and a fair growth of pinyon pines. Along the trail to Telescope Peak—at 10,000 feet—appear thin stands of limber pine and the short, massive, all-enduring bristlecone pine, more ancient than the Book of Genesis. Timberline.

There is no forest here. And fifty or sixty airline miles to the west stands the reason why—the Sierra Nevada Range, blocking off the sea winds and almost all the moisture. We stand in the rain shadow of that still higher wall.

I walk past three wild burros. Descendants of lost and abandoned prospectors' stock, they range everywhere in the Panamints, multiplying freely, endangering the survival of the native bighorn sheep by trespassing on the latter's forage, befouling their springs. But the feral burros have their charm too. They stand about a hundred feet from the trail watching me go by. They are quite unafraid, and merely blink their heavy eyelashes like movie starlets when I halt to stare at them.

However, they are certainly not tame. Advance toward them and they trot off briskly.

The bray of the donkey is well known. But these little beasts can make another sound even more startling because so unexpected. Hiking up some arid canyon in the Panamints, through what appears to be totally lifeless terrain, you suddenly hear a noise like a huge dry cough behind your shoulder. You spring ten feet forward before daring to look around. And see nothing, nothing at all, until you hear a second cough and scan the hillsides and discover far above a little gray or black burro looking down at you, waiting for you to get the hell out of its territory.

I stand by the cairn on the summit of Telescope Peak, looking out on a cold, windy, and barren world. Rugged peaks fall off southward into the haze of the Mojave Desert; on the west is Panamint Valley, the Argus Range, more mountains, more valleys, and finally the Sierras, crowned with snow; to the north and northwest the Inyo and White mountains; below lies Death Valley—the chemical desert—and east of it the Black Mountains, the Funeral Mountains, the Amargosa Valley, and farther mountains, wave after wave of wrinkled ridges standing up from the oceanic desert sea until vision gives out somewhere beyond the curving rim of the world's edge. A smudge hangs on the eastern horizon, suggesting the presence of Death Valley's counterpart and complement, the only city within one hundred miles: Las Vegas: Glitter Gulch West.

Echo Canyon, November 30. A hard place to love. Impossible? No, there were a few—the prospectors, the single-blanket, jackass prospectors who wandered these funeral wastes for a century dreaming of what? Sudden wealth? Not likely. Not Shorty Borden, for example, who invested eight months of his life in building by hand a nine-mile road to his lead and silver diggings in Hanaupah Canyon. Then discovered that even with a road it would still cost him more to transport his ore to the nearest smelter than the ore itself was worth.

Echo Canyon. We are deep into the intricacies of the Funeral

Mountains. Named not simply for their proximity to Death Valley, but also for shape and coloration: lifeless escarpments of smoldering red bordered in charcoal, the crags and ridges and defiles edged in black and purple. A primeval chaos of faulted, uplifted, warped, and folded dolomites, limestones, fanglomerates of mud, sand, and gravel. Vulcanism as well: vesiculated andesite, walls embellished with elegant mosaics of rose and yellow quartz. Fool's gold—pyrite—glittering in the black sand, micaceous shales glinting under black light, veins of pegmatite zigzagging and intersecting like an undeciphered script across the face of a cliff; the writing on the wall: "God Was Here." Shallow caves, holes in the rock, a natural arch, and the canyon floor littered with boulders, deep in coarse gravel.

Nowhere in Echo Canyon can I find the slightest visible trace of water. Nevertheless, it must be present under the surface, at least in intermittent or minute amounts, for here and there stand living things. They look dead but are actually dormant, waiting for the resurrection of the rain. I mean the saltbush, the desert fir, the bladderweed, a sprinkling of cottontop cactus, the isolated creosote bush. Waiting.

You may see a few lizards. In sandy places are the hoofprints of bighorn sheep, where they've passed through on their way from the high parts of the range to the springs near Furnace Creek. Sit quite still in one spot for an hour and you might see a small gray bird fly close to look you over. This is the bird that lives in Echo Canyon.

The echoes are good. At certain locations, on a still day, one clear shout will create a series of overlapping echoes that goes on and on toward so fine a diminuendo that the human ear cannot perceive the final vibrations.

Tramp far enough up Echo Canyon and you come to a ghost town, the ruins of a mining camp—one of many in Death Valley. Deep shafts, a tipple, a rolling mill largely intact, several cabins—one with its inside walls papered with pages from the *Literary Digest*. Half buried in drifted sand is a rusted model-T Ford without roof or motor, a child's tricycle, a broken shovel.

Returning through twilight, I descend the narrow gorge between flood-polished walls of bluish andesite—the stem of the wine glass. I walk down the center of an amphitheater of somber cliffs riddled with grottoes, huge eyesockets in a stony skull, where bats hang upside down in the shadows waiting for night.

Through the opening of the canyon I can see the icy heights of Telescope Peak shining under the cloud-reflected light of one more sunset. Scarlet clouds in a green sky. A weird glow pervades the air through which I walk; it vibrates on the canyon walls, revealing to me all at once a vision of the earth's slow agony, the convulsive grinding violence of a hundred thousand years. Of a million years. I write metaphorically, out of necessity. And yet it seems impossible to believe that these mountains, old as anything on the surface of the planet, do not partake in some dim way of the sentience of living tissue. Geologies: From these rocks struck once by lightning gushed springs that turned to blood, flesh, life. Impossible miracle. And I am struck once again by the unutterable beauty, terror, and strangeness of everything we think we know.

Furnace Creek, December 10. The oasis. We stand near the edge of a grove of date palms looking eastward at the soft melting mudhills above Texas Spring. The hills are lemon yellow with dark brown crusts on top, like the frosting on a cake. Beyond the hills rise the elaborate, dark, wine-red mountains. In the foreground, close by, irrigation water plunges into a pool, for which it is diverted into ditches that run between rows of date palms.

The springs of Furnace Creek supply not only the palms but also the water needs of the hotel, the motel (both with swimming pools), Park Service headquarters and visitor center, an Indian village, and two large campgrounds. I do not know the output of these springs as measured in gallons per minute. But I do know that during the Christmas and Easter holidays there is enough water available to serve the needs of ten thousand people. Where does it come from? From a natural reservoir in the base of the bleak, fatally arid Funeral Mountains. A reservoir that may be joined to the larger underground aquifers beneath the Amargosa and Pahrump valleys to the east.

This does not mean that the Furnace Creek portion of Death Valley could support a permanent population of ten thousand drinking, back-scrubbing, hard-flushing suburbanites. For the water used here comes from a supply that may have required twenty thousand years to charge; it is not sustained by rainfall—not in a country where precipitation averages two inches per year.

That's the mistake they made in central Arizona—Tucson and Phoenix—and are now making in Las Vegas and Albuquerque. Out of greed and stupidity, but mostly greed, the gentry of those cities overexpanded their investment in development and kept going by mining the underground water supply. Now that the supply is dwindling, they set up an unholy clamor in Congress to have the rest of the nation save them from the consequences of their own folly. Phoenix might rise again from ashes—but not, I think, from the sea of sand that is its likely destiny.

There are about two hundred springs, all told, within the boundaries of Death Valley National Monument, counting each and every tiny seep that produces any flow at all. None except those in the northeast corner of the park are comparable to the springs at Furnace Creek. In addition to the springs, there are the heavily saline, undrinkable waters of Salt Creek, Badwater, and the valley floor itself.

All this water is found in what meteorologists believe to be the hottest place on earth, year in and year out hotter than the Sahara, the Great Karroo, the Negev, the Atacama, the Rub' al-Khali ("Empty Quarter") of Arabia, or the far-outback-of-beyond in central Australia. The world's record is held by Libya, where a temperature of 136 degrees Fahrenheit was once recorded at a weather station called Azizia. Death Valley's high so far is a reading of 134 degrees at Furnace Creek. But Azizia has been unable to come near repeating its record, while temperatures at Furnace Creek consistently exceed the mean maximums for Azizia by ten percent. And Badwater, only twenty miles south of Furnace Creek, is on the average always 4 degrees hotter. It follows that on the historic day when the thermometer reached 134 at Furnace Creek, it was probably 138 at Badwater. But there was nobody around at Badwater that day (July 10, 1913).

Official weather readings are made from instruments housed in a louvered wooden box set five feet above the ground. In Death Valley the temperature on the surface of the ground is ordinarily fifty percent higher than in the box five feet above. On a normal summer's day in Death Valley, with the thermometer reading 120 degrees Fahrenheit, the temperature at ground surface is 180.

Curiosities: There are fish in the briny pools of Salt Creek, far out on the hottest, bleakest, saltiest part of the valley floor—the inch-long cyprinodon or pupfish. There is a species of soft-bodied snail living in the Epsom salts, Glauber's salt, and rock salts of Badwater. There are fairy shrimp in the *tinajas* or natural cisterns of Butte Valley in the southwest corner of the park: estivating beneath the clay most of the year, they wriggle forth to swim, rejoice, and reproduce after that rarest and most wonderful of Death Valley events, a fall of rain.

More curiosities: Blue herons enter the valley in winter; also trumpeter swans; grebes, coots, and mallards can by seen in the blue ponds of Saratoga Springs; and for a few weeks in the fall of one year (1966) a real flamingo made its home among the reeds that line the shore of the sewage lagoon below Park Village. Where this flamingo came from no one could say; where it went the coyotes most likely could testify. Or perhaps the lion.

A lean and hungry mountain lion was observed several times that year during the Christmas season investigating the garbage cans in the campgrounds. An old lion, no doubt—aging, possibly ill, probably retired. In short, a tourist. But a lion even so.

But these are mere oddities. All the instruments agree that Death Valley remains the hottest place on earth, the driest in North America, the lowest in the Western Hemisphere. Of all deathly places the most deadly—and the most beautiful.

Badwater, January 19. Standing among the salt pinnacles of what is called the Devil's Golf Course, I heard a constant tinkling and crackling noise—the salt crust expanding in the morning sun. No sign of life out there. Experimentally I ventured to walk upon, over, among the pinnacles. Difficult, but not impossible. The formations are knee-high, white within but stained yellow by the dusty winds, studded on top with sharp teeth. Like walking on a jumble of broken and refrozen slabs of ice: At every other step part of the salt collapses under foot and you drop into a hole. The jagged edges cut like knives into the leather of my boots. After a few minutes of this I was glad to return to the security of the road. Even in January the sun felt uncomfortably hot, and I was sweating a little.

Where the salt flats come closest to the base of the eastern mountains, at 278 feet below sea level, lies the clear and sparkling pool known as Badwater. A shallow body of water, surrounded by beds of snow-white alkali. According to Death Valley legend the water is poisonous, containing traces of arsenic. I scooped up a handful and sampled it in my mouth, since the testing of desert waterholes has always been one of my chores. I found Badwater lukewarm, salty on the tongue, sickening. I spat it out and rinsed my mouth with fresh water from my canteen.

From here, the lowest point in all the Americas, I gaze across the pale lenses of the valley floor to the brown out-wash fan of Hanaupah Canyon opposite, ten miles away, and from the canyon's mouth up and up and up to the crest of Telescope Peak with its cornices of frozen snow 11,049 feet above sea level. One would like to climb or descend that interval someday, the better to comprehend what it means. Whatever it means.

I have been part of the way already, hiking far into Hanaupah Canyon to Shorty Borden's abandoned camp, up to that loveliest of desert graces, a spring-fed stream. Lively, bubbling, with pools big enough and cold enough, it seemed then, for trout. But there are none. Along the stream grow tangles of wild grapevine and willow; the spring is choked with watercress. The stream runs for less than a mile before disappearing into the sand and gravel of the wash. Beyond the spring, upcanyon, all is dry as death again until you reach the place where the canyon forks. Explore either fork and you find water once more—on the right a little waterfall, on the left in a grottolike glen cascades sliding down through chutes in the dark blue andesite. Moss, ferns, and flowers cling to the damp walls—the only life in this arid wilderness. Almost no one ever goes there. It is necessary to walk for many miles.

Devil's Hole, February 10. A natural opening in the desert floor; a queer deep rocky sinkhole with a pond of dark green water at the bottom. That pond, however, is of the kind called bottomless; it leads down and down through greener darker depths into underwater caverns whose dimensions and limits are not known. It might be an entrance to the subterranean lakes that supposedly lie beneath the Funeral Mountains and the Amargosa Valley.

The Park Service has erected a high steel fence with locked gate around the hole. Not to keep out tourists, who only want to look, but to keep out the aqualung adventurers who wish to dive in and go all the way down. Within the past year several parties of scuba divers have climbed over and under the fence anyway and gone exploring down in that sunless sea. One party returned to the surface one man short. His body has not been found yet, though many have searched. If supposition is correct, the missing man may be found someday wedged in one of the outlets of Furnace Creek springs.

Death Valley has taken five lives this year—one by water, two by ice, and two by fire. A hiker slipped on the glazed snow of the trail to Telescope Peak and tumbled a thousand feet down a steep pitch of ice and rock. His companion sent for help; a member of a professional mountaineering team, climbing down to recover the victim, also fell and was also killed.

Last summer two young soldiers from the Army's nearby Camp Irwin went exploring in the desert off the southwest corner of Death Valley. Their jeep ran out of gas, they tried to walk home to the base. One was found beside the seldom-traveled desert road, dead from exhaustion and dehydration. The body of the other could not be found, though two thousand soldiers hunted him for a week. No doubt he wandered off the trail into the hills seeking water. Absent without leave. He could possibly be still alive. Maybe in a forgotten cabin up in the Panamints eating lizards, waiting for some war to end.

Ah to be a buzzard now that spring is here.

The sand dunes, March 15. At night I hear tree toads singing in the tamarisk along the water channels of Furnace Creek Ranch. The days are often windy now, much warmer, and rain squalls sail north through the valley, obscuring both sky and sun. The ground squirrels scamper from hole to hole in the mud hills, the Gambel's quail swoop in flocks low over the ground, alight, and run in unison through the brush, calling to one another. Tawny coyotes stand bold as brass close to the road in broad daylight and watch the tourists drive by. And the mesquite thickets, black and lifeless-looking since last fall, have assumed a delicate tinge of spring green.

Death Valley's winter, much too lovely to last, is nearly over.

Between winds and storms I walk far out on the dunes. How hot and implacably hostile this sea of sand appeared last June when we saw it for the first time. Then it seemed to be floating in heat waves, which gathered among the dunes and glistened like pools of water, reflecting the sky.

I bear for the highest of the dunes, following the curving crests of the lesser dunes that lead toward it. On the way I pass a few scraggly mesquite trees, putting out new leaves, and a number of creosote shrubs. No other plants are deep-rooted enough to survive in the sand,

and these too become smaller and fewer as I advance and the dunes rise higher. On the last half mile to the topmost point there is no plant life whatsoever, although in the sand I find the prints of ravens, coyotes, mice, lizards. The sand is firm, rippled as the seashore, and virginal of human tracks; nobody has come this far since the last windstorm a few days ago.

Late in the afternoon I reach the summit of the highest dune, two hundred feet above the valley floor. Northward the sand drops abruptly away to smaller dunes, mud flats, a scatter of creosote and mesquite—and what looks to be, not a mirage, but a pond of real water encircled by the dunes.

Glissading down the hill of sand, climbing another, and down the far side of that, I come to the margin of the pool. The sandy shore is quick, alive, and I sink ankle deep in the mud as I bend to taste the water and find it fresh, cool, with hardly a trace of salt—fit to drink. The water must be left over from the recent rain.

I struggle out of the wet sand onto the dunes. Here I'll make camp for the evening. I scoop a hole in the sand, build a tiny fire of mesquite twigs, and sear a piece of meat on the flaming coals. Mesquite makes excellent fuel—burns with a slow hot flame, touching the air with a nut-sweet fragrance, and condenses as it burns to a bed of embers that glow and glimmer like incandescent charcoal. Fire is magic, a purifying and sanctifying magic, and most especially a mesquite fire on a sand dune at evening under desert skies, on the shore of a pool that gleams like polished agate, like garnet, like a tiger's eye.

The sun goes down. A few stray clouds catch fire, burn gold, vermillion, and driftwood blue in the unfathomed sea of space. These surrounding mountains that look during the day like iron—like burnt, mangled, rusted iron—now turn radiant as a dream. Where is their truth? A hard clean edge divides the crescent dunes into black shadow on one side, a phosphorescent light on the other. And above the rim of the darkening west floats the evening star.

Overlooking Carrizo Gorge

Susan Zwinger (b. 1947) is an author and naturalist whose fiction, poetry, and scholarly articles have been featured in numerous magazines and journals. Following the tradition of her mother, Ann Zwinger, she has also written several books about her wilderness journeys, including Still Wild, Always Wild: A Journey into the Desert Wilderness of California *(1997), from which this piece is excerpted.*

I gaze out from Carrizo Gorge above Interstate 8 and piece together the new Sonoran wilderness where I will hike and backpack over the next two weeks. On foot, I will cover sixty miles of the pristine yet long-traveled desert sands. It's the edges and borders and ecotones that drive me wild. I need to know how the Mexican Sonoran melts into the United States' Sonoran, how the Peninsular Mountains of coastal California melt into the Sonoran Desert floor, and how Anza-Borrego State Park flows into its adjacent wild lands: Carrizo Gorge Wilderness, 15,700 acres of deep canyons; the Jacumba Wilderness, 33,670 acres of rugged waterless mountains; and the Coyote Mountains, 17,000 acres of outrageously colored rock.

Far to the north, the cobalt ridge of the Santa Rosa Mountains entices me to backpack deep into an ancient Cahuilla village in Rockhouse Canyon. Closer to me stand the Fish Creek Mountains, full of pure gypsum, and the Coyote Mountains, with their sediments of a six-million-year-old sea. In between the Carrizo Badlands: I ache to explore their four-hundred-foot cones of gold, red, green, and purple remnants of marine reefs, lake deposits, and ancient Colorado River deltas. Within the badlands, I will tromp along with mastodons, early llamas, horses, tapirs, and saber-toothed tigers, or hang with giant sloths—twenty thousand years too late.

The Sonoran Desert is the youngest North American desert, having existed for only the last twelve thousand years. It stretches from 23 degrees north in Baja California, Mexico, to 35 degrees north on the border with Arizona. Mostly lying in Mexico, it spills over the U.S. border with its lush variety of bizarre life forms—twenty-foot-tall cacti, raucous carrion-eating birds, wily reptiles, and plants endemic only to the southernmost edge of the United States. As a subtropical desert, it tends to have a greater number of species than do the more temperate desert habitats

I have driven fifteen hundred miles from my rainy home in Washington State, longing for the Sonoran's magic—life forms and weather distinctly different form those found in any other desert. Here, the unique pattern of rainfall creates the largest cactus in the world—the saguaro, strange trees with green bark; the palo verde; and bizarre forms of the lily family, the yucca and nolina. Long, gentle winter rains from the coast and the shorter more intense summer rains from the southeast make possible the outlandish ocotillo, the eight-foot-high teddy bear cholla, the fragrant desert lavender shrub, and the elephant tree with its water-swelled, rhinoceros-skinned trunk and lemon-smelling leaves.

I throw my worn-out army poncho, Therm-a-Rest mattress, and twenty-seven-year-old sleeping bag on the sandy, dry ground because I want to wake with the breath of the Sonoran in my nostrils. In the damp morning or after rain, odors of incredible intensity emanate from desert plants that have evolved volatile oils to prevent desiccation: vivid lemons, pungent pines, lavender, mint, sage, rosemary, creosote, and intoxicating earth smells.

It is early February, and Carrizo Gorge Overlook is an ideal place for my exploration to begin. Below me, dropping three thousand feet down, the In-ko-pah, Carrizo, and Bow Willow Gorges look like arid crevices of rock boulders. I know that a hike up from the bottom of Bow Willow will reveal hidden palm oases, waterfalls, and cool pools after a rain, yet because of this barren view I don't believe it yet. This overlook straddles the transition between the peninsular zone's moist mountain climate and the dramatic Sonoran Desert. I stand at the serrated knife-edge of two ecosystems and their exceptionally rich variety of species. Last night I slept half a mile back from this escarpment under lush old madroñas, huge manzanitas with thick trunks, and deep green oak trees. Yet here, the lush foliage of ocean cliffs dovetails with the scrub of desert floor: *Ephedra viridis* (bright green Mormon tea), desert scrub oak, rabbit brush, sage, and oval-leaved buckwheat. Nuttall's woodpecker, scrub jay, and chickadee of the mountain chaparral mix air waves with Cooper's hawk, turkey vulture, and a magnificent eagle with a flashing golden head.

To the east-northeast, the whiter-than-white Salton Sea shimmers below sea level. Far to the southeast, Picacho Peak Wilderness drops toward the Colorado River; I plan to go there next. To the southeast, the Mexican border's steep mountain terrain, the Jacumba Wilderness, sinks from high coastal mountains on the west to sea level in a matter of miles. The U.S. Border Patrol sits outside the waterless wilderness and waits for thirsty illegal aliens.

Directly below me is the infamous Carrizo Corridor. I stare at this barren—or so it seems from up here—desert strip, which was an obvious route for Native Americans traveling by foot between the interior and the coast. Because they knew how to listen to the desert, what to eat, where to look for water, and sought the guidance of shamans, the ancestors of the Cahuilla would pass through with relative ease, taking notice of the great beauty around them.

Beauty, however, was not the preoccupation of the first Europeans who passed through this rugged, "impenetrable" topography. Here, where less than an inch of rain per year may fall and the temperature day after day may soar to 108 degrees, thousands of soldiers, miners, settlers, Spanish friars, snake oil peddlers, outlaws, and dreamers crossed this dry expanse, passing from palm grove to palm grove, spring to spring. Their bodies, composed of 92 percent water, would be incapacitated by a 2 percent water loss; at 8 percent loss they were dead. Death from dehydration is awful, slow, and torturous, with swollen tongue and hallucinations.

I imagine each of these Native Americans and European travelers leaving a different colored ribbon behind them in their wanderings. Then, in my mind's eye, I add the silver cross-hatching of railroad, the powder blues and pale greens of 1930s Chevys along old Route 99, and the strong reds, dark greens, and blacks of sport utility vehicles on State Route 2. Their intersections weave an intricate crochet of hope, intent, and culture.

Many of the threads, however, end abruptly—explorer or pioneer fallen, desiccated hands outreached toward springs, men slumped over fried radiators, miners picked clean by coyotes, ill-prepared pioneers carried off in the guts of vultures. Just so much dried, bleached detritus on the desert pavement.

Bow Willow Gorge to Carrizo Gorge Overlook

Before dawn the next morning I drive an hour, through the dramatic Jacumba boulders and into the bottom of Bow Willow Gorge in Anza-Borrego State Park. Soon after dawn, there on the Sonoran Desert floor, I look up again to the Carrizo Gorge Overlook where I stood yesterday and have a burning desire to make my way up there on foot— four thousand feet above. I want to know intimately, increment by increment, plant by plant, how such an enormous ecological-altitudinal change unfolds.

At the lower end, Bow Willow Wash begins as a groggy, quarter-mile-wide, deep sand arroyo where creosote and mesquite are half buried in the debris of the last flash flood. Shiny black phainopeplas—cardinal-shaped, obsidian-black birds—start up from their bushes like black holes in the air.

At thirteen hundred feet the day is heating up: no shade and no sign of water. It is my first day back in the desert. I feel anxious. To take my mind off my hot feet, I notice the bright chartreuse and red balls of mistletoe beginning to bloom in the dull brown shrubs. Dripping with sweat, miserably hot, I hear a sudden swell of bird chirruping.

One hundred feet below me, the shrub down in the arroyo appears gray in color. Now that I am closer I see its color is bright green. Water? The first surface water has appeared where there has been no water for almost a year. It has instantly created a stream habitat: water beetles and algae asleep for months have sprung to life. The multitude of desert seeds, such as chia, sleeping dry and "dead" for years, have swollen and surrounded themselves with sticky mucilage to protect the life within them as they sprout. The boulders suddenly are slick with algae strands which undulate in the current. Water striders, insects which walk on surface tension, have suddenly found water where water was not. Bird volume has increased tenfold.

I am down there in an instant. On my hands and knees, armpit-deep, I plunge my whole skull in. Cold water goes up my nose, down my neck. Cold desert water!

Cooled down, finally, I scramble with all four limbs up through shed-sized boulders and native palms. I watch the water pulse below me through eight-foot-tall carrizo reeds. Bow Willow Canyon narrows darkly; on its steep sides, talus teeters straight up for hundreds of feet. I scramble, up and down, over and through these great stone slabs. A pearly gray California tree frog sits perfectly camouflaged on the quartz monzonite stone; I have heard their lovely Ukrainian choir at dusk.

At sixteen hundred feet, something is happening to the vegetation—the higher I climb, the more plants come into bloom. A Costa's hummingbird zaps by me at impossible velocity, stopping where it finds a solid profusion of red-orange tube flowers—a chuparosa shrub, *Justicia californica*.

At seventeen hundred feet, I discover something amazing.

Mountain chaparral—a sugar bush, deep and shiny green like manzanita—which grows at thirty-five hundred feet in the coastal mountain transition zone, appears down here at seventeen hundred feet. I am in a classic ecotone, a transition between one ecosystem and another. In the middle of the steep canyon, rock pools, cool temperatures, and tall reeds have created a microclimate.

After the dry, pricking tans of the desert arroyo, suddenly I'm walking into a Technicolor land of the living. I find a misted hanging rock garden next to a seven-foot waterfall lush with chuparosa, desert apricot, desert rockpea, water-logged mosses, a California cloak fern, *Notholaena californica*. Ferns are supposed to exist in moist forests, yet here they are in glorious desert conditions. I strip off my pack, stinky bandanna, and boots, then lie back in the waterfall's spray and dibble my toes in the lucid brown pool. Up close to my eyeballs, ferns studded with water have sprung from cracks in solid stone. To protect themselves from summer's harsh heat, they grow furry white hairs on top and exude wax underneath.

Paradise at eighteen hundred feet. The next twenty-two hundred feet promise to be a bleak boulder-scramble. Wisdom is the better part of desert travel. This is as far as I'm going.

Colorado Desert

The Palms in Our Hands

Gary Paul Nabhan (b. 1952) is an ethnobiologist, plant ecologist, and author who has devoted his career to advocating the preservation of desert plants and the lifestyles of native desert people. In Gathering the Desert *(1985) he wrote about a dozen of the more than 425 edible wild species found in the Sonoran (Colorado) Desert, including the palm tree.*

Around Palm Springs, California, half of the sixty thousand residents are over sixty years old. In August, the asphalt running in to the various retirement subdivisions drives the thermometer up over 170 degrees. The pavement is so hot, you can fry a snowbird's egg on it—if you can find one. Most of the old birds who stay year-round stay inside during the summer. They may take a couple of showers a day to stay fresh. Many of them pay Southern California Edison a thousand dollars a month or more to keep their air conditioners running straight through the summer.

Outside, there is little shade you can sit under. Carports or porches, if those can be considered "outside." A eucalyptus in the backyard, perhaps. A couple of lollipop-shaped citrus trees or an African sumac, though they are seldom manicured so that you can fit a warm body beneath their canopies. The Hollywood junipers in the front may throw a shadow on the wall, but they don't shade a soul.

Then there are the palms. All the planned adult communities have broad streets lined with widely spaced palms. They are lucrative commodities in the landscape-nursery industry of southern California, sold by the foot, hauled by truck, and propped up in yards as if a motion picture studio were making an instant oasis movie right there in the new neighborhood. Introduced date palms are placed in strategic locations, but they usually have a big puddle of irrigation water at their bases which keeps folks from sitting beneath them. And there are the lines of native palms, the shorter "California fan palms" with petticoats of dead fronds trimmed halfway down their stout trunks, interspersed every sixty feet with tall, slender "Mexican skydusters." Landscape architects love how these two variants of *Washingtonia filifera* "rise out of the bare earth" on the curbs of urban boulevards, either in monotonous rows "for cadence" or singly, "like an exclamation point." They are planted in these subdivisions to make each landowner feel that he is living within his very own "oasis paradise." Yet these palms are stuck out on the side of the street where hardly anyone walks. Separated from one another by irrigated lawns of empty space, each throws a tiny oval shadow down on the ground. Torn from their evolutionary history of being densely clustered with other palms of various ages, each is as lonesome as a fish out of school.

When the more speculative subdivisions dry up economically, the faucets close, and the flow of water from some subterranean aquifer slows. The billboard showing a life of leisure played out beneath a palm grove cracks in the wind, then blows over. On one abandoned boulevard near Palm Springs, a starved *Washingtonia* finally curls down, fronds gone, dead growth tip touching the dust. The whole plant makes a big, sad U. It looks like a lean-legged ostrich hiding its head in the ground.

Nearby, a speculator leaves his office—a mobile trailer—and heads into town for a noonday drink. Parking his air-conditioned Oldsmobile, he locks the doors and walks, sweating, across the superheated paved lot. A palm silhouette shaped of menthol-green neon lights the window of the entrance to the Oasis Tap, promising paradise and lunch inside. His arms quiver and he makes a quiet grunt while pulling open the heavy door. Coldness rushes out. He enters. He can hardly see anything except for the flashing lights of the electric Coors ski-slope sign on the far wall. He takes off his sunglasses and his eyes adjust to the dimly lit tavern. He is glad to have taken refuge in this little electrically simulated oasis, away from business, bright lights, and the blazing sun. He finds a stool. Perspiration cools quickly on his arm.

"Whatchou guys been up to, huh? Hey," he pants, "gimme a cold one. Hey, what they got on the tube today? Are the Padres gonna let the Goose pitch today? Is that game on? What time is it anyway?"

He reaches for the icy Coors in front of him and takes the first gulp. A chill hits his chest. He gasps. Staring at the TV, still sweating, he can't see a single Padre.

He never walks out of the Oasis Tap.

Three women ascend from a hole in a mound near their house as the shade begins to side up the Sonoran barranca slope. It is after four on a June afternoon. They have been in the shelter of their *buki* since eleven or so. The two younger women joke while casually stripping palm fiber for the rectangular-shaped *petaca* baskets that they will begin the next day. The older woman, plaiting a new palm sombrero for her husband, is quiet, thoughtful. The last double-weave sombrero like this one lasted her husband for four years; his newer, store-bought plastic fiber hat hardly weathered seven months of his constant use. So she starts twilling its roundish crown, working down toward the pliant brim, and tomorrow will weave back to the top and tie it in. It will take several days of work for something that most people now buy at the store. But then again, having a durable hat is important. It is all that stands between her husband and the scorching sun on these June days when he has to work long hours to prepare his fields for the rainclouds that will soon cross central Sonora.

By noon on most days since early May, she has been retreating with the other women into the huki, a semi-subterranean shelter where a roof of logs, palm fronds, dirt, and brush covers a shallow excavation into a hillside. There, with her bare feet on the earthen floor, she hums quietly to herself while weaving, or giggles at the jokes the other two make about the men. There, in the musky dark, the frond fibers of the Sonoran palmetto, *Sabal uresana*, remain moist and workable. There, too, she has a break after helping her husband do the milking, after making breakfast and cheese, after sweeping the house and the ramada. Her thoughts are her own in the huki. Although she continues to work, the shadowy solitude somehow restores her freshness.

Huki. Perhaps it means "basket-house," or possibly "menstrual hut." Whatever the derivation, it is an ancient word among the Uto-Aztecan languages, and *huki* is a term still shared by Mountain Pima, Cahitan, and a few Warihio in Sonora and adjacent Chihuahua. The structures remain in use in the foothills of the sierras of east-central Sonora, but most hukis have fallen into abandonment in the lowlands. South of 30 degrees latitude, and below 1,000 meters in elevation in eastern Sonora, the Sonoran palmetto has been among the major weaving fibers for utility baskets, hats, sleeping mats, and other household articles for centuries. Two other palm species, beargrass, sotol, and agaves are also woven into baskets or cordage, but their association with the huki is not as strong.

Sonoran palmetttos are used for myriad purposes. The fronds are employed for thatching the sides and roofs of Warihio and Pima homes, ramadas, and A-frame shelters. Sections of the trunks serve as uprights and crossbeams in houses. Whole lengths are stacked up to make corrals. The hearts of palm seedlings are infrequently roasted and eaten like agave hearts. Yet this practice apparently has not been too intensive or widespread in Sonora during recent times. The density and areal extent of certain palm stands in fairly accessible areas suggest that they have escaped overexploitation. *Sabal uresana* grows in extensive stands near

Opodepe, Onavas, Sevepa, Mazocahui, and other ancient pueblos in central Sonora, well within reach of where thousands of people have lived for centuries. Perhaps only "surplus" palm hearts were used in years when there was an abundance of young plants resulting from the beneficial effects of burning the palmetto oases and savannas. Piman speakers are well aware that the whole palm dries up if the bud is used. Palm fronds are too important to let a whole plant be lost in just one meal.

Palms may have appeared as far north as central California more than seventy million years ago, based on reports of pollen similar to that of *Sabal* and *Washingtonia* found in Late Cretaceous sediments. Fossilized imprints of palm fronds have been found embedded in Californian limestone strata twenty-five to thirty feet below the present surface of the ground. Sometime less than five million years ago other tropical plants such as wild figs began to drop out of sight of these northern palms as summer rains decreased and winter temperatures lowered. For some reason, the *Washingtonia filifera* palms have persisted in more northerly, winter rainfall–dominated localities than those of *Sabal uresana* and *Erythrea* palms in Baja California or in Sonora. By themselves, the northern palms are considered relicts left over from earlier climates that were more favorable for your average palm.

They too may have been occasionally extirpated on a local basis from small canyons within their range by floods, freezes, borers, droughts, or disease. Later they could have been dispersed to some of the same sites again as seeds in the feces of wandering coyotes. For periods prior to human habitation of the continent, *Washingtonia* palms had already earned the status of survivor, persisting in areas over long stretches of time, through varying climates, while other early-established plants were lost from the region's flora.

After people came upon palms in the western Sonoran Desert, it must have been difficult for them to conceive of a life in which these palms were absent. Before A.D. 1500, there may have been a period of a couple of centuries when *Washingtonia* lined the shores of prehistoric

Lake Cahuilla in the Salton basin, if Richard Felger's hypothesis is correct. Prehistoric Indians harvested nearly forty species of plant and animal foods along the shores of Lake Cahuilla, and contemporary palm
oases are situated close to this ancient shoreline. These shady oases
would have been ideal sites for processing such foods, and many bedrock mortars used for grinding are found in the washes running
through them. Virtually every palm oasis in southern California has
prehistoric pottery or petroglyphs associated with it. Scratched and
painted glyphs tell us of giants, big-horned animals, and solar visions
dreamed by our antecedents. Under the tallest palm in North America
dreams grew large.

The Aguas Calientes group of Cahuilla Indians at Palm Springs tells
a story about the creation of the first palm. As Francisco Patencio
recalled, it began when one of the head men realized that his life as one
of the People was about done, and that he should prepare to go:

> The man wanted to benefit his people, so he said, I am going to be
> a palm tree. There are no palm trees in the world. My name shall
> always be Palm. From the top of the earth to the end of the earth
> my name shall be Palm. So he stood up very straight and very
> strong and very powerful, and soon the bark of the tree began to
> grow around him. And so he passed from the sight of his people.
>
> Now the people were settled all about the country in many
> places but they all came to Indian Wells to eat the fruit of the palm
> tree. The meat of the fruit was not very large, but it was sweet like
> honey, and was enjoyed by everybody—animals and birds too. The
> people carried the seed to their homes and palm trees grew from
> this seed in many places. The palm trees in every place came from
> the first palm tree, but, like the people who change in customs and
> language, the palms often were somewhat different . . . all, every
> one of them, came from this first palm tree, the man who wanted
> to benefit his people.

The benefits? Food from buds, flowers, and fruit. The fruit are produced on as many as thirty-one stalks per tree, with each fruit cluster

weighing from five to twenty pounds. Fiber for sandals, skirts, trays, and baskets. Petioles for spoons and bows. Fronds for thatched ramadas. Wood for innumerable needs. The pithy wood from the branches of the palm fruit clusters was used as tinder when fires were started by friction-spinning. Home, hearth, cloth, food, and fiber—the palm was to the Desert Cahuilla what the bison was to the historic Sioux.

The Cahuilla and other tribes probably dispersed palms to other canyons, both unintentionally like the coyotes and intentionally like the Early People. Stands high in the San Jacinto Mountains have been traced back to Cahuilla plantings. The seeds are easy to germinate in moist soils, and young plants, carefully transported, could have been transplanted. *Washingtonia* palms, now found at the Papago oasis of Quitovac, Sonora, may have arrived on that scene in historic times via aboriginal trade routes. It could have easily been maintained there where western Papagos continue to transplant, burn, and irrigate various plants much the same way historic Cahuilla did.

Palm seed gets around, whether in guts of wildlife, in human guts, or in human hands.

In truth, the fate of various palms has been in our hands for centuries. Humans have longed changed the age structure of "wild" palm stands by increasing the frequency of burning and by management practices such as irrigation and clearing of ground-covering plant litter. Go to nearly any palm stand in Baja California, Sonora, or Arizona and you will see some blackened trunks that are the evidence of fires, often ones intentionally initiated by local residents. In 1909, botanist Parish saw that "it is almost impossible to find mature indigenous palms from which the leaves have not been repeatedly burned." Such torched oases have irked many a purist naturalist wishing to visit palms in their presumed natural state, with long skirts of fronds tapering down toward the ground. Instead they see charred, bared trunks that are ugly as plucked chickens.

However ugly they may have looked, only a small percentage of plants died in each oasis fire set by historic Indians. At the same time, brush, debris, and competing plants were killed back. Water and nutrients were freed. Ecologist Richard Vogl estimates that Indian-managed oases were burned nearly every four years, and each fire stimulated a subsequent bumper crop of fruit to be produced. In one of his study sites, palms surviving a burn averaged twenty-one stalks of fruit after a fire, as opposed to twelve in the unburned control. Following a fire, fruit are so abundant that the surplus falling to the open ground may produce thousands of new seedlings. These bumper crops attract birds and larger mammals, some of whom were hunted. The fires also improve the nutritional value of oasis understory plants such as saltgrass and rushes.

If you live within a palm oasis for any period of time, you find reasons to burn, to clear away dead fronds and the creatures associated with them. Early Anglo-American naturalists claimed that the Cahuilla had spiritual reasons for burning oases—because dry fronds were the hiding place of spirits, or to offer fire to the dead and to send messages to departed friends. Cahuilla have also offered much more mundane reasons for setting fires in the palms near where they lived. Patencio remembered that "the bugs that hatched on top of the palm trees made the fruit sick, and no fruit came. After the trees were set afire and burned, the bugs were killed and the trees gave good fruit." Long after the Cahuilla began such a practice, the USDA undertook studies which confirmed that periodic burning is the most effective way to eliminate scale and spider mite pests, thereby increasing palm fruit harvests.

There are other motives for burning dried fronds. They get in the way of harvesters, and fallen ones provide shelter for rodents and other camp-robbers. Wasps and yellow jackets often hang their nests among drooping fronds, and fires dispel them as well.

Such human modifications of palm populations probably began in prehistoric times, but the palms remained reproductive. All ages of one or two palm species could be seen clustered together in canyons where springs or seeps fed them, forming oasis microhabitats that sheltered cultures from the extremes of the open desert environment. . . .

In April, 1782, the soldier-explorer Pedro Fages encountered two small oases of *Washingtonia filifera* around pools of water as his party traveled northwest out of the Imperial Valley. Numerous palm springs such as these had been used by the Kumeyaay ancestors since at least A.D. 1000. Yet one of the spots that Fages visited was singled out in the next century as the southern Palm Springs, owing to its accessibility to a foot trail that grew into the Butterfield Stage and Overland Mail Line.

Another, northern Palm Springs grew from campsite to stagestop to artists' colony to resort to unwieldy retirement community in less than a century. But it was the southern site that was more frequently visited earlier. In the 1840s, the Mormon Battalion recorded twenty to thirty native palms at this southerly oasis. These palms did not survive for more than a decade.

In 1833, Dr. W. P. Blake of the Pacific Railway Survey unknowingly stopped at the same site that the Franciscans and Mormons had camped on in earlier years. He commented upon the destruction left in the wake of careless Forty-niners:

Three or four palm trees, each about thirty feet high, are standing on the bank from which the springs issue. They are much injured by fire and persevering attacks of emigrants who have cut down many of the finest of the group, as if determined that the only trees that grace the sandy avenue of the Desert, and afford a cool place for the Springs, should be destroyed.

Just five years later, J. M. Farwell rode the Butterfield Line to the southern Palm Springs:

This place takes its name from a species of palm trees which formerly grew here, and which within a few years were standing, as I saw the trunks as they lay upon the ground, and the stumps

228 / Gary Paul Nabhan

from which they were cut. . . . It was bright moonlight while we remained here, and the beauty and singularity of the scene will not soon fade from my memory.

Recalling these events a century later, historian E. I. Edwards lamented that the "picturesque oasis [had been] stripped of its crowning glory. The palm trees had been cut down. All of them." At the time of his visit to the site in 1959, "only one isolated stump remained as a visible reminder of the palms." Two other trunk fragments were uncovered within a mound of dirt. The springs had become seasonally dry.

In the meantime, the northern town of Palm Springs prospered. By the mid-1880s, Anglo-American settlers had begun to build irrigation ditches from other springs to support agricultural development. These ditches later fed not farms but urban landscaping. There are perhaps more cultivated palms today in *the* Palm Springs—the northern one— than in all the historic canyons of Alta California. Something different from mainstream agriculture developed—a myth of idyllic oasis life. Here in the Perfect Land, you could live and breathe and, if you were so inclined, plant a backyard orchard. The *San Bernardino Weekly* ran this notice of a land auction in October 1887:

> Invest at Palm Springs, where there is NO FROST! NO HEAVY WINDS! NO FOG! THE HOME OF THE BANANA, DATE AND ORANGE! Only spot in California where frost, fog and windstorms are absolutely unknown. . . . Best Opportunity for Men of Moderate Means.

Plans for the Perfect Land were, at that time, built on the presumption of Perfect Access to Water. Such perfect access remained in the bush, never quite coming securely into hand. Anglos and the Aguas Calientes branch of the Cahuilla Indians fought over water rights for three decades. During the 1894–1905 drought, agriculture in the valley almost turned belly-up under the hot, dry sky. But the government finally led the Indians into a complex settlement that returned to them certain water rights plus a checkerboard of land tracts in Palm Valley that they could then lease to non-Indians for ninety-nine-year periods. Most of the Aguas Calientes families joined in the rush for the Perfect Deal and soon became prominent developers. Aguas Calientes descendants now have interest in condominiums, tract housing, hotels, and unrestricted bingo-game bonanzas. Once posing for tourist photos in bedouin garb on the backs of camels, welcoming visitors to the "New Araby," some of the Aguas Calientes people have turned their dromedaries in for Mercedeses.

This is not to say that agriculture failed to develop in the region. On the contrary, southeastern California is among the four richest agricultural zones in the United States. Yet the natural attributes that once attracted men of modest means to the area are now largely gone. The air is often dull gray in color, a stifling haze. Highway signs reading "Daylight Test Area" and "Keep headlights on for the next 50 miles" perplex unacquainted travelers. Surface water resources are overallocated. Groundwater overdraft per year has become so great that it would take decades without pumping to return the water table to its pre-1900 levels. The Coachella Valley's groundwater quality has also worsened. High levels of total dissolved salts, boron, fluoride, and sulfates severely constrain the future uses of this resource.

Is there negative feedback between southern California's Idyllic Oasis myth and natural oases left in the region? At first it appears as if the Coachella Valley's prosperity simply allows more people to appreciate the native oases—many are now protected, and they are elegantly interpreted at the Palm Springs Museum by enthusiastic, competent naturalists. It is believed that the number of palms in southern California canyons may be on the upswing. Most of these canyons are above the valley, in the zone of groundwater recharge, so that they are minimally affected by groundwater pumping on the plains below.

But it is the oasis as a unique microenvironment that has suffered, through fire suppression, exclusion of Native American gardening, and locally within the valley, changing water relations. Less than four hundred hectares of native palm oasis habitat persist in the wilds of the American Southwest.

Ecologist Richard Vogl has eloquently written of how "empty" southern Californian palm stands feel today:

> The original oases were largely open and foot-worn, free of accumulated plant debris. Springs were clear and impounded water holes were maintained for bathing and washing. In addition, hand-dug channels shunted water to small garden patches. Today's oases are usually cluttered and choked with plant accumulations, springs are silted in or taken over by emergent aquatic plants, and unimpeded streams tumble down to sink into the desert floors.
>
> Oases formerly smelled of charred wood, camp fires, burned grass, and moist soil, occasionally interrupted by cooking food. In some instances, oases could be smelled before they were seen. Today's oases take on the more subtle odors of the existing vegetation, they smell of willows, of mule fat, or of desert lavender, but seldom of smoke, char and fire.

Years of fire suppression allow the buildup of tinder to the extent that when a fire does occur, it damages many more palms. Similarly, there have always been flash floods in southern California, but their frequencies and intensities have changed with urbanization. At Willow Hole near Palm Springs, twenty-one palms were evident in 1961. A 1969 flash flood, intensified by the amount of runoff rapidly dumped into washes from a paved housing development upstream, downcut the wash running through Willow Hole, dropping the water table there by six meters. By 1983, only nine palms were left, all scattered along the edge of surrounding dunes, where moisture bleeds out of their sandy shoulders.

Not too far away, the celebrated Thousand Palms oasis sits beside a series of sedimentary hills. Its three groves look fine from the summits of these hills. But when you meander under the palms you see that a number of them have been saved by supplemental water provided to

them by a trickle irrigation system. It is like seeing someone fed intra-
venously, knowing that he might not survive without this lifeline. The
smallest of the three groves, Powell Palms, has been particularly vulnerable to arroyo downcutting and water table droppage over the last
decade. Groundwater use at nearby housing developments can only
aggravate this situation.

It has become clear that no oasis is an island unaffected by surrounding land uses and abuses. Northeast of Palm Springs in the Mohave
Desert, the National Park Service created Joshua Tree National
Monument to preserve palm and yucca stands. Groundwater consumption in nearby fields and military bases has caused a five-meter drop in
the groundwater over the last four decades. Spring-fed pools dried up
in the Oasis of Marah (Twenty-nine Palms) over a decade ago. To avoid
desiccation of the tourist attraction there, the wild *Washingtonia*, the
National Park service is running a pipeline up to the palms to keep
them irrigated. With what? Pumped groundwater.

Somewhere within this rapidly changing scene, a man emerged who
truly loved palm oases, as they have been and should be. Randall
Henderson was born in the late 1880s in Ohio, but by the end of World
War I he was firmly planted in the deserts of southern California. From
1920 up until his death on the Fourth of July 1970, Henderson visited
eighty-eight native palm oases in Alta California and Arizona, and no
less than eight oases in Baja California. Using a hand-held counter, he
individually tallied the number of *Washingtonia* palms in natural habitats north of the border (11,000) as well as some 4,500 of the estimated
18,000 palms of three species found within the first eighty kilometers
south of the international boundary.

His quest for understanding the context of palms took him into
remote areas with the likes of renowned botanist Liberty H. Bailey and
the Pai-Pai Indians, seasoned oasis dwellers. The astonishing amount of
information that he published on oases in his twenty-one years as editor
of *Desert* magazine continues to dwarf that contributed by any trained
scientist. His notes and photos form a baseline from which we can

record change in their habitats. His compulsiveness for counting palms did not, however, diminish his wonder that any are able to grow in such an arid environment: "I have never ceased to be amazed and delighted at the paradox of palms growing wild in the desert, for this tree must have abundant water at its shallow roots."

What Henderson recognized is that much of the natural elegance of palms has to do with their specificity to certain kinds of places, their geological, hydrological, and microclimatic conditions. Most of the California palm oases are situated where springs and seeps well up at fault lines, such as the San Andreas, that are part of tectonic-plate intersection. Hillside seeps caused by water outflow from exposed geological strata provide habitats for palms in Fishtail Canyon in the Kofa Mountains of Arizona and in Horseshoe Palms in the Indio Hills of California. Where water bubbles up on floodplains or in canyons due to impervious bedrock reaching the surface, oases such as Pushwalla Palms are formed. These islands of greenery float like mirages on the edge of sand seas surrounding the Salton Sea and Colorado River delta. Their beauty is in part due to contrast with their surrounding environment. Oases cannot occur just anywhere, for the natural habitats within which palms can persist for centuries are few and far between. Once established, the palms help create soil conditions and a buffered microclimate that encourage future generations of palms.

Henderson detailed the uniqueness of nearly every oasis he visited and pointed out differences and similarities with others nearby. Late in life, he became greatly disturbed that each oasis was rapidly becoming like every other in southern California, that suburbanization was making the landscape more homogenous. The town of Palm Desert that he founded in 1948 currently houses more than 11,000 people. It now suffers from the same trappings that most post–World War II instant cities do.

One thing eventually saddened Henderson even more than the cancerous growth in his own backyard; it was the repercussions from a stripped-down jalopy that he adapted in the 1930s to drive down sandy

washes during his oasis explorations. His modest homemade contrap-
tion became the prototype for the modern dune buggy.

When he realized what destruction off-road vehicles would cause, he
retired from tourist-oriented *Desert* magazine in 1958 and poured his
energies into the Desert Protective Council. He had hoped to put constraints on the all-terrain vehicles that were flooding the Mohave and
Sonoran Deserts, but he was too late to turn the tide. By the time he
died there were an estimated five million off-road vehicles in the United
States. Many of their western owners had access to Henderson's earlier
publications on how to get to remote places, including oases. For a conservationist loving tranquillity, it was the equivalent of creating a
Frankenstein. In his last days, he wondered when society would realize
that it was "time to see what could be done about tooting auto horns,
badly muffled exhausts, blatant radios . . . and the prattle of garrulous
and ill-tempered humans."

Traveling over a wide washboard road on the edge of Laguna Salada,
Paul Mirocha and I inadvertently ended up at one of Henderson's
favorite oases, Guadalupe Canyon. We had missed the ill-defined intersections with two roads leading toward more northerly canyons in the
Sierra Juarez of Baja California. Our road was considerably better than
the winding course of dry arroyo that Henderson had used as a path,
but still it rattled our kidneys. When we reached sight of the first palms,
we stopped in the middle of the road, emptied the truck cab and ourselves, and watched the sun go down behind the Sierras.

We were relieved to reach any oasis by sunset, let alone one where
we turned out to be the only visitors. Not that we were the only people
evident, for caretaker Arturo Loya Espinosa lives half a kilometer
upstream from where we camped. We heard his dogs and chickens all
night. He rents out primitive huts and camping spaces with fire pits,
charges fees to enter the swimming pool and hot springs, and rakes up
beer cans and plastic bags after visitors leave. He knows where the
ancient fire pits are, and the bedrock mortars, the petroglyphs. He also

knows the way to a cave containing clay ollas and palm sandals, but he won't take anyone there. He concedes that there is virtually no place near the oasis that you can go without finding evidence of human activities, camping debris, ancient or otherwise.

Yet palms, not public paraphernalia, dominated the habitat and consumed our attention. The last light glinted off the Virgin of Guadalupe, a rock outcrop high above us. We sat down amidst a dense clump of *Washingtonia* and *Brahea* palms.

What music to wash the road-roar out of our ears! The flower stalks drooped down like streamers, rattling in the wind against the half-burned miniskirts of old fronds. From the background noise of the canyon bottom below, the rush and bubble of spring water wafted in. I looked up: a quarter moon, the Virgin, and the free flight of western yellow bats leaving their roosts beneath the fronds.

As an inky darkness steeped into the canyon, my eyes worked harder. On a bench across the arroyo bottom, several hundred palms of all ages gathered around seeps. Arrowweed, carrizo reeds, screwbeans, and saltgrass grew in their shadows. Climbing down across the mineral-rich stream and up toward the bench, I found raccoon and skunk tracks in the mud. The best find, though, was as I approached the heart of the palm stand. There, in the ashes below a fire-tumbled giant, were palm seedlings. Scattered around in the darkness, there were densely toothed new palm sprouts and seedlings of various sizes and ages, manelike hairs emanating from their young, tender fronds. They were growing in the protection of their elders, where the earth gave freely of its waters. They would offer to future generations the chance to see an oasis as it should be, where it should be.

THE COAST

Gaviota Coast Trails

J. Smeaton Chase (1864–1923) emigrated to Los Angeles from England in 1890. He traveled throughout California, and wrote half a dozen books about its natural wonders. In California Coast Trails *(1913) he recounts his 1911 horseback trip up the coast, including his adventure on the Gaviota coast, south of Point Conception.*

The coast road from this point west for ten or twelve miles is little more than a track, and that of the roughest kind, quite impossible for wheeled vehicles. There was a fence across the path, and a notice was posted that travelers must take the beach. I rode down to the shore, but when I saw that a little farther on the tide was washing up to the base of the cliffs I turned back, found a way through the fence, and trespassed on my way.

The country hereabout is monotonous and unattractive. Low undulating hills run for mile on mile, treeless, and scanty even of brush, and the cañons are dry and shadeless. We marched some miles before finding water, and I resolved to camp at the first creek I should see. At last I came to one, which afforded good pasturage also; and, dismounting, I led Chino down toward the beach, where I noticed a little bench of green grass at the mouth of the cañon and on the very edge of the shore sand.

Here the expedition narrowly escaped disaster. The inwash of the tide, meeting the water of the creek, had formed an area, a sort of pit, of quicksand. This we had to cross in order to reach the beach, and in a moment, without warning, I was up to my middle, and Chino, following close behind, plunged in beside and almost upon me. On the instant I threw myself backward, and tried to work myself out, but the sand clogged me as if it were liquid lead, and I could not reach back with my hands to where the solid ground would give me support. Chino, meanwhile, was struggling desperately but helplessly, the heavy saddle-bags and other articles of his load weighing him down so that he was already half covered.

By great good fortune the cañon wall was nearby, not over eight feet away. It was of weathered rock, soft and shaley, and I though that if I could anyhow work over to it I could get grip enough on it to support myself. It seemed an impossible thing to do, with the fatal sand clasping and weighing me down, but I attempted it.

I remember that, as I struggled, a horror of the commonplace sunlit evening flashed over me and, with it, the thought that no one would ever know what had happened to me, for there would be no trace, no clue. That horrible sand would close over me, the sun would shine on the spot, the roar of waves would go on unbroken; I should simply cease to be. I think I wondered whether there would not be any way of telling my friends; but I am not sure whether that thought came then, or in thinking it over afterward.

All this can only have taken a very short time, during which I was struggling to reach the rocky wall. At last my fingers scraped the rock, and gradually I was able to draw myself backward to firm ground. Then I ran round by the solid beach sand, crossing the creek, and came back to Chino. He had stopped struggling, but lay over on his side, and had sunk so that one of the saddle-bags was quite out of sight. Blood, too, was spattered all about him.

Coming as close as was safe behind him, I gradually loosened as much of his load as I could reach. Then I caught his rope and tried to get him to exert himself. For some time he made no move, and I thought he must have broken his off-side foreleg on a half-buried snag of dead wood that projected above the sand. Again and again I tried to get him to move, but he still lay on his side, drawing great gasping breaths, and I about decided I should have to shoot him where he lay. But I made a last effort, shouting and hauling at him with all my strength, until I literally forced him to bestir himself: when, putting my last ounce into it, I pulled and shouted, refusing to allow him to relax his efforts for a moment and gradually working his head round somewhat toward where I stood. With a final wild spasm he scrambled up onto the dry, hard sand and stood snorting and trembling pitifully, bespattered with blood and utterly exhausted.

I was vastly relieved to find that the blood was coming from his mouth and nostrils. He had broken some small blood vessel in his first struggles. I took off the saddle and led him carefully over to a grassy spot, where I washed out his mouth and then gave him a thorough rubbing down; and within half an hour I had the satisfaction of seeing my staunch companion of so many days and nights feeding with equanimity and even enthusiasm.

The incident was sufficiently dangerous to give me a lesson in caution, as well as cause for hearty thankfulness. There was not the slightest hint of treachery in the appearance of the sand, but thereafter I went warily in all doubtful places. I ransacked my rescued saddle-bags and made a rare supper to celebrate the adventure. As the bags were strongly made, and waterproofed, the contents had not been much damaged. Then I ran up my sleeping tent, in view of the fog which I could see advancing from the sea. I chose a place on a little shelf of dry sand, sheltered by the angle of the cañon wall, and apparently above high-water mark by a safe though narrow margin. Then in the dusk I gathered a pile of driftwood and made a royal fire, by which I sat until long after dark, listening with more than usual enjoyment to the tinkle of Chino's bell and the manifold voices of the sea.

There seemed that night to be an unusual variety in the sound of the surf. Intervals of dramatic silence were broken suddenly by roars as if huge bodies of water were being dropped from some great height. Then would come a long, sibilant swish, which, after subsiding to rippling murmurs, ended smartingly with a *thump, fortissimo*. Occasionally, in the midst of a long whisper there would come a smart clap, followed by little quarrelings, and shudderings, and sighs, almost of human quality of tone. The ordinary sounds of the breakers, the steady pound, boom, and clatter, pound, boom, and clatter, seemed not to be in evidence.

The entertainment was so interesting that it drew me down to the water's edge. When I passed beyond the light of the fire, I found a new fascination in the pale sea-flame that hovered and raced up and down my quarter mile of beach as the rollers broke in ghostly phosphorescence. Then a steamer, three or four miles out, passed on her way upcoast, her lights shining genially across the black void of water. I fancied that some lover and lass, leaning together over the bulwarks, might be watching my twinkling beacon, and I went back and threw on another log to brighten the blaze, in the hope that the beam might stimulate my swain to some urgency, or some pretty fancy, that should bring a happy climax to his wooing.

When at last I felt in mood to turn in, I noticed that the tide had made a long advance toward my tent; but I felt sure that it was close upon its turn and that I could hold my ground. Still, as there seemed just a possibility of trouble, I did not undress to my usual camping limit, but got into my blankets partly dressed, and soon fell asleep. I suppose I had slept about half an hour when I awoke with an uneasy feeling that the water was coming too near. Looking out, I saw that the stronger waves were sending their fans of foam quietly up to within a few feet of me, leaving a very slight rise of beach before they would wash against and undermine my little shelf of sand. There seemed to be still a "sporting chance" that I should be safe, and I lay down again; but the thought of awaking next time to find myself swamped and the tent collapsing over me was so annoying that I could not sleep and resolved to move.

To go farther back was impossible, for the stream ran only a few yards behind me, so I gathered an armful of my traps and made a bolt in the darkness across the creek, which was already flooding with seawater, and found a level place among the grass near my horse. I had to make two more flights to and fro to bring over the rest of my belongings, and then, too disgusted to set up the tent again, I made a windbreak of the saddle-bags, rolled myself up in the blankets, and finally got to sleep. My last glance across at the red embers of the fires showed an ambitious wave in the act of washing it out of existence.

In spite of mishaps, the place was so attractive, in its close proximity to the sea and its complete retirement, that I decided to remain for another day. The swallows that haunted the cliffs made the pleasantest of company, flying happily about me, and pursuing the sand flies almost into the coffee. The weather, too, supplied the one desirable thing, namely, shade, which the camp otherwise lacked; for the fog of the night, lifting but not passing off all day, afforded a delightful temperature, with restful tones of color. It is so that I best love the sea. Its grandeur, its significance, its solemnity, are far more felt than "'neath the all revealing sun"; and the water itself, deeply, darkly clear, seems more aqueous and elemental.

There was an unusual number of seabirds hereabouts, and in a walk down the beach I came upon the rocky point which was their home. Hundreds of them sat ranked in demure hierarchy, the shags, who were the most numerous, taking the lowest place, then the white-backed gulls, and, presiding over all with an air of burlesque dignity, a dozen or so pelicans. At my approach the whole company took flight, and in a moment "the winged air was darkened with plumes." The clatter of wings was bewildering as they circled once or twice and then streamed off to settle on the belt of kelp which here forms a floating reef unbroken for mile on mile. The flight of the pelican is a wonderful exhibition of ease in motion. I was never tired of watching them gliding in file, smooth, swift, and silent, with no movement of wing for great distances. If ever men attain to such perfection of aeronautics (though that is impossible), I mean to sell my belongings, to my boots, if necessary, and purchase the magic machine.

Returning from my walk, I almost stepped upon a rattlesnake that lay coiled among the driftwood which I had been drawing upon for my fire. He was not a large one, and the calendar in his tail marked only four changes of skin; but I judged that he must die. Mr. Muir, I remember, deprecates killing these creatures, and says that, having once put one to death, he felt himself "degraded by the killing business, farther from heaven." On the other hand, I recalled that when, on the island called Melita, a viper bit the shipwrecked apostle in the hand, he unceremoniously "shook off the beast into the fire." My little reptile was a potential evil-doer also, and on the whole I saw no reason for trying to better such a notable example as that of St. Paul.

At evening the cloud curtain to the south lifted a little from the horizon, and one of the islands of the Channel Group shone out like a great jewel in the light of the setting sun. It was very beautiful, and rather solemn—the slow lifting of the veil; the magic of the revelation; the silent passage through tone on tone of ethereal color until, when the sun had sunk, the distant isle stood marked in soft dense purple on a glowing belt of yellow, the only object between gray cloud and gray of sea. Then came the gradual lowering of the veil again over all. There was something unearthly in the quiet color-action, as if an angel had managed the heavenly display. Indeed, perhaps one had.

Malibu

Where the Mountains
Meet the Sea

Lawrence Clark Powell (b. 1906) was Chief Librarian (1944–1961) and Dean of the School of Library Services (1960–1966) at UCLA. He is also the author of a number of books about his life, his travels, and literature, including the following selection from The Little Package *(1964), about his days living in Malibu in the late 1950s and 1960s.*

M y boyhood and youth were nourished by the San Gabriels and the San Bernardinos, which ranges wall out the desert from southern California. It was not until I went to work at UCLA and moved near to the campus that allegiance was transferred to the Santa Monicas, a less spectacular range that rises in Hollywood and extends fifty miles to a marine ending at Point Mugu.

From living in Beverly Glen, I came to love the surrounding range of chaparral, oak, and sycamore. It was a good place for our sons to live as boys, and now that they are grown to manhood they find their sub-conscious minds full of memories of their mountain boyhood.

Although . . . I discovered the westernmost part of the range in the poems of Madeleine Ruthven, it was not until a decade later, in 1944, that I came actually to know this remote area. At war's end my friend Gordon Newell, the sculptor, acquired land on the north slope of the mountains, overlooking Seminole Hot Springs, and it served me as a kind of retreat from too much city. From driving and walking and talking to Newell, I came to know and love his land and the sea of chaparral that enislanded it. The north slope of the Santa Monicas is green the year round from springs, one of which he had deepened and rock-lined, so that it was an unfailing source of cold water, even in the driest summer. Through the years I watched him quarry honey-colored flagstone, sift and sack leaf-mold, breed Nubian goats, keep bees, carve wood, and cut stone, while his wife Emelia fashioned delicate jewelry and airy mobiles, and their children thrived in a kind of twentieth-century Theocritean idyll.

It takes time to assimilate the essences of a land. When after years of residence in Inyo County Mary Austin wrote *The Land of Little Rain*, her publishers wanted her to move around the country, writing similar books about other places of residence. Her reply was that it would take her ten years in a locale to be able to evoke its spirit, as indeed she did later for Arizona–New Mexico in *The Land of Journeys' Endings*.

Thus, although we moved to the Malibu, in the seaward lee of the Santa Monicas, as recently as 1955, I brought to the land years of slow-growing knowledge and deepening love for this country "where the mountain meets the sea"; and I was ready to write about it not as a stranger. In fact, it was this long background of reading and seeing that motivated our move—that and the feeling we have always had for the seashore. Plus something else, instinctive, mysterious, and right.

So it was a kind of magnetic homecoming, this move to the Malibu, and now our leisure time is divided between shoreline walks and mountain drives.

On this coast the seasons merge imperceptibly into each other. When the rainy season is regular, then it is easier to know the time of year. When drought comes, how is one to know summer and fall for winter and spring? By the stars to be sure, and the position of the sun—those heavenly clockworks that transcend earthly times of wet and dry.

In the late autumn the evening wears Vega like a blue-white diamond. Arcturus has set long before the sun. Capella comes up over the mountain, brightest of the northernmost stars, and toward midnight, when Sirius is well risen, there directly below it, just above the horizon, appears the sky's number-two glitterer, the southern star Canopus, never rising high enough to get beyond the city's atmosphere, which lends it a baleful light.

The sun, which in summer sets behind the mountain, has moved out to sea, dropping from sight at the point where San Nicolas Island lies, if we were high enough to see it. See it we did from the crest of the mountains, on one of the day's-end drives that conclude our otherwise stay-at-home Sundays, lying between Santa Barbara Rock and the Santa Cruz–Anacapa conjunction, eighty miles out, dark whale on the blue sea, never to be seen from shoreline.

Living on the Malibu one can choose between many peaceful things to do—stay at home and read or write or garden and other chores, or just sit; or drive in the hills; or walk on the beach. There is choice too among the hill drives—whether it be up the Decker Road along Mulholland, and down the Arroyo Sequit to the sea again, or up Little Sycamore Canyon on the Yerba Buena Road, over Triunfo Pass with a view to Lake Sherwood, then down past the lake, through Hidden Valley, over the hills and down Long Grade Canyon to Camarillo and the coast highway; or west from Little Sycamore along narrow roads leading into cul-de-sacs, where one sees foxes and hawks, and water flowing out of rock face—all of this within fifty miles of Los Angeles, unknown to the millions.

In the autumn of 1955, when the first of two fires swept over the mountains from the valley, leaped the crest of Boney Ridge, and devoured the forest of red shanks which graced that mountain's southern slope, we feared a long bareness for the burned flanks. Winter rains brought a myriad of flowers in places where the sun had not penetrated for years, and then in the spring we rejoiced to see rise from the base of the burned chaparral delicate new growth. The fire had not proved mortal; though ten years would be needed for the forest to recover.

Summer's flowers succeeded spring's pinks and blues and whites—orange monkey flower, red gooseberry, and larkspur, and the purple sage, bee heaven on earth—while the arroyos became *seco* and sand choked the creek mouths.

By summer the winter's creek wood had all been gathered, and the gleaning was again of plank wood cast up by the sea, that and shells and fragments to serve as gravel on the garden paths. All these years I had remembered the crushed abalone shells with which Una and Robinson Jeffers graveled their paths at Tor House, and now I began to strew our walks with shells and bones and jeweled bits from the seashore.

The Chumash who dwelled here were jewelry makers, and the Southwest Museum [in Los Angeles] preserves examples of their necklaces of tide-line treasures. Now I see why. The wash of water renders all things smooth, and after high tide recedes one finds the bench strewn with beautiful fragments. Westward I walk, stooping, picking, filling a cloth bag, until it becomes leaden and the way back weary. And when at last I empty it out on the path at home, the scattering iridescences and pearly bits—blue black of mussel, flesh pink of cowrie, purple of abalone—make a display Tiffany's should envy, and I am moved to acquire a polishing wheel, a cutter and a borer, a ball of cord, and become a necklace maker. The abalone shells of this coast were prized by the Hopis far to the east, who ground them for dye tincture. These Mollusca are rarely exposed by even the lowest tide, seeking the safety of deeper water, and even then skin divers need powerful leverage to pry them loose, and woe to the man whose hand is caught. Freshly caught and sauteed in butter they are delicious, and their shells remain forever beautiful.

Indians are buried everywhere from Mugu Lagoon to Malibu Creek. Every bulldozing operation brings their bones and artifacts to light, as one did just across Broad Beach Road from us—a dozen huddled skeletons, four or five hundred years old, taking no notice of their noisy resurrection. Our geranium garden, falling to Encinal Creek, is sure to be a burying ground, the diggers tell us. Mary Austin writes of the residue of personality that always haunts a place once inhabited by man. Jeffers's poetry is full of these hauntings. But I cannot say that I have encountered spirits here on the Malibu. Perhaps the diesels drive them away. I have no fear of them, however. The Chumash were a gentle people, living on shellfish, roots, and acorn meal. We who are carnivorous may leave a different residue. Sometimes I wonder who will follow us here, and what they will make of our artifacts—books and disks and Scriptos and, less tangible though perhaps more lasting, our love for this marine mountainscape called the Malibu.

Along the Malibu there has been good aftermath of the storm, and the coast has been gathering manna. Mushrooms and other edible fungi rose overnight, and lived briefly in the light of day before consummating a buttery union in the skillet. Mustard greens likewise had a short life span before they too yielded up on the stove. Last year's stalks were rooted out by the wind and spilled like skeletons against the fences, to make room for the new growth now in its head-high yellow prime.

Mussels also are in season—no delicacy, true, but few meals are more satisfying than a mess of them, gathered at ebb tide in the twilight, then steamed open and dunked in lemon butter, salty, sandy, tough little guys, tasting of kelpy iodine, an atavistic feast linking us with our predecessors on this coastal shelf, who gave names to many of the places, from Anacapa and Hueneme to Mugu, Malibu, and Topanga.

Now we know why they inhabited the lagoons at the creek mouths, for when the rainy runoff swells these *arroyos secos* to savage streams, the rivers break their summer sand bars and run to the sea, bearing treasure to the tidelanders. We live on the cliff by the estuary of Encinal Creek, and at the height of the storm, when we went down with shovels to divert ravenous runoffs, we saw the little watercourse, long barred from union with the ocean and held in stagnant continence, changed to a torrent and raging out of the Santa Monicas to an eager consummation with the sea.

The Pacific was belying its name, roiled up for a mile offshore, windblown, coffee-colored, perilous to all but its native denizens—and I doubt they were pleased with the turmoil. We dwell on an open coast, with few shelters for small craft, and the shoreline is that seen by Cabrillo, Drake, Vancouver, and Dana, and in our day by the crews of purse seiner, tuna clipper, and tanker. The Catalina and Santa Barbara channels afford scant protection from southwesterlies, and the islands themselves are mostly steep and forbidding on both their leeward and windward sides.

Life on the Malibu is richest at the creek mouths, the Chumash knew; and so did we, after the storm was over and the runoff from the mountain washed upon the beaches. What a haul of firewood for the gleaning! We envy our neighbors the Brents, whose open fireplace will take logs up to ten feet in length. Ours is only twenty-four inches wide, which means that sawing, chopping, and splitting must follow gleaning and hauling.

It is years since the hills received such a scouring, yielding logs and stumps, burned roots, and rotting branches of oak, sycamore, red shank, and chamisal, much of it smashed to fireplace length in its fall down the stream beds, and sculptured into beautiful shapes.

The sea itself casts up wood, smoothed by wind and wave—empty packing cases of water chestnuts from Hong Kong and ammunition boxes from navy vessels, flawed planks of pine, Douglas fir, oak, and redwood, cast overboard from lumber schooners, flotsam, corks from fishermen's nets, an occasional Japanese glass float, battered lobster traps, and sundry jetsam not worth its salt.

The first step is to cache the wet wood and let it dry, before carrying it up the path to the cliff top. If one posts his pile with a sign reading, "Blest be he who leaves my logs; curst be he who steals my sticks," he is certain to find it when he returns, and just half its weight.

The joy of gathering beach wood is matched by that of burning it, although an occasional twinge is felt, like eating one's pet rabbit, when a shaft of skin-smooth chaparral is reduced to silvery ash. This wild wood's smoke has its own smells, different from those of domestic firewood—oak and walnut perfumy, eucalyptus acrid, orange bitter-sweet, and juniper like incense—and unless it has been submerged a long while, it does not burn with a blue flame. One twelve-foot length of a 2-by-4 was difficult to identify. From its weight and grain and color I called it oak. When I began to saw it, I realized my error. The fragrance was like the interior of our clothes closet. Cedar! The smoke from its burning was even sweeter. Once I found a broken mast or boom, stamped with Chinese characters. On sawing, it proved to be camphor wood, so pungent that I kept a section of it in my clothes closet.

Characteristic of this coast is the offshore wind that blows after dark, very faintly, a mere breath of mountain air suspiring delicately toward the sea, bearing smells of sun-warmed brush and stream bed with smoke from our chimney, ghosts of the beach wood, drifting down over the dark sand and water, residue of fire, liberated energy, sweeter far than incense of cathedral.

Now winter's constellations are risen high, Sirius ruling the zenith and fiery Canopus, describing his short arc above the southern horizon. In the west the lighthouse opens like an eye, then closes, leaving the night darker than before. In the east, when it is very clear, the Point Vicente light can be seen on the Palos Verdes and, nearer, the light buoy off Point Dume. These smells and sights assure one that one can leave the world to the wakeful and seek one's bed, with the final thought that another storm will find us in the wood business.

Big Sur Coast

Big Sur

When he moved to Big Sur in 1944, Henry Miller (1891–1980) had already achieved some notoriety with the publication in the 1930s of his Paris novels, including Tropic of Cancer *(1934). Ensconced atop Partington Ridge, he became the center of an artists' colony and continued to write—and to paint. His book of ramblings about California,* Big Sur and the Oranges of Hieronymous Bosch—*from which this excerpt is taken—was published in 1957.*

I t was twelve years ago on a day in February that I arrived in Big Sur—in the midst of a violent downpour. Toward dusk that same day, after a rejuvenating bath outdoors at the hot sulphur springs (Slade's Springs), I had dinner with the Rosses in the quaint old cottage they then occupied at Livermore Edge. It was the beginning of something more than a friendship. It would be more just, perhaps, to call it an initiation into a new way of life.

It was a few weeks after this meeting that I read Lillian Bos Ross's book *The Stranger.* Till then I had been only a visitor. The reading of this "little classic," as it is called, made me more than ever determined to take root here. "For the first time in my life," to quote Zande Allen's words, "I felt to home in the world I was borned in."

Years ago our great American poet Robinson Jeffers began singing of this region in his narrative poems. Jack London and his friend George Stirling made frequent visits to Big Sur in the old days; they came on horseback, all the way from the Valley of the Moon. The general public, however, knew almost nothing of this region until 1937 when the Carmel–San Simeon highway, which skirts the Pacific for a distance of sixty miles or more, was opened up. In fact, until then it was probably one of the least known regions in all America.

The first settlers, mountain men mostly, of hardy pioneer stock, came around 1870. They were, as Lillian Ross puts it, men who had followed the buffalo trails and knew how to live on meat without salt. They came afoot and on horseback; they touched ground which no white man had ever set foot on before, not even the intrepid Spaniards.

So far as is known, the only human beings who had been here before were the Esselen Indians, a tribe of low culture which had subsisted in nomadic fashion. They spoke a language having no connection with that of other tribes in California or elsewhere in America. When the padres came to Monterey, around 1770, these Indians spoke of an ancient city called Excelen which was theirs but of which no vestiges have ever been found.

But perhaps I should first explain where the Big Sur region is located. It begins not far north of the Little Sur River (Malpaso Creek) and extends southward as far as Lucia, which, like Big Sur, is just a pinpoint on the map. Eastward from the coast it stretches to the Salinas Valley. Roughly, the Big Sur country comprises an area two to three times the size of Andorra.

Now and then a visitor will remark that there is a resemblance between this coast, the South Coast, and certain sections of the Mediterranean littoral; others liken it to the coast of Scotland. But comparisons are vain. Big Sur has a climate of its own and a character all its own. It is a region where extremes meet, a region where one is always conscious of weather, of space, of grandeur, and of eloquent silence. Among other things, it is the meeting place of migratory birds coming from north and south. It is said, in fact, that there is a greater variety of birds to be found in this region than in any other part of the United States. It is also the home of the redwoods; one encounters them on entering from the north and one leaves them on passing southward. At night one can still hear the coyote howling, and if one ventures beyond the first ridge of mountains one can meet up with mountain lions and other beasts of the wild. The grizzly bear is no longer to be found here, but the rattlesnake is still to be reckoned with. On a clear, bright day, when the blue of the sea rivals the blue of the sky, one sees the hawk, the eagle, the buzzard soaring above the still, hushed canyons. In summer, when the fogs roll in, one can look down upon a sea of clouds floating listlessly above the ocean; they have the appearance, at times, of huge iridescent soap bubbles, over which, now and then, may be seen a double rainbow. In January and February the hills are greenest, almost as green as the Emerald Isle. From November to February are the best months, the air fresh and invigorating, the skies clear, the sun still warm enough to take a sun bath.

From our perch, which is about a thousand feet above the sea, one can look up and down the coast a distance of twenty miles in either direction. The highway zigzags like the Grand Corniche. Unlike the Riviera, however, here there are but few houses to be seen. The old-timers, those with huge landholdings, are not eager to see the country opened up. They are all for preserving its virginal aspect. How long will it hold out against the invader? That is the big question.

The stretch of scenic highway referred to earlier was cut through at enormous expense, literally blasted out of the mountainside. It now forms part of the great international highway which will one day extend from the northern part of Alaska to Tierra del Fuego. By the time it is finished the automobile, like the mastodon, may be extinct. But the Big Sur will be here forever, and perhaps in the year A.D. 2000 the population may still number only a few hundred souls. Perhaps like Andorra and Monaco, it will become a Republic all its own. Perhaps the dread invaders will not come from other parts of this continent but from across the oceans, as the American aborigines are said to have come. And if they do, it will not be in boats or in airplanes.

And who can say when this region will once again be covered by the waters of the deep? Geologically speaking, it is not so long ago that it rose from the sea. Its mountain slopes are almost as treacherous as the icy sea in which, by the way, one scarcely ever sees a sailboat or a hardy swimmer, though one does occasionally spot a seal, an otter, or a sperm whale. The sea, which looks so near and so tempting, is often difficult to reach. We know that the Conquistadores were unable to make their way along the coast, neither could they cut through the brush which covers the mountain slopes. An inviting land, but hard to conquer. It seeks to remain unspoiled, uninhabited by man.

Often, when following the trail which meanders over the hills, I pull myself up in an effort to encompass the glory and the grandeur which envelops the whole horizon. Often, when the clouds pile up in the north and the sea is churned with whitecaps, I say to myself: "This is the California that men dreamed of years ago, this is the Pacific that Balboa looked out on from the Peak of Darien, this is the face of the earth as the Creator intended it to look." . . .

Here at Big Sur, at a certain time of the year and certain time of the day only, a pale blue-green hue pervades the distant hills; it is an old, nostalgic hue which one sees only in the works of the old Flemish and Italian masters. It is not only the tone and color of distance abetted by the magic fall of light, it is a mystic phenomenon, or so I like to think, born of a certain way of looking at the world. It is observable in the work of the older Breughel, for one. Strikingly present in the painting called "The Fall of Icarus," in which the peasant with his plough dominates the foreground, his costume just as enchanting and obsessional as the enchanting and obsessive sea far below him.

There are two magic hours of the day which I have only really come to know and wait for, bathe in, I might say, since living here. One is dawn, the other sunset. In both we have what I like to think of as "the true light"—the one cold, the other warm, but both creating an ambiance of super-reality, or the reality behind reality. At dawn I look out to sea, where the far horizon is painted with bands of rainbow tints, and then at the hills that range the coast, ever entranced by the way the reflected light of dawn licks and warms the "backs of the drugged rhinoceroses." If there is a ship in sight the sun's bent rays give it a gleam and sparkle which is utterly dazzling. Once can't tell immediately that it is a ship; it seems more like the play of northern lights.

Toward sundown, when the hills in back of us are flushed with the other "true light," the trees and scrub in the canyons take on a wholly different aspect. Everything is brush and cones, umbrellas of light—the leaves, boughs, stalks, trunks standing out separate and defined, as if etched by the Creator Himself. It is then one notices rivers of trees catapulting down the slopes! Or are they columns of soldiers (hoplites) storming the walls of the canyon? At any rate, at this hour one experiences an indescribable thrill in observing branches, between the leaves. It is no longer earth and air, but light and form—heavenly light, celestial form. When this intoxicating reality reaches its height the rocks speak out. They assume more eloquent shapes and forms than the fossils of prehistoric monsters. They clothe themselves in vibrant-colored raiment glittering with metallic residues.

Fall and winter are the best times to get the "revelation," for then the atmosphere is clear, the skies more full of excitement, and the light of the sun, because of the low arc it describes, more effective. It's at this hour, after a light rain, that the hills are ringed with fuzzy trails which undulate with the undulating golds of the hills. Turning a bend, the hill before you stands out like the coat of an Airedale seen through a magnifying glass. So hoary does it look that one scans the horizon in search of a shepherd leaning against his crook. Memories of olden times return, the leavings of childhood reading: illustrations from story books, first gleanings of mythology, faded calendars, the chromos on the kitchen wall, bucolic prints on the walls of the man who extracted your tonsils. . . .

If we don't always start from Nature we certainly come to her in our hour of need. How often, walking the barren hills, I've stopped to examine a twig, a dead leaf, a fragrant bit of sage, a rare flower that has lingered on despite the killing heat. Or stood in front of a tree studying the bark, as if I had never before noticed that trunks are covered with bark, and that the bark as well as the tree itself leads its own life.

It's when the lupine has run its course, as well as the bluebonnets and the wildflowers, when the foxtails are no longer a menace to the dogs, when there is no longer a riot and profusion assailing the senses, that one begins to observe the myriad elements which go to make up Nature. (Suddenly, as I put it down now, Nature seems like a strange new word to me. What a discovery man made when he found the word, just one, to embrace this indescribable thesaurus of all enveloping life!) . . .

There are . . . times when I seem to be in what I can only call an autodidactic mood. At such times I am instructing myself in the art of seeing with new eyes. I may be in a painting phase or getting ready to enter one. (These phases come over me like a sickness.) I will be on the Angulo trail, facing the gigantic ten-gallon rock at Torre Canyon, with a dog on either side of me . . . and look and look and look at a blade of grass, a deep shadow in the fold of a hill, a deer standing motionless, no bigger than a speck, or turn my gaze upon the churning lace which the sea makes around a clump of rock, or that white collar of foam which fastens itself to the flanks of the "diplodoci," as I sometimes call the half-submerged beastlike mountains that rise up out of the ocean bed to bask in the sun. It's quite true, as Lynda Sargent used to say, that the Santa Lucia range is hermaphroditic. In form and contour the hills and mountains are usually feminine, in strength and vitality masculine. They look so very ancient, especially in the early morning light, and yet they are, as we know, only newly risen. The animals have done more to them than man, fortunately. And the wind and rain, the sunlight and moonlight, still more. Man has known them only a short while, which accounts perhaps for the pristine quality which they still preserve.

If it be shortly after sunup of a morning when the fog has obliterated the highway below, I am then rewarded with a spectacle rare to witness. Looking up the coast toward Nepenthe, where I first stayed (then only a log cabin), the sun rising behind me throws an enlarged shadow of me into the iridescent fog below. I lift my arms as in prayer, achieving a wing-span no god ever possessed, and there in the drifting fog a nimbus floats about my head, a radiant nimbus such as the Buddha himself might proudly wear. In the Himalayas, where the same phenomenon occurs, it is said that a devout follower of the Buddha will throw himself from a peak—"into the arms of Buddha." . . .

When first I beheld this wondrous region I thought to myself—"Here I will find peace. Here I shall find the strength to do the work I was made to do."

Back of the rise which overshadows us is a wilderness in which scarcely anyone ever sets foot. It is a great forest and game reserve intended to be set apart forever. At night one feels the silence all about, a silence which begins far back of the ridge and which creeps in with the fog and the stars, with the warm valley winds, and which carries in its folds a mystery as deep as the earth's own. A magnetic, healing ambiance. The advent of city folk, with their cares and worries, is pure dissonance. Like the lepers of old, they come with their sores. Whoever settles here hopes that he will be the last invader. The very look of the land makes one long to keep it intact—the spiritual reserve of a few bright spirits.

Of late I have come to take a different view of it. Walking the hills at dawn, or at dusk, looking over the deep canyons or seaward toward the far horizon, absorbed in reveries, drowned in the awesome beauty of it all, I sometimes think how wonderful will be the day when all these mountainsides are filled with habitations, when the slopes are terraced with field, when flowers burst forth everywhere, not only wildflowers planted by human hands for human delectation. I try to imagine what it may be like a hundred, five hundred, years hence. I picture villas dotting the slopes, and colossal stairways curving down to the sea where boats lie at anchor, their colorful sails unfurled and flapping listlessly in the breeze. I see ledges cut into the sharp flanks of the cliffs, to give purchase to chapels and monasteries suspended between heaven and earth, as in Greece. I see tables spread under brilliant awnings (as in the time of the Doges), and wine flowing into golden goblets, and over the glitter of gold and purple I hear laughter, laughter like pearling rapids, rising from thousands of jubilant throats. . . .

Yes, I can visualize multitudes living where now there are only a few scattered families. There is room here for thousands upon thousands to come. There would be no need for Jake to deliver food and mail three times a week. There would be ways and means undreamed of today. It could happen, in fact, in a very few years from now. What we dream is the reality of tomorrow.

This place can be a paradise. It is now, for those who live it. But then it will be another paradise, one in which all share, all participate. The only paradise, after all.

Peace and solitude! I have had a taste of it, even here in America. Ah, those first days on Partington Ridge! On rising I would go to the cabin door and, casting my eyes over the velvety, rolling hills, such a feeling of contentment, such a feeling of gratitude was mine that instinctively my hand went up in benediction. Blessings! Blessings on you, one and all! I blessed the trees, the birds, the dogs, the cats. I blessed the flowers, the pomegranates, the thorny cactus. I blessed men and women everywhere, no matter on which side of the fence they happened to be.

That is how I like to begin each day. A day well begun, I say. And that is why I choose to remain here, on the slopes of the Santa Lucia, where to give thanks to the Creator comes natural and easy. Out yonder they may curse, revile, and torture one another, defile all the human instincts, make a shambles of creation (if it were in their power), but here, no, here it is unthinkable, here there is abiding peace, the peace of

God, and the serene security created by a handful of good neighbors living at one with the creature world, with noble, ancient trees, scrub and sagebrush, wild lilacs and lovely lupine, with poppies and buzzards, eagles and hummingbirds, gophers and rattlesnakes, and sea and sky unending.

The Sundown Sea

T. H. Watkins (b. 1936) was born in Loma Linda, where he spent his sum-
mers at the beach; these experiences are eloquently recounted in On the Shore
of the Sundown Sea *(1973). Widely published in the fields of history and the*
environment, Watkins was for many years associated with American
Heritage *and* Wilderness *magazines.*

Y
ou ran, dog at your side, not just to keep warm or for the simple
joy of it, but because you wanted to take advantage of every
secret moment of this time. Your parents had not forbidden
these unsupervised expeditions; they simply did not know about them,
and you wanted to keep it that way. God knew, it was dangerous enough
a business, clambering barefoot over rocks polished by centuries of
beating surf, made slick, smooth, and wet. One slip, and you could
break an arm or leg, or even crack your skull. And if you were injured as
far out on those rocks as you frequently ventured, you could lay immo-
bilized until the tide returned and the sea washed your body away—and
no one to know where you were. If you thought about it, it could all be
pretty frightening—but of course you did not think about it. Your step
was sure and unhesitant, your confidence boundless, your good luck
remarkable.

And it was worth it, for this rocky landscape, stripped of the sea which kept it hidden for most of the day, vibrated with a secret, mysterious, unimaginable life that creeped and crawled in its pools, its dark nooks and crannies, like a population straight out of dream. Where else but out of the mists of dream could a hermit crab have been spawned? Barely an inch in length, he scrabbled and lurched among the rocks, seeking an unoccupied shell to inhabit; without it, he was a pitiful, helpless creature, his pink lower body curled under his torso like a tiny coil of rope; with it, he lurched along as before—quite as helpless, but at least granted the illusion of security. Starfish, too, were dreamlike, inching through life on those impossible arms, changing colors to match their surroundings, their mouths a tiny slit in the bottom center of their bodies, where mouths had no business being. And more: crabs, pink ones the size of dinner plates with pincers that could hurt, if not maim; mottled yellow ones as broad as the palm of your hand, little sand-colored ones no larger than your thumbnail; mussels and sea-snails clustered on the sides of rocks, extensions of the stone itself, immobile, hiding from the light, waiting for the return of the tide and their real world; the occasional landlocked ray trying to hide itself behind a rock in a tide pool, and once in a while a smelt or a rock fish, or a gang of herring that had become similarly trapped; nearly invisible sea worms that squiggled along the bottom of pools like miniature snakes; and, most wondrous of all, the rainbow-colored anemones, half-animal, half-flower, lurking in rock crannies with poison at the heart of their beauty. Over it all the ubiquitous gulls wheeled and screamed, small shadows of death that harvested what they could of that abundance of life.

You were entranced, utterly. Leaping from rock to rock, tide pool to tide pool, you poked and probed and watched everything you could watch. Lying on your belly at the edge of a particularly rich pool, you would be driven by the small boy's insatiable need to know, to understand, to experience—in short, to meddle. You would take out your little tin shovel from the sand bucket and use it to stir up a sleeping ray, if you could reach him. You would use it to stroke the petals of a crimson anemone, shuddering as the petals convulsed in an attempt to draw the shovel into its maw; thus you discovered that beauty could be a trap—a very large thing to learn at so young an age. You would seek out a large crab and toy with it until in its rage and fear it gripped the shovel firmly. You would then lift it out of the pool and dump it in your bucket, captured, helpless to escape the mindless cruelty of your curiosity. For you it was a game, for him a death struggle.

No matter how often or how long you visited this secret world, the potential for surprise was never absent—and it could sometimes be a large surprise indeed. Once you discovered the body of a sea lion stranded on the edge of a tide pool far out among the rocks. You came upon it suddenly, unexpectedly, while crawling over the lip of a rock, and at first you thought it was alive. But no; the gulls had already been at its eyes. It was a huge mound of blue-black flesh, perhaps six or seven feet from nose to tail. You poked at the still resilient flesh with your shovel—gingerly, and a little fearfully. This was not your first dramatic encounter with death; after all, you had watched gulls hammering and picking at still-living crabs, a grisly and unforgettable spectacle. But never before had you realized the sheer power of a force that could destroy even this human-sized creature, leaving it to be picked at by gulls and crabs and whatever other scavengers there were who did the sea's bone-cleaning. To stand too close to it was to stand too close to your own end. You left it finally, left if for the sea that would reclaim it in a few hours.

Perhaps it was nothing more complicated than your stomach-clock sounding an alarm for food, but you always seemed to know when it was time to head back to camp. You dumped whatever creatures you might have in your bucket back into their tide pool and scrambled back across the rocks to the beach where your dog would be waiting (she possessed no measurable interest in tide pools or slippery rocks). Running along the beach (when did you not run?) you stopped now and then to scoop up a few shells, for you had to have some reasonable excuse for your long absence. *Where in the world have you been? Shells?* you could say, holding out your bucket. *I've been collecting shells.* The answer would suffice, for there was neither danger nor mystery in shell-collecting.

Mystery and danger were the very elements of a small boy's life then—certainly the elements of this small boy's life. A ten- or eleven-year-old boy is the essential Romantic, a creature riveted by wonder most of the time, driven by the need to challenge the very heart of life the rest of the time, a confused and confusing mix of Don Quixote, Tarzan, and Neil Armstrong. Parents sometimes mistake his dreamy-mindedness for stupidity, his daredevil antics for willful attempts to gray the hair of his elders. Not so. He is simply doing what his genes have programmed him to do, which is to learn the mystery and test the danger of life. Most of us get over this, sooner or later; we acquire wisdom and caution, become bank managers or real estate salesmen or book writers, ultimately reaching that point in life when we are certain that all the mysteries have been learned, all the dangers tested. Others are not so fortunate, but they are to be pitied, not censured.

There was both danger and mystery enough in my world by the sun-down sea—more than enough, more than could be learned, or tried. Take the mystery of the Sound, for instance. I have only heard it three times in my life, and those three times when I was a boy, but the memory of it has not diminished since, and I think I will be remembering it when my nerveless fingers are plucking at my last coverlet. The first time was pure accident, as discoveries usually are. Involved in my usual afternoon wave-chasing, I selected a towering devil of a wave to ride; it may have been twelve feet or more from base to crest, and definitely was not the sort of wave to try to ride. I realized my mistake almost immediately, but even then it was too late to do anything about it, for I was caught in its curl and would have to ride it out. The lip of the wave curved over my head, and for one brief instant I found myself in a long, green translucent tunnel that stretched forty or fifty feet on either side of me. That moment was when I heard the Sound, a high, hollow, almost metallic keening that cut through the outside roar of the surf until it was all that could be heard. It seemed to come from a great distance, like a cry out of the ancestral night, then swept over me and moved on just as the wave seized my helpless body and plunged it through the water and into the sand, where I gouged out a good-sized trench. The Sound could not have lasted for more than two seconds, but when I finally surfaced I was certain that I had been privileged to experience one of the essential mysteries. I tried again and again over the years to re-create the circumstances of that moment, but was able to do so only twice, each time as much by accident as by design. I suppose the phenomenon could be explained away by various acoustical laws having to do with decibels and the Doppler effect, but I remain as convinced today as I was then that I had heard nothing less than the voice of the sea itself.

There were other things to know, less intense, perhaps, but no less wondrous in their own right. Not far from the point where the rocks and the tide pools lay was the canyon that Salt Creek had cut into the bluffs on its way to the sea (it was no more than an outsized gulch, of course, but it served my purposes to think of it as a canyon). Salt Creek was just a trickle by normal creek standards, but this was sandstone country—even the soil was little more than well-packed sand—and the canyon it had cut into the bluffs was deep and narrow and dark, running perhaps two hundred and fifty or three hundred yards back to the Coast Highway, and filled with a strange mix of coast chaparral, ice plant, Scotch broom, wild mustard, and occasional clusters of iridescent ferns in little dells where the creek had formed pools. And there were caves. The first time I ventured into the canyon, I counted seven open caves, ranging in size and shape from a nichelike hole that could barely shelter a child to a commodious little cavern that could have held half a dozen adults or more. How they got there I had no idea, whether carved by wind and weather, by Indians (although I found no bones, no skulls, no pottery shards to suggest it), or by those who followed. I immediately peopled them with all manner of types from my imagination, not excluding pirates, and fancied myself the first person to see them in generations. . . .

As anyone who has ever watched the adventures of Jacques Yves Cousteau (or even those of Lloyd Bridges) must know by now, one of the most compelling wonders of the sea is not what is on it or around it, but what is under it. I found some of that wonder in my tide pool explorations, but only that part which the sea itself chose to reveal. To know it truly, you had to enter the undersea world without passport and explore it on your own. My expeditions along these lines were fairly limited, I have to admit. It was not yet an age when the aqua-lung was standard equipment for weekend hobbyists (nor could I have afforded one, in any case), and I had to make do with the basics, which were pretty basic: one rubber face mask that always seemed to leak just a little, one pair rubber flippers that never fit quite right, one plastic snorkel which I never did learn how to use properly. This was skin diving just one step removed from skin, but it was enough to give me at least partial entrance into a world I could not otherwise have known, that dim, green world where light entered in slanting, mote-filled rays, where rocks that were gray or black in the sunlight took on a spectrum of shadings from some dark rainbow, where dangling kelp became a coral jungle, murky, tangled, and dangerous, where the bottom sand was impossibly white, impossibly smooth, where the commonest fish acquired a mystery and dimension that transcended everything you had always believed you knew about fish.

In time, I took possession of a spring-powered aluminum speargun, one of the most deadly looking instruments man has devised since the invention of the crossbow. As my mother took pains to remind me, it was deadly, capable of piercing the midsection of a fully grown man at a distance of several feet—*under* water. I promised faithfully never to aim it at the midsection of a fully grown man, or even a half-grown man, and with my face mask, my flippers, and my snorkel I entered the water as a Mighty Hunter of the Deep.

What a fraud that pose was. In the two summers I sported around with that speargun, I did not fire it once at any living target. It was not as if I had never killed fish before. I had killed hundreds. Standing at the gunwales of a deep-sea boat, I had cheerfully hauled in barracuda, shovel-nosed sharks, sand sharks, halibut, sculpin, and once—almost— a sea bass so huge it bent my rod double before carrying my tackle back to the deep. Sitting in a rowboat on a lake, I had caught sacks full of bluegill, crappie, sunfish, and bass. Tramping the bouncing stream of Bear Creek in the San Bernardino Mountains, I had put limits of trout in my creel. Leaning on the rail of the pier at Newport Beach during the no-limit seasons of the mackerel run, I had pulled in dozens of the shining, muscular beasts, then gutted them, cleaned them, and beheaded them with the aplomb of an Elizabethan executioner. No, I was a fully accredited fish killer of no little experience.

But I could not kill a fish swimming under water, nor did I ever try. It puzzled me then, and it has puzzled me periodically since, although I think now that I may be close to an answer. It was not that I was incompetent, and therefore afraid to try my skill. I had practiced assiduously, and was good—well, adequate. It was not that the fish were beautiful, particularly (although they were beautiful, as only a creature in his nautical environment can be beautiful). It certainly was not that I had an aversion to killing: I had done enough of that, God knows. It was a kind of fear, I think the fear of an alien in a world that neither welcomes him nor understands him. I could be tolerated as an observer, perhaps, but the moment I chose to kill, or try to kill, I would have chosen to become part of that world, to accept it on its own terms, to be fully vulnerable to all the laws which governed it, unto death itself. And some part of me must have known, or suspected, that the attempt could destroy me, for it was not my world. It would never be my world.

So I did not kill fish under water. And in the process of not killing fish, and questioning why, I must have gained a hint, however subconscious, of a very important truth: that the mysteries we explore in the world around us (or below us) very often turn out to be mysteries within ourselves, that the challenge to test and know is a challenge to test and know ourselves first, the world second. I came much closer to realizing this truth the day I climbed Dana Point.

My father and I and a friend and his two boys had been out in Dana Cove all afternoon, diving for abalone (paradox: I would strip abalone from their rocks with a tire iron, but I could not kill fish). After we had paddled back to the beach where our two families waited for us, my father's friend suggested that the five of us men (or so he called us) try climbing the old hand-and-knee trail etched into the leeward face of the point, which rose straight above us like a wall. I was then, and am now, terrified of any significant height, and the idea appalled me. I assumed that my father felt the same, since to the best of my knowledge, in my presence or otherwise, he had never climbed anything higher than a ten-foot ladder, solidly planted. Yet he accepted the idea, for reasons which I still believe were not entirely rational. The man who suggested it was his friend. The friend was blond, brown, muscular, and agile, while my father was black-haired, red more often than brown, generally slender (although he filled out nicely in later years), and stiff in his movements when not in the water. The friend was a back-slapping extrovert, while my father chewed his meditative cud. The suggestion was unmistakably made as a kind of challenge, and I suppose there was nothing my father could do but accept it, pride being the heedless thing it is.

Normally, my mother would have raised holy hell at any such idea, and I looked to her with a hopeful heart. But she was a very smart wife, and knew when to shut up. She said nothing. The thought of objecting personally, myself, never entered my mind. How could I shame my father? We climbed Dana Point.

Possibly because I was the smallest of the bunch—and therefore the most easily caught in the case of a violent backslide—I was put in the head of the line, with my father behind me, and behind him the other two boys and their father. We had only about 130 feet to climb, but I never traveled so long a distance in my life. The first fifty or sixty feet were not so bad, for they were up a little ravine that was blocked off left and right as if it were a tunnel; I could see only ahead of me or behind me, neither of which views were particularly alarming. Then the ravine ended, and I ventured out on the surface of the cliff itself. This was not good, for the higher I climbed, the more a sense of proportion I acquired. Height developed real meaning, because I could look off the left edge of the trail and see below me the rocks and surf of the beach, which became smaller and smaller the more I scraped and scrambled up the cliff. At one point, perhaps seventy or eighty feet up, I looked over the side and saw my mother, who waved unenthusiastically, a pinched and worried look on her face. I froze momentarily, for I had never seen my mother from such a height. She was a doll, an ant, and I knew suddenly, inarguably, that I was going to fall. I only prayed that I might land smack on my head, to keep the pain brief.

"C'mon, Tommy, let's get going." Behind me, my father's face was as shriveled and white as I was sure my own must be. But behind him, the two boys waited impatiently, fearlessly, as brainless as their father who had insisted on this whole business. I moved on, somehow, knowing perfectly well that at any moment I would make a fatal slip, or the ledge would give way beneath me, or a monstrous rock would crash down on me from above, punching me into the abyss where the waves made spiderweb patterns on the sand.

Suddenly, before I knew it, I was at the top. Above and to the left of me was the little wooden observation tower. One more series of carved footholds and I was over the edge, standing safe in the middle of several square feet of flat ground. Behind me, my father popped over the edge with a relieved and only slightly hysterical laugh, and after him came the two boys and their father, all laughing, as if they were ready to do it again. The idiots.

Standing there, both feet spread wide, the wind in my hair, looking down on the miniature cove, I felt huge, Olympian. In spite of myself, I had met my fear and survived it. I had come to a working compromise with one of my deepest personal mysteries, for I knew as I stood there that my fear had been a very real and reasonable one, and should have been respected. I did not regret climbing Dana Point; I may even have celebrated it. But I knew that I would never do it again.

A Certain Moment

Russell Chatham (b. 1939), a native of San Francisco, began fishing, painting, and writing at an early age. His essays have appeared in such publications as the Atlantic *and* Esquire. *His books include* Dark Waters *(1988) and* The Angler's Coast *(1990), from which this essay about bass fishing in Marin County's Tomales Bay is taken.*

The fisherman's day began before daylight. Roads were lightly iced where water had seeped from a rain earlier in the week, and a dense tule fog hugged the valleys. Eaves were white with frost in San Anselmo, and the vague predawn light showed Fairfax utterly deserted. The landscape surrounding the rest of the drive lay pristine beneath a silver mantle: White's Hill, San Geronimo Valley, Samuel P. Taylor State Park, Tocaloma, and, finally, the Olema Grade, giving rise at its crest to the full sweep of Inverness Ridge and Tomales Bay, where the fisherman was going after striped bass.

Near the town of Point Reyes Station the road branched left, and at White House Pool steelhead fishermen were beginning to gather. Beyond Inverness Park, past Willow Point, the road skirted the bay, and the angler pulled onto a wide shoulder. As he stepped from the car and walked to the water's edge, ice and frost crunched beneath his feet.

Dawn was breaking and the brittle air hung still, with mingled scents of the marsh and wet farmland. Except for the distant rumble of the sea at Point Reyes and the intermittent call of a mallard out on the nearby moor, the landscape was silent. Over the water itself a light mist spiraled gently toward a clear azure sky in which the morning star was quickly dimming.

A light eight-foot boat soon sat ready at the water's edge. There had been a choice in launching locations: here, to fish the morning high water without having to row for an hour first, or down at the Golden Hind dock, which later would be convenient—necessary, actually—on the minus tide when it was time to come in. The fisherman had chosen the former, deciding to come ashore at the yacht club or wherever he could, then walk back to his car.

The rod was strung, a momentarily appealing fly tied on, and the tackle set on the seat, tip over the stern. In minutes the trim El Toro was rhythmically disturbing the surface with a wake of foam and bubbles. Ahead, behind his back, the fisherman heard the cries of water birds as they took flight. He chose a likely area on the flooding water and drifted with the tide, casting at random. An hour passed. There were baitfish everywhere, and when the sun had risen well in the sky, little Bonaparte's gulls started fluttering and diving to feed. Several bass surfaced but on such widely divergent tangents that it was useless to try to discover a pattern. All he could do was fish the vicinity and hope.

The day grew sublime, one that winter sometimes offers as counterpoint. The cloudless air was pure, almost fragile, the temperature hovering in the sixties. Earlier it had been cold enough for wispy sheets of ice to form against the shoreline, but now the sun was at its winter zenith. The angler had reason for remaining confident even though the morning's initial enthusiasm had long waned. In previous weeks he'd caught enough fish so that, as the hour or tide changed, he could always recall a success during conditions similar to the present moment. Nearby, a flock of bluebills circled, set their wings, and alighted. The myriad bay ducks—scoter, mud hen, bufflehead, goldeneye, ruddy—

were moving continually, and it was impossible to distinguish between their rings and those made by surfacing bass. Overhead, great Vs of pintails whistled, and once, very high, he saw geese.

Low water would be at sundown. The tide, which had started to fall at noon, ran rapidly. Wind blew against tide, causing the boat to drift at an angle across the bay, rather than with either wind or tide alone. By casting to one side and then the other as the boat moved, great swaths of water were probed. Assuming an average cast to be seventy feet, each pass ate up a ribbon of territory a hundred and forty feet wide. Using a floating head and dark streamer, the angler confined his drifts to areas no more than four feet deep, as the stripers seemed to maintain this level while the tide fell.

All during the afternoon he found nothing, and his casts occasionally failed to straighten, causing irritation. The flats had not produced as they should have and the tide was steadily drying them up. As he turned to watch a backcast fling spray into the afternoon sun he knew it was time to move. The sun was lowering against the peninsula and soon the short twilight of winter would gather.

The angler had thought of a particular oyster bed during the morning but not as the last resort it had now become. He'd fully expected to catch fish at intervals throughout the outgoing tide, then move to the bed on the low water. He knew the cove near the fence held bass on a minus tide when the broad expanse to the south was completely dry. As he rowed from near the yacht club over to Millerton Point, the breeze died and the air became icy still as it had been at dawn. The many birds so obvious earlier could no longer be seen clearly and the shoreline was becoming indistinct behind a bluish haze through which only an occasional light sparkled. The earth was immersing itself into the pearly liquid of dusk. Exposed shoreline crackled and Inverness Ridge loomed black, its forest of ancient pine standing in sharp contrast to the sensual, easy slopes of the hills to the east. In the distance a chain saw whined, and behind Inverness thin columns of smoke eased skyward as night began to fall.

The oyster fence lent a certain definition to the otherwise undefined basin where the angler hoped to fish. Like sentinels, the long row of slender eucalyptus poles stretched to the north, guarding vulnerable crustaceans against the appetites of the many large bat rays that inhabited the cove. In places the fence suffered the disrepair of time, which gave it a particular attraction.

Nearing the stakes, the fisherman carefully drew his oars back through the locks after a final stroke, which sent the little boat surging forward. The boat drifted slowly on the glassy water, then stopped. Picking up the fly rod, he took the slender bucktail from the cork grip, dropped it over, and watched it vanish into the green, past the faintly reflected rose sky. Downward thrusts laid a pattern of loose monofilament in the boat. A tentative false cast followed before the rod hissed a clean delivery eighty feet toward the fence. As the fly settled he imagined its descent into dimness. The next cast straightened several yards to the right of the first, beginning a radius that would eventually strike all the water.

When nearly half of the second cast was recovered, he saw a boil behind the fly. Had the surface not been still it would have gone unnoticed; in fact, so subtle was this evidence of a missed strike that it was at once undeniable and unbelievable. The fish had stayed deep; cruising, it had arced beneath the bait, making the surface well up in a restrained convulsion. The disturbance has scarcely dissipated when the next cast was formed of slow, mannered loops that slid smoothly forward, back, then far forward to the bass again. Sensing the lethargy of the season, the angler slowed the retrieve, inducing several more passes. Near the boat the line tightened, but when he struck there was nothing. He began to strip in line for another cast.

It seemed inevitable that the line should pull up again as it just had, but his first strip met with solid resistance and the long rod curved fully, its tip low. Momentarily unbalanced, at the top if his vision he saw the water open and churn, then bulge as the fish moved off. Loose line, which had been coiled haplessly in the boat, snapped against the guides until it was taut to the reel, then released in spasms as the bass surged away. Fifty yards of line hummed under the strain of the fish's pulsing attempts to free itself as it circled widely. The boat returned and moved with the bass, but even so, recovered line was soon lost. This was the linear fight of the shallows. When the fish ran, the rod plunged but came back as the reel gave line until the run ceased. Then the rod went down again as line went back onto the spool.

Soon the bass was thrashing nearby, turning, boring down and away. It seemed so dark, its green back glistening, its stripes sharply defined. It thrust its tail, sending a crescent of water over the angler. In a moment the striper lay motionless off the transom. But it dived beneath the boat and then away in a tight arc, which brought it to the surface again a few feet out. This time, in a quick succession of moves, the fisherman took the leader in his left hand, set the rod down, grabbed the hook shank with his right, clamped his left on the fish's jaw, and, using this paralyzing grip, lifted twenty pounds of striped bass over the gunwale.

There was still enough light in the afterglow to have fished longer, but he didn't. It had been a difficult day, and this was, he thought, its proper conclusion. He snipped the leader and wound in his line.

The sky was pale lemon toward the ocean, and a light was on at the oyster company. Stars were coming out strongly above, and Inverness glimmered from across the bay as the angler started the long row back. Settling into the rhythm of it, he glanced behind him to look at the fish, but saw first a three-quarter moon rising over the gently rolling hills to the east. In the magic, almost colorless light, the bass glinted from the bow, its lifeless form stretched over coils of rope. He felt mutely accused and melancholy over this complicated yet unplanned death. The perfect eye, which moments earlier had guided the fatal chase, no longer saw. But the decision was final, the memory forever etched; he had done as he would do, and in the morning would perhaps arise again before dawn to begin another day of fishing.

Central Coast

Tapping the Source

Kem Nunn (b. 1948) attracted critical attention in 1984 with his first novel, Tapping the Source, *set mostly in the surf culture of Orange County's Huntington Beach. The following scene, however, is set at an isolated beach near Santa Barbara's Hollister Ranch, where the novel's protagonist, Ike, is taken by his friend, Preston. Nunn's latest novel is* The Dogs of Winter *(1997).*

The night was filled with the song of insects, the earthy scents of grass and sage, the damp salt smell of the sea. The moon lit the road and threw a silver light upon the blades of grass, the polished rails of the boards. They walked for what seemed to Ike a long time. His arms ached and each felt about a foot longer when they finally put everything down. They rolled the bags out between the roots of some thick trees on the side of a hill. The ground fell away into darkness, more trees. The moon was straight overhead now. In the distance Ike could hear the sound of surf. . . .

In the morning Ike saw that the hillside was higher and steeper than he had guessed in the night. A clump of trees obscured the view directly in front of them, but off to the left the ground dropped away to reveal other hills, great patches of mustard and wildflowers, green grass and dark trees, and below it all, the sea.

The beaches here were different from those Ike had gotten used to. The beaches in Huntington were wide and flat, colors kept to a minimum. Here the scenery was wild, the colors lush, varied. Long lines of hills rolled toward the sea then broke into steep tumbling cliffs, patchworks of reds and browns. Below the cliffs were thin white crescents and rocky points that reached into the Pacific. There were no traffic noises here, no voices. There were only the calls of the birds, the breeze in the grass, and the surf cracking far below them.

They pulled on trunks and wet suits in the crisp morning air. They knelt on the rocky soil beneath the trees and waxed their boards. The smells of rubber and coconut mixed with the smells of the earth and grass. "We'll get some morning glass," Preston told him. "Surf till ten or eleven, then back here for some food and sleep, surf again around sunset."

They stashed the bags and gear and started down the slope. . . . When they had cleared the trees, they stopped and looked down. "Look at that," Preston told him, and he did: the unmarked crescent of white sand, the rocky point, the perfect liquid lines waiting to be ridden, and he figured that perhaps he knew after all why they had come. He touched Preston's arm as they started down. "Thanks," he said. "Thanks for bringing me." Preston just laughed and led the way, and his laughter rang among the hills.

They entered the water near the middle of the crescent-shaped beach. Ike followed Preston, and when they had pushed through the shore break, Preston angled his board toward the point. Ahead of them the horizon was a straight blue line. The sun sparkled on the water and the water was like glass, smooth and clear so you could look down and see small schools of fish and tendrils of seaweed reaching for the sun. Soon they were paddling over shoulders, the waves lifting and lowering them, and Ike could feel his heart beginning to thump against the deck of his board. He had never paddled out this far or been in waves like these.

At last Preston dug his legs into the water and drew himself up to straddle the board. Ike did the same and together they looked very far away. . . .

"This is what it's all about," Preston said. "You know, there used to be places like this all up and down the coast. Surf 'em with your friends. They're gone now. Fucking developers. People. Fuckers'll all drown in their own garbage before it's over, wait and see." He seemed a little winded from the paddle, as if it was something he had not done in a long time. He swung his arms and rolled his thick neck, then squinted out to sea as the next outside set began to build. Ike forgot about the coastline and began to paddle. It looked like they were still too far inside, but Preston called him back: "Just stick with me, hot shot; set up like I tell you to."

Ike did set up as Preston told him. The set was moving past them now and Preston began paddling hard to the left, paddling closer toward the center of the peaks. Ike paddled after him. As each wave reached them it lifted them high into the air and as it passed there was fine white spray blown back from the lip and there were rainbows caught in the spray. Suddenly Preston turned to him and shouted: "Your wave, ace. Dig for it."

Ike swung the board around and began to paddle and almost at once, without time for a second thought, he was in the grip of the wave. He could hear Preston yell behind him. He could hear the wind and a funny kind of swishing sound. He gripped his rails and swung himself up and there he was, at the top, the wave a great moving hill beneath him, and he was amazed at the height, amazed at how different this was from the short, steep faces he had ridden at Huntington. He was dropping and picking up speed. His stomach rose in his chest. The wave face grew steeper, a green wall that went on forever. The board pushed against his feet. There was a feeling of compression, as if he stood on the floor of a speeding elevator. And then it was over. He made a bit of a turn at the bottom, come to a dead stop. He left the deck as if catapulted, skidded once on his face and stomach before going under, and that was when the whole Pacific Ocean came down on top of him. He had no idea of where he was in relation to the surface. His head filled with salt water. He could feel the leash that connected his ankle to his board dragging him beneath the water. He tried to relax, to go limp, but what he kept seeing was the way Preston would find his body, bloated and discolored, half eaten by crabs, caught between the rocks. He began to claw with both hands, to fight for the surface, and suddenly he was there, the sea a mass of swirling white water all around him, the sunlight dancing in the foam, and he was sucking in great lungfuls of air and blinking the salt out of his eyes and marveling at the beauty of the sky. . . .

They surfed until the sun was overhead and Ike's arms were so weary he could barely lift them out of the water. But he had begun to catch waves, to paddle for them, make the drop, the turn. He was also beginning to see that the wipe-outs wouldn't kill him, not these waves, not today.

They did as Preston had suggested, surfed until noon then returned to the camp, where they ate canned peaches and drank water, slept in the shade of the trees with the hills and ocean spread out below them. Near sunset they surfed again. The water passed like polished glass beneath their boards. Once Ike turned to see Preston sitting on his board maybe fifty yards away. The sea was dark and all around him slivers of sunlight shimmered and vanished like darting schools of fish. On the horizon, the sun had begun to melt, had gone red above a purple sea. The tide was low and the waves turned crisp black faces toward the shore while trails of mist rose from their feathering lips in fine golden arcs. The arcs rose into the sky, spreading and then falling back into the sea, scattering their light across the surface like shards of flames. There was a cyclical quality in all of this, in the play of light, in the movement of the swell. It was an incredible moment and he felt suddenly that he was plugged into all, was part of it in some organic way. The feeling created an awareness of a new set of possibilities, a new rhythm. He wanted to laugh, or to shout. He put his hand in the air and waved at

Preston across the dark expanse. It was a crazy kind of wave—done with the whole arm, his hand swinging at the end of it, full of childish exuberance. And as he watched, Preston raised his own arm and waved back. . . .

By midmorning Ike was alone with the waves. . . . The morning, the surf, could not have been more perfect. A clean swell, three to five feet out of the southwest. Paper-thin walls with long workable faces turned toward the sun. While he surfed, a school of porpoise arrived to join him for a time in the waves, passing in a leisurely fashion, slapping at the water with their bodies, calling to one another with strange sounds. They passed so close he could have reached them in a single stroke. A group of pelicans cruised by in formation, their bodies within inches of the sea. They circled the point and passed him once more, this time just inside the lineup, actually skimming along the faces of the waves, the last bird just ahead of the falling crest so it was like they were surfing, at play on the empty point, and he joined them in the waves, letting jewel-strung faces slip beneath his board, carving lines out of crisp morning glass.

He did not have to rush, to worry about beating anybody back outside, or watch for someone dropping in on him. He could paddle out slowly, take as much pleasure in watching the empty liquid lines as he did in riding them. It was something he had not fully appreciated on his first visit, how surfing was not just about getting rides. It struck him this morning that what he was doing was not separated into different things. Paddling out, catching rides, setting up. Suddenly it was all one act, one fluid series of motions, one motion even. Everything coming together until it was all one thing: the birds, the porpoise, the leaves of seaweed catching sunlight through the water, all one thing and he was one with it. Locked in. Not just tapping the source, but of the source.

Channel Islands

Santa Rosa

Gretel Ehrlich (b. 1946) is usually associated with Wyoming, the setting of her best-known book, the acclaimed The Solace of Open Spaces *(1985). However, she grew up in Santa Barbara, where she continues to live part of the year, and of which she has written, as in this essay about neighboring Santa Rosa Island.*

Green, no one here remembers when it started. Maybe three days ago, after seven months of brown. "It comes on like blindness," one of the cowboys says. "One day the green puts your eyes out, and you didn't even see it coming." I'm standing on the mountainous top of Santa Rosa island off the Santa Barbara coast. Out across the channel waters—white-capped, big-swelled, and shark-glutted —I can see, on the California mainland, the ridge where my house is perched. From there, the view down a canyon perfectly frames Santa Rosa. It is as if this marine shard were the missing half of the land where I live, the other side of my green mind. Santa Rosa island is shaped like a four-pointed star plucked in the middle and dropped. The east and west arms reach for the shore of the next islands in the chain. They were once linked together in a sixty-mile-long island: now the passages between them are cross-currented, choppy, wild, and dangerous, churning gyres rotating counterclockwise, mixing warm water into the cold and bathing the islands in clear seas. At 53,000 acres, Santa Rosa is the second largest of the eight Channel Islands and has been run as a cattle ranch for almost a hundred years by the Vail and Vickers families. Plunging down a rough dirt track in the Vails' battered pickup truck, we go east toward Bechers Bay, the steep land splaying out into broad coastal grasslands. Two foxes, endemic to the island, pounce on a field mouse, oblivious to our passing, reminding me that the four northern islands—Anacapa, Santa Cruz, Santa Rosa, and San Miguel—are sometimes called the Galapagos of the Northern Hemisphere.

We pass a stand of Torrey pines. Tall and thin-limbed, they are pruned by the raging winds that have driven some people on this island crazy. We cross a creek, and the land grows broader. Salt grass tightens its hold on sandy coastal bluffs as a hard northwesterly wind surges our way. Below us the bay is held by a wide curve of sand where snowy plovers nest, and to the southeast a stream widens into a freshwater estuary where egrets and herons prance and stalk, performing their near-motionless ballets. As we descend to the lee side of the island, a feeling of calm engulfs me.

Islands remind us of our intrinsic solitude, yet they usually stand in relationship to a greater body of land and so also teach us about relatedness, just as the islands in a Japanese garden must rest in harmony with the garden.

In our travels we are lured to islands, as if crossing their watery boundaries will endow us with a more vivid sense of ourselves set apart from the maddening fray. But once there, the plangent wholeness of the place blossoms forth: grasses, flowers, birds, trees, streams, animals all distinguished by having gotten there and survived, having been bound together by the frame of limited space.

We follow a long narrow barranca called the Wreck because the British ship *Crown of England* went aground here in 1894. Swales of green flatten out near shore as waves break with sharp reports, as if to say: "Home at last. I have come such a long way."

Near a set of sorting corrals for cattle, a meandering stream is still mostly dry, and a single tree's tortured trunk twists upward from bedrock.

"There never was much in the way of vegetation in this canyon," foreman Bill Wallace tells me, "and after last year's floods, even that was swept away."

We cross the creek and follow the coast west to a beach where cattle take their morning rest on the sand. At low tide, eelgrass is swept up on brown rock, and jade green waves break like windowpanes on the bare bones of the island.

Beyond, a black ridge bends down to the sea, and from around its snout a plug of fog spews continually, never coming onto land.

Another day, the green has intensified. "Who needs a damned watch around here?" one of the men says. "The grass grows an inch every minute."

The southwest coast of the island is paradisiacal. Accordioned by a winter storm in Hawaii, I am on my favorite part of the island, China Camp, once an abalone camp of Chinese fishermen. A set of corrals and a small two-room cabin on the coastal plain overlook the ocean.

"Used to camp here when we were gathering," Russ Vail says. "I've traveled around some, and I guess this is one of the most beautiful spots in the world," he adds quietly, then looks west toward San Miguel. "The other one is next door."

As we come down off the mountain, hundreds, maybe even thousands, of western meadowlarks fly up, land, and throw their heads back in ecstatic song. This whole island is musical, a meadowlark orchestra.

Now the thick roll of fog that pulled past black rock yesterday twists overhead, and I feel as if I were riding a sea turtle, a great green back floating in mist. Waves that are lapis and foam break through the fog at the fringes of this tiny universe, and a seal observes me from the trough between sets of waves.

In Arlington Canyon we come across the site of Phil Orr's camp. An archaeologist with the Santa Barbara Museum of Natural History, Orr did research on early man here on Santa Rosa for twenty years, from 1947 to 1967.

"He was a little crazy," Al Vail says, bemused. "Lived in a cave, fed the damned foxes, and spent years looking around for bones."

Orr theorized that hunter-gatherers lived on these islands as long ago as 35,000 years, though current thinking dates humans here to less than a third of that. Before those people, there were dwarf mammoths, giant mice, sea otters, and flightless geese. Even though the geology of the West is relatively new, the island seems old, having weathered continuous habitation by animals and humans for more years than we know.

Down by the shore Arlington Creek empties out into another estuary loaded with ducks. Huge beams from a wrecked boat are strewn in grass, and an elephant seal, his face and neck scarred from a lifetime of fighting, is slumped across a hummock of kelp, dead.

Fog billows over us and San Miguel disappears. An island may represent apartness and isolation, but that too is only an aspect of its stepping-stone unity with the whole. How do you know you are apart if you do not know there is something other—other islands, a mainland?

When Juan Cabrillo sailed into the Santa Barbara Channel in 1542, the Chumash people greeted him in their plank canoes, called *tomols*. They called what we know as Santa Rosa by the named Wi'ma—driftwood.

Each island had its own dialect, and the island tribes remained distinct from the Chumash who lived in villages along the mainland from Malibu to San Simeon.

They thought of the channel as a stream to step over. "I make a big step," one Chumash islander song goes. "I am always going over to the other side. I always jump to the other side, as if jumping over a stream of water. I make a big step."

With these words, sung in Santa Rosa island dialect, the Fox Dance began, the participants moving in a circle from fire to fire taking up offerings of *islay*, wild cherries. At the end, when the fox dancer whirled around and around under his weighted headdress, another song was such in Cruzeño—the language of Santa Cruz island: "March! There comes the swell of the sea, and the wood tick is drowning."

There were many dances—the Swordfish, Barracuda, Arrow, and Skunk, and the haunting chant of the Seaweed Dance: "I walk moving my brilliance and feathers. I will always endure in the future. . . . "

But they did not endure. They were gone—moved to the mainland—by 1817.

"There are many ghosts on this island," Nita Vail, Al's daughter, tells me.

On Bechers Bay is the main ranch house, the oldest standing house in Santa Barbara County, built in 1865. It is plain and rickety.

When I slept there, the winds seized and shook it, and two elegant Torrey pines outside the door swayed with the house's shaking.

Behind the house two red barns are still standing, but the original bunkhouse is gone. An old cook named Henry fell asleep with a cigarette in bed, burning it down, with himself and his dog in it. For years afterward the Vails said they could hear Henry walking around, clanking pots and pans in the middle of the night.

All afternoon we stroll luxuriant Lobos Canyon, one of the deepest and most unusual barrancas of them all. Year-round springs feed watercress, reeds, and sedge grasses. A snipe flies up as I splash through the stream, and an orange-crowned warbler sings in a small tree. As we tunnel down, the canyon walls grow taller; they are sheaves of sandstone, carefully etched with fine lines as if music had been written on them, the notes erased by wind. Here and there shallow caves have been smoothed out by the island's hard winds, and in one amphitheater, a long tooth of rock hangs down from the roof of a cave, as if from the roof of some orange giant's mouth.

Downstream. More green: reeds, grasses, ferns, Toyon—California holly—and willows grow tall, and even the colonies of lichen on boulders stand up as if starched. A forty-foot-high wall is feathered into delicate filaments that look like the underside of a mushroom, sunsplashed and edible.

"I would like to die here," Nita says, "except I love this canyon so much, I'd want to stay alive to savor it."

As would I.

Lost Coast

John McKinney (b. 1956), award-winning nature writer, conservationist, and Los Angeles Times *hiking columnist, is the author of several walking guides as well as* A Walk Along Land's End: Discovering California's Unknown Coast *(1995), a narrative of a journey inspired by J. Smeaton Chase's 1912 trek. A native of southern California, the author has long been active in the effort to save the region's and the state's environment.*

It doesn't get any wilder than this.

California has a very long coastline, and millions of acres of wilderness, but it has only one wilderness coast.

The Lost Coast.

A day's walk north of Fort Bragg I'm greeted by towering shoreline cliffs, rising abruptly like volcanoes from the sea. I get just a glimpse of the two-thousand-foot-high cliffs before the morning mist turns to heavy fog and the coast is lost to my view. The Lost Coast is so rough—rougher even than Big Sur's coast—that it even thwarted California's highway engineers; much to their frustration, they were compelled by geography to route the Coast Highway inland more than twenty miles.

The Lost Coast is black sand beaches strewn with patterns of driftwood and the sea's debris, a mosaic of small stones. On grassy blufftops, sheep and cows turn tail to angry winds blowing in from Siberia and the Bering Sea. Canyon mouths fill with fog, nourishing the redwoods within.

Abandoned barns and failed fences record the efforts of settlers who tried, but failed, to tame this land. Nowhere is the Lost Coast blighted by transmission lines, oil wells, power plants, RV parks, or fast-food franchises.

As traced on the map, the Lost Coast's northern boundary is the Eel River in Humboldt County, its southern boundary Usal Beach in Mendocino County. Much of the Lost Coast is in public ownership as part of the King Range National Conservation Area in the north and Sinkyone Wilderness State Park in the south.

But "Lost Coast" is not a place name found on any map.

Except mine.

One January, a few years back, I served as volunteer ranger/camp-ground host for Sinkyone Wilderness State Park. I cared for a couple of horses, gave directions to the very few visitors who braved the rain and miserable park road to get to the coast, read and wrote in the ranch house that serves as the park's visitor center on those days when it rained hard, and wandered the trails on those days when it rained less. I hiked all the Lost Coast's trails, mapped the territory, then supervised production of a map called "Trails of the Lost Coast."

The word *lost* on a map has long been a call of the wild to me. Lost Palms Oasis and Lost Horse Mine in the Mojave Desert, Lost Valley in Big Sur, and Lost Lake in the High Sierra are just a few of the lost places I've found.

A fifty-five mile footpath—Lost Coast Trail—traverses the Lost Coast. To reach the trailhead, from Wages Creek Beach outside the hamlet of Rockport, where I camped in a private campground, I must walk seven miles along the beaches and bluffs, then another seven miles up Usal Road. The road, a muddy thoroughfare not pictured on most maps, hasn't changed much since Jack London and his wife, Charmian, drove it in a horse-drawn carriage on a trip to Eureka in 1911, or since

J. Smeaton Chase rode it in 1912. I'm not surprised that after two hours of hiking the road, not a single car has passed me.

Usal Road, with a couple of name changes, follows the crest of the ocean fronting Lost Coast peaks. It doesn't offer much in the way of coastal views, but winds through some wild country. Chase followed roads the length of the Lost Coast. He and I will part company, so to speak, at Usal Beach, where I will join the Lost Coast Trail, a pathway of late 1980s vintage.

"Actual, rosy, purple-blotched foxgloves, such as I last saw in the lanes of Surrey and Devon," he exults.

Chase, two decades removed from an England he would never see again, was understandably nostalgic. But for what exactly? The Britain of his youth? Would Chase have enjoyed a 1912 ride around Britain's coast more, or less, than his ride along California's? Would he have been inspired by Mother England's tidy fields and hedgerows or appalled by the motorcars, mines, mills, and other manifestations of the Industrial Age?

As I walk Usal Road, maybe there's a better question to ponder: Would I—or a reborn Joseph Smeaton Chase—better enjoy a modern-day adventure along land's end in Britain or in California?

These days about 80 percent of Californians and a like percentage of Brits live within thirty miles of coast. But while sharing a common proximity to the ocean, we do not share a common coastal view. In England, the coast is where one gets rid of things—power plants, resorts, gun emplacements, oil refineries, sewage plants—presumably to keep the interior looking pastoral. We Californians, while guilty of placing (more than) our share of horrors on the coast, attempt to locate the worst of our architectural and ecological atrocities some distance inland.

In Britain, the Countryside Commission, so successful at preserving the nation's hills and dales, has not had similar success along the coast. In California, the Coastal Commission has waged a foot-by-foot battle for public access and the preservation of beauty, but its legal powers end a quarter mile inland.

At several locales along Britain's coast, I've felt myself a witness to the last gasp of an empire. Fortress Britain, whose castellated coast has long been a defense against barbarians, is still repelling invaders, this time with ramparts of uglification. Walking Britain's coast left me with the impression of a nation looking inward, determined to take care of its own.

We Californians, by contrast, appear worried what people sailing in from the Pacific Rim will think when they see our coast. And we seem to care not a whit what other Americans, or anyone arriving from the East, will see as they cross the interior on their way to the coast.

After his brief look backward to Britain, Chase looks ahead. He tells us for the first time that he always planned to finish his ride by November 1, and that he has but ten days or so to make the Oregon line.

Despite the rude and crude Californians met during the latter part of this journey, despite witnessing the great tracts of land laid waste by lumbermen, Chase is as plucky, as indefatigable, as ever as he rides the Lost Coast. His "There-will-always-be-a-California" point of view is as unshakable as the "There-will-always-be-an-England" belief held by generations of traveling scribes.

I arrive at Usal Camp on the banks of Usal Creek, select a campsite (I can choose from among fifteen sites in the fifteen-site camp), and set up my tent. Sunset draws near, though I know this only by consulting the moist face of my watch, not by any glimpse of the day star, which has been absent all day.

I follow Usal Creek to its mouth at Usal Beach, a dramatic, dark sand-and-gravel strand backed by tall cliffs whose tops are lost in the fog. Scattered at the base of the eroded cliffs are huge boulders. Such rocks falling from the bluffs make me glad Lost Coast Trail stays atop the bluffs rather than below them.

Usal Beach is not a friendly place. Not only do huge rocks rain on the beach, but huge rogue waves frequently surprise-attack the shore. The surf pounds offshore rock pillars, socks Usal Creek in the mouth.

However, these adverse conditions that discourage even walking Usal Beach did not discourage capitalists of a hundred years ago.

During the 1890s, Captain Robert Dollar regularly navigated his steamship, *Newsboy*, in and out of the treacherous doghole port of Usal in order to transport logs sawn by the Usal Redwood Company. The aptly named Dollar went on to greater fame as founder of the Dollar Steamship Line, later the President Line. The sawmill closed in 1900, and Usal became a near–ghost town, largely because the timber in these parts was inferior. The redwoods' timber prospects looked good to the loggers, but the tall trees never yielded board-feet commensurate to their great size, and produced a lesser grade of lumber. Nevertheless, Georgia Pacific Company resumed logging after World War II and continued until 1986, when, after cutting down most of the trees, it sold its land to the park. In 1969, the company burned Usal to the ground, to avoid what it termed "liability problems."

I lug some driftwood back to my camp and, after much coaxing, get the wet wood to burn. When the fire offers more heat than smoke, I put my pot of macaroni and cheese on the fire. As my hands and face warm and my damp clothes dry, my thoughts turn from California's wettest land to its driest.

After Chase finished his long coastal ride, he began exploring the desert, wrote desert books, moved to Palm Springs and married. No doubt after an upbringing in the England damp, and his excursion along this coast, he was ready to live out his remaining days where it was warm and dry.

The Lost Coast is said to have two seasons: six months of rain and six months of fog. It's very foggy again today. The ocean below and the sky above are a single shade of gray. The tall grass covering the coastal slopes and the Douglas fir that border the meadowland are dripping. Lost Coast Trail is muddy, and populated by so many earthworms that the earth itself seems alive and wiggling.

I enter Dark Canyon, a rainforest-like environment of bay laurels draped with moss, maple, and alder. The fog lingers in this canyon, so that the land never seems to dry. The fog tarries too in Anderson and Northport gulches. The Lost Coast's canyons and gulches, from Usal to Bear Harbor, were logged not so many years ago, but the fog softens the scars, hides the stumps. Wrapped in mist, the forest is healing.

Along Little Jackass Creek grows one of the few surviving old-growth redwood groves, the Sally Bell Grove, named for the last full-blooded Sinkyone. She survived a massacre of her people to become a woman of strong will and strong medicine.

Near the grove, I hail state park ranger John Jennings, an easygoing mustachioed fellow who has patrolled here almost since the beginning. "Here" is Sinkyone Wilderness State Park; "the beginning" was in 1975, when the state park opened.

He spent the afternoon finding and cleaning up a marijuana garden, he reports. The grower had harvested his plants, but not his trash, and Jennings hauled away beer bottles and a hammock. "A lot of trash for just two plants."

While the marijuana industry here is small-scale compared to elsewhere in Humboldt County, the weed and its growers nevertheless invade the state park.

The Lost Canyon is part of the so-called Emerald Triangle, the name given to an area of Humboldt, Mendocino, and Trinity counties where many a marijuana garden grows. Indeed, the sinsemilla flourishes.

In the good old days of 1960s and 1970s, big growers harvested huge fortunes—crops of hundreds of plants grew along the Lost Coast on such places as the banks of the Mattole River and Ettersburg. But growers have fallen on hard times, particularly on the coastwood side of the isosceles. The CAMP (Campaign Against Marijuana Plants), complete with helicopter surveillance and trucks full of heavily armed men running through the woods, has been effective in reducing the number of growers. So have stiffer jail sentences and fines, not to mention confiscation and forfeiture of their land.

Now growers have taken up guerrilla gardening—cultivating perhaps a half dozen, sometimes only one or two, plants in dispersed locations on public land. Still, a single sinsemilla plant is a cash crop for several thousand dollars, making it worth the risk to many.

As a peace officer—a term that better describes his job than that of his city cop counterparts—Jennings must protect the Lost Coast from the locals, who, like the native Sinkyone who preceded them, could be said to be a family-oriented loosely organized tribal group that lives off the land. But many locals are attracted to the Lost Coast because it's long been a place for people to escape tax collectors, the criminal justice system, and most conventional forms of personal and social responsibility.

"John, there are three seasons," Jennings tells me.

"No way, John. You told me two the last time I was here: the foggy season and the rainy season."

"That's the weather. The humans around here observe three seasons: hunting season, fishing season, and growing season."

These three seasons make it rough for Jennings in a park designated "wilderness." A wilderness is by definition off-limits to vehicles, which severely restricts what locals call "traditional uses" of the land.

"Traditional uses" is a motto that plays well with the conservative board of supervisors and county government, but in practice is quite different. Traditional wood gathering means four-wheeling it up to a tree and chain-sawing what you need. Traditional fishing is backing up to the river and fishing off the back of a truck. Traditional hunting is blasting at critters from a pickup trucks. Traditional agriculture is planting pot on public land.

In the minds of many locals, the gun is an integral part of the coastal system, and they want to solve these traditional problems in their traditional manner.

Problem: Too few steelhead

Solution: Shoot the sea lions

Problem: Too few trout

Solution: Shoot the merganser ducks

Problem: Too few quail to shoot

Solution: Shoot the bobcats

Problem: Too few deer to shoot

Near sunset—or more precisely, about when the sun sets, since I have not glimpsed the orb all day—I reached Wheeler, where some cement foundations mark what was a company town, from 1950 to 1960. Near the ruins grow spearmint, alyssum, and other domestic plants gone wild. During the Lost Coast's logging decade, diesels hauling 120,000 pounds of logs thundered along Usal Road from Wheeler, a modern town of thirty families, with electricity and phones.

Wheeler, one of the last company towns (and maybe the newest ghost town) on the California coast, was established by the Wheeler family. The Wheelers renamed Jackass Creek "Wolf Creek," probably so they could call their business Wolf Creek Timber Company rather than Jackass Creek Timber Company, no doubt preferring to name their company after a predator rather than a nitwit.

One of mapmaking's great joys is choosing geographical names among contenders. I figured that Jackass Creek was so named before the Wheelers and their timber company came, so Jackass Creek it should be henceforth, and Jackass Creek it is on my Lost Coast Map.

I pitch my tent by Jackass Creek beneath two large redwoods. The redwoods remind me that tomorrow I will visit a very special stand of the tall trees—the J. Smeaton Chase Grove, a grove that I named for my trail companion.

From Wheeler, I ascend steep switchbacks, then wind through a grassland at the edge of a forest. Among the blue-eyed grass and monkey flowers are the foxgloves so beloved by Chase.

I reach Duffy's Gulch, a garden of rhododendrons, head-high ferns, and vines climbing redwoods to the sky. Splashing color about the gulch are Indian paintbrush, dandelions, huckleberry, Douglas iris, Calypso orchid, and some bright red poison oak. The trees in J. Smeaton Chase Grove are towering thousand-year-old redwoods, some ten feet in diameter, surrounded by a multitude of ferns—sword, lady, five-finger, and woodwardia.

Doubtless Chase would have frowned at me for naming a grove for him. He was a modest man (far more photographs of his horse survive than of him) and in *California Coast Trails* wrote of the vanity of naming groves of the tallest living things for men of questionable stature.

But Chase also wrote of the rest that comes with an eternal sleep in the woods: "Every good man loves the woodland, and even if our concerns keep us all our lives out of our heritage we hope to lie down at last under the quiet benediction of slow-moving branches." . . .

It is a miracle the redwoods of J. Smeaton Chase Grove escaped the ax and saw, I think as I tramp under ever gloomier skies to Bear Harbor, the main port for southern Humboldt and northern Mendocino counties from the 1860s to the turn of the century. This onetime timber shipping point isn't much more than a mile from the grove's virgin redwoods. . . .

It begins to rain and I decide not to stop at Railroad Creek trail camp, but to push on for the relative comfort of Needle Rock Ranch House. Just offshore, a strange cloud formation, like a blackened teapot, pours water from the ocean onto the land.

An hour's walk in the rain (a relief, actually, from the incessant fog,) brings me to the ranch house, a combination visitor center/hostel, where I unpack my things. . . .

The dark clouds vanish and the rain ceases. I step out onto the porch to see the sun, low over the water, struggling against the gloom. An isolated, lone eucalyptus shines ghostly white against the dark, storm-tossed sea.

It is this special, brooding light that intrigued the great Catholic theologian Thomas Merton when he visited here and talked of establishing a monastery for Trappist monks. He thought the Lost Coast shores around Needle Rock an ideal location for a life of prayer and contemplation—high praise indeed for one who believed so strongly in the power of physical silence and seclusion. . . .

Above the roar of the breakers I hear what sounds like the crack of a bat meeting a baseball, like someone taking batting practice on the bluffs. I walk up the coast one hundred, two hundred yards, following my ears until I spot an amazing sight. Two bull Roosevelt elk paw the ground, lower their heads, butt antlers. Around them, grazing on the bluffs, are two dozen females, by all outward appearances utterly disinterested in the result of this combat.

Again and again the elk circle, feint, clash. From a distance they look evenly matched, but up close it's apparent that a young bull, strong but outweighed, is challenging an older bull. No blood is drawn. This is more ritual, than actual, combat.

Roosevelt elk are enchanted-looking creatures, with chocolate-brown faces and necks, tan bodies, and dark legs. The California natives look like a cross between a South American llama and a deer. In truth, the elk are more awesome when they butt heads than when they call. I always figured elk had a majestic call, a trumpet to arms, but these Roosevelts have a funny little call more like the wee-wee of a pig than the bugle of a powerful thousand-pound elk.

The younger bull may successfully challenge his elder next year or the year after, but this evening the older bull, with his fuller antlers and more clever moves, and still very much in his prime, is a sure bet to keep his harem. Sunset (the first I've seen in days) casts an orange glow over the clifftop combatants, like a floodlight on a stage. When the light finally fades and darkness falls, the duel ends.

Dark shapes gather together, protection against the enemies of the night, but if the elk intend to be inconspicuous they had better stop eating. The ruminants tear at the grass, an aggressive munching, like a lion ripping into a kill.

The next morning I hike up Whale Gulch on the Lost Coast Trail, leaving behind the state park and entering King Range National Conservation Area. Its one of the wettest spots in America, with over a hundred inches of rain annually, but today the weather seems most indecisive. Black clouds hover offshore to my left, the sun rises over the King Range to my right. The radio in the ranch house predicted a 50 percent chance of showers.

Soon after the boundary between state park and U.S. Bureau of Land Management territories, I cross another boundary, the line between Mendocino and Humboldt counties. The county line is another boundary of sorts—the fortieth parallel of latitude.

The change in latitude heralds a change in attitude.

In the sharp morning light, the land shows its scars. The King Range is chain saw country, Utah with fog. The magnificent coast is visible, and files of Douglas fir, but so also are clear-cut ridges, overgrazed slopes, and silted streams. Some of this land looks like the "Before Rehabilitation" pictures in the Boy Scouts' Soil and Water Conservation merit badge pamphlet.

I think of yet another boundary I've crossed—this one wholly in my mind. After all this coast walking, I've decided there are three Californias: Smog Land, Fog Land, and Log Land. This beginning of BLM land, this fortieth parallel, this Mendocino-Humboldt county line: this is clearly the start of Log Land.

As I climb Chemise Mountain the vegetation changes. Most of the firs have been logged, and it's tan oak and madrone that cling to the steep hillsides. Near the top of Chemise Mountain is some chemise (greasewood), as well as chaparral bushes and lots of manzanita; the presence of drought-resistant plants only a mile or so from a thick rainforest is truly bizarre. The difference in ecology has to do with elevation. Chemise Mountain, at 2,596 feet, is about two thousand feet higher than the rainforest. I enjoy the view from atop the mountain: King's Peak, the dominant promontory to the north, a half dozen ridges of the Sinkyone to the south, Shelter Cove on the coast far below. The view doesn't last long; it closes like a storm window.

As I descend Chemise Mountain Trial toward the coast, the weather has decided to be—indecisive. The sun warming the King Range from the east meets the storm brewing on the western horizon, and the result is neither rain nor sun but a dense fog.

Here on these very steep slopes, exposed to the full fury of Pacific storms, the firs grow grotesque, their massive trunks short and twisted. Only the patter of condensed fog dripping from the branches breaks the silence.

I hurry through the dark, spooky forest. The reason for my hustle down the knee-jarring decline is that I have an appointment with Point No Pass on the beach below at precisely 2:53 P.M., and I must not be late. Such punctuality is critical because rounding the aptly named point is only possible at a rare minus tide, which, luckily for me, happens to occur this afternoon. If I can't round Point No Pass and walk the beach to Shelter Cove, I will have to ascend this brutal slope of Chemise Mountain and hike over the crest of the King Range to continue north.

About a quarter mile from the beach I reach the end of Chemise Mountain Trail; it's been buried by a landslide, as if a giant bulldozer has scraped the side of the mountain. I slip-slide on feet and butt through the slide zone, hoping the mountain doesn't slide with me to the sea. When I reach the beach, I walk a mile to Point No Pass and, thanks to my watch and tide table, am able to round the point and reach Shelter Cove. . . .

An elderly couple walks the black sand beach patrolled by swifts and swallows and . . . I can't believe my eyes . . . trucks and off-road vehicles. . . . Rifles hang in gun racks in the cabs of the passing pickup trucks, fishing poles in the beds behind them. The Lost Coast locals are ever ready to practice their traditional hunting and fishing techniques.

The beach, twenty-five miles from Shelter Cove to the mouth of the Mattole River, is the longest roadless stretch in California. Something of the thrill of knowing this, of walking this coast, is diminished when, road or not, vehicles are permitted on the beach for the first three and a half miles.

Dodging cars and trucks, I walk the beach to Gitchell Creek, just beyond the boundary, separating beaches that allow vehicles from

beaches that forbid them. Just in case one of the locals decides to practice some traditional drunk driving on the beach tonight, I pitch my
tent behind a massive log that seems guaranteed to stop even a tank.

As I gather driftwood for my evening fire, I nearly step on a rattlesnake. As lethargic a creature as I've ever seen, the timber rattler
manages one flick of the forked tongue at me before uncoiling itself
from a piece of wood and crawling deeper into the woodpile. I manage
to work up some sympathy for a snake in such a cold and wet part of the
world. The Lost Coast belongs to amphibians, not reptiles.

The next morning I'm off into the fog, and in a few miles reach Buck
Creek, where a steep trail leaves the beach and climbs into the King
Range. This is my only chance to leave the beach and hike along the crest
of the King Range. But now that I've left civilization—and vehicles—
behind, I want to stick with the beach.

And a magnificent beach it is—rock, pebbles, and coarse black sand
strewn with great logs, as if the sea, not the land, had been logged. And
water, water, everywhere; the ocean, deep and wide and restless on my
left, the fog all around me, creeks trickling, waterfalls tumbling from
the rainforest above to the beach below. High above me, at the limits of
vision, where the green slope meets the gray sky are seeps and springs
nurturing hanging wildflower gardens, scattered like Easter eggs in the
forest.

After a long day, I make another beach camp, another driftwood fire,
at Cooksie Creek. Then back to the beach the next morning.

I hear the residents of Sea Lion Rocks before I see them—two dozen
Steller's sea lions. A mile beyond the big creatures is the abandoned
Punta Gorda lighthouse. In 1911, after several ships were wrecked on
the rocks and reefs of the Lost Coast, a lighthouse was built a mile
south of Punta Gorda, a name meaning "massive point."

The mouth of the Mattole River, a complication of gravel bars,
marks the northern end of the Lost Coast. Seagulls and osprey circle
above me as I watch the harbor seals bob in the tidal area where the river meets the ocean. I look back into the mist at the King Range, at

slopes that seem so much steeper than the angle of repose, and that are kept from collapsing into the sea only by some hidden force deep within the earth.

It is not really the coast that is lost, but ourselves. If we cannot find the coast because of the smoke of our cities, the walls we build to keep one another out, the industries we run that run us, it is surely we who are lost.

We all need one place on the map, one place in our hearts that is lost. In a wild place, lost from the mean streets, we can find ourselves, our best selves. A place that is peaceful, for prayer and for contemplation, is good; a place that is wild, for challenge and confrontation, is better; and a place that is both peaceful and wild, for the love of life and the lust of living, is best.

EARTH, WIND, RAIN, AND FIRE

San Andreas Fault

Continental Drift

James D. Houston (b. 1933) is California born and educated. He has taught writing for a many years and has written several novels, a collection of short stories, and several works of nonfiction. The following is the prologue to his 1978 novel Continental Drift.

From high above, say gazing down from one of our tracking satellites, he can see it plain as an incision, a six-hundred-mile incision some careless surgeon stitched up across the surface of the earth. It marks the line where two great slabs of the earth's crust meet and grind together. Most of North America occupies one of these slabs. Most of the Pacific Ocean floats on the other. A small lip of the Pacific slab extends above the surface, along America's western coastline, a lush and mountainous belt of land not as much a part of the rest of the continent as it is the most visible piece of that slab of crust which lies submerged. The line where these two slabs, or plates, meet is called the San Andreas Fault. It cuts south from San Francisco, past San Jose, underneath the old San Juan Bautista Mission, on down behind Los Angeles, and back under water again at the Gulf of California.

The Pacific plate, he will tell you, is creeping north and west at about two inches per year, an example of the movement geologists call continental drift. Our globe, which appears to be divided into continents and bodies of water, is actually a patchwork of these vast plates, all floating around in a kind of subterranean pudding. What it resembles most is a badly fractured skull. From time to time the towns and cities along the fault line have been jiggled or jolted by temblors large and small, when sections of it buckle or lock, and then unbend, release, or settle. There are people who predict that one day the ultimate quake is going to send a huge chunk of California sliding into the ocean like Atlantis. They foresee this as one of the worst disasters in the history of the civilized world. They sometimes add that in a land as bizarre and corrupt as California is reputed to be, such a fate has been well earned.

Montrose Doyle will tell you all that is poppycock. Both the physics and the prophecy. He will tell you that the earth's crust is three hundred miles thick, whereas the fault line only cuts down for thirty of those miles. He will tell you that if anything is going to undo this piece of coast it will be the accumulated body weight of all the people who have been moving into his part of the world at a steady rate since 1849. But it won't be the San Andreas. He has made it his business to find out what he can about this creature, because he owns fifty-five acres of orchard and grazing land that border it. He grew up on this ranch, will probably die here, and during his forty-six years he has seldom felt more than a tic across the earth's skin, an infrequent shiver in the high cupola which serves as his personal antenna and seismograph.

Montrose has studied with fascination the photographs of rotundas upended in the streets of San Francisco during the famous quake of 1906. He has corresponded with experts. And he has escorted visitors over to Hollister, twenty-five miles east of where his own house stands. An otherwise neat and orderly farm town, Hollister happens to be gradually splitting in two, because it sits in the fracture zone, like an Eskimo village caught on a cracking ice floe. By following cracks you can trace the subtle power of the fault as it angles under the town, offsetting sidewalks and curbstones and gutters, an effect most alarming in the house of a chiropractor which you pass soon after entering Hollister from the west. One half of a low concrete retaining wall holding back the chiropractor's lawn has been carried north and west about eight inches. The concrete walkway is buckling. Both porch pillars lean precariously toward the coast. In back, the wall of his garage is bent into a curve like a stack of whale's ribs. The fact that half his doomed house rides on the American plate and the other half rides the Pacific has not discouraged this chiropractor from maintaining a little order in his life. He hangs his sign out front, he keeps his lawn well mowed and the old house brightly, spotlessly painted.

One afternoon Montrose leaned down to talk with a fellow in Hollister who was working on the transmission of a Chevy pickup. The curb his truck stood next to had been shattered by the ageless tension of those two slabs of earth crust pulling at each other. Five inches had opened in the curb, like a little wound, and someone had tried to fill it with homemade concrete, and that had started to split.

Monty said, "Hey!"

The grease-smeared face emerged, irritably. It was hot. The man said, "Yeah?"

"Hey, doesn't the fault line run through this part of town?"

"The what?"

"The San Andreas . . . "

"Oh, that damn thing." The man waved his wrench aimlessly. "Yeah, she's around somewhere," and he slid back out of sight underneath his pickup.

Montrose regards that man with fondness now. He voiced Monty's own attitude pretty well, which is to say, none of this really troubles him much. Is he a fatalist? Yes. And no. He anticipates. Yet he does not anticipate. What he loves to dwell on—what he savors so much during those trips to Hollister—is that steady creep which, a few million years hence, will put his ranch on a latitude with Juneau, Alaska. He admires the foresight of the Spanish cartographers who, in their earliest maps, pictured California as an island. Sometimes late at night, after he has been drinking heavily, he will hike out to his fence line and imagine that he can feel beneath his feet the dragging of the continental plates, and imagine that he is standing on his own private raft, a New World Noah, heading north, at two inches per year.

Most of the time he doesn't think about it at all. It is simply there, a presence beneath his land. If it ever comes to mind during his waking hours, he thinks of it as just that, a presence, a force, you might even say a certainty, the one thing he knows he can count on—this relentless grinding of two great slabs which have been butting head-on now for millennia and are not about to relax.

San Andreas Fault

The San Andreas
Discrepancy

John McPhee (b. 1931) is one of the most highly regarded writers in America, whose books on a wide variety of subjects usually first appear as essays in the New Yorker. *Over the span of fifteen years McPhee explored the San Andreas Fault with Eldridge Moores, a tectonist at the University of California, Davis; the result was* Assembling California *(1993), a historical and geological cross-section of the state.*

Farther north [of Los Angeles], it loses, for a while, its domestic charm. Almost all water disappears in a desert scene that, for California, is unusually placed. The Carrizo Plain, only forty miles into the Coast Ranges from the ocean at Santa Barbara, closely resembles a south Nevada basin. Between the Caliente Range and the Temblor Range, the San Andreas Fault runs up this flat, unvegetated, linear valley in full exposure of its benches and scarps, its elongate grabens and beheaded channels, its desiccated sag ponds and dry deflected streams. From the air, the fault trace is keloid, virtually organic in its insistence and its creep—north forty degrees west. On the ground, standing on desert pavement in a hot dry wind, you are literally entrenched in the plate boundary. You can see nearly four thousand years of motion in the bed of a single intermittent stream. The bouldery brook, bone dry, is fairly straight as it comes down the slopes of the Temblor Range, but the San Andreas has thrown up a shutter ridge—a sort of sliding wall—that blocks its path. The stream turns ninety degrees right and explores the plate boundary for four hundred and fifty feet before it discovers its offset bed, into which it turns west among cobbles and boulders of Salinian granite.

You pass dead soda ponds, other offset streams. The (gravel) road up the valley is for many miles directly on the fault. Now and again, there's a cattle grid, a herd of antelope, a house trailer, a hardscrabble ranch, a fence stuffed with tumbleweed, a pump in the yard. A daisy wheel turns on a tower. Down in the broken porous fault zone there will always be water, even here.

With more miles north come small adobes, far apart, each with a dish antenna. And with more miles a handsome spread, a green fringe, a prospering ranch with a solid house. The fault runs through the solid house. And why should it not? It runs through greater San Francisco.

Of the two most direct routes from southern to northern California, always choose the San Andreas Fault. If you have adequate time, it beats the hell out of Interstate 5. Nearly always, some sort of road stays right in the fault zone. Like a water-level route through rough country, the fault is a place to find gentle grades and smooth ground. When the fault makes minor turns, they are nothing compared to the bends of a river. With more distance north, the desert plain yields to hay meadows and then to ever lusher country, until vines are standing in the fault-trace grabens and walnuts climb the creaselike hills. Ground squirrels appear, and then ever larger flocks of magpies, and then cottonwoods, and then oaks in thickening numbers, and velure pastures around horses with nothing to do. In age and rock type, the two sides of the fault are as different as two primary colors. Strewn up the west side are long-transport gabbroic hills and deracinated ranges of exotic granite. Just across the trough is Franciscan melange—stranger, messier, more interesting to Moores.

Near Parkfield, you cross a bridge over the San Andreas where Cholame Creek runs on the fault. The bridge has been skewed—the east end toward Chihuahua, the west end toward Mt. McKinley. Between Cholame and Parkfield, plate-shattering ruptures have occurred six times since 1857, an average of one every twenty-two years, and the probability that another will occur before 2003 has been reckoned at ninety-eight percent. Thirty-four people live in Parkfield. If the population is ever to increase, seismologists will be the first to know it, for the valley here is wired like nowhere else. Parkfield has attracted earthquake-prediction experts because the brief interval time on this segment of the fault suggests that if they monitor this place they may learn something before they die. Also, the Parkfield segment has—in Moores's words—"relatively simple fault geometry." And the last three earthquakes have had a common epicenter and have been of equal magnitude.

An average of one plate-shattering earthquake every twenty-two years works out to 45,000 per million years. The last big Parkfield event was in 1966. It broke the surface for eighteen miles. Words on the town's water tower say "Parkfield, Earthquake Capital of the World, Be Here When It Happens." The actual year doesn't matter much. The instrumentation of Parkfield assumes that a shock is imminent. Its purpose is not to confirm the calculated averages but to develop a technology of sensing—within months, days, hours, or minutes—when a shock is coming. Even a minute's warning, or five minutes', or an hour's, let alone a day's, could (in highly populated places) save many lives and much money. Accordingly, the Cholame Valley around Parkfield—between Middle Mountain, in the north, and Gold Mountain, to the south—has been equipped with several million dollars' worth of strain gauges, creepmeters, earth thumpers, laser Geodimeters, tiltmeters, and a couple of dozen seismographs. It is said that the federal spending has converted the community from Parkfield to Porkfield. Some of the seismographs are in holes half a mile deep. Experience suggests that rocks creep a little before they leap. The creepmeters are sensitive to tens of millionths of an inch of creep.

If ever there was a conjectural science, it is earthquake prediction, and as research ramifies, the Tantalean goal recedes. The maximum stress on the San Andreas Fault—the direction of maximum push—turns out to be nearly perpendicular to the directions in which the fault sides move, like a banana peel's horizontal slip when pressure comes upon it from above. A fault that moves in such a manner must be weak enough to slide—must be, in a sense, lubricated. Among other things, the pressure of water in pores of rock in the walls of the fault has been mentioned as a lubricant, and so has the sudden release of gases that may result from shaking. Such mechanisms would tend to randomize earthquakes, diminishing the significance of mounting strains and temporal gaps. Those who practice earthquake prediction will watch almost anything that might contribute to the purpose. A geyser in the Napa Valley inventively named Old Faithful seems to erupt erratically both before and after large earthquakes that occur within a hundred and fifty miles—an observation that is based, however, on records kept for scarcely twenty years. In 1980, the United States Geological Survey began monitoring hydrogen in soils. Two years later, near Coalinga, about twenty miles northeast of Parkfield, the hydrogen in the soil was suddenly fifty times normal. It appeared in bursts, and such bursts became increasingly numerous in April 1983. In May 1983, a 6.5 earthquake occurred on a thrust fault under Coalinga. Releases of radon are watched. So are patterns and numbers of microquakes, especially those that are known as the Mogi doughnut. In the mid-1960s, a Japanese seismologist noticed on his seismograms that microquakes occurring in the weeks before a major shock sometimes formed rings around the place that became the epicenter. Mogi's doughnut is a wonderful clue, but—like hydrogen bursts and radon releases—before most major shocks it fails to appear.

People who live in earthquake country will speak of earthquake weather, which they characterize as very balmy, no winds. With prescient animals and fluctuating water wells, the study of earthquake weather is in a category of precursor that has not attracted funds from the National Science Foundation. Some people say that well water goes down in anticipation of a temblor. Some say it goes up. An ability to sense imminent temblors has been ascribed to snakes, turtles, rats, eels, catfish, weasels, birds, bears, and centipedes. Possible clues in animal behavior are taken more seriously in China and Japan than they are in the United States, although a scientific paper was published in *California Geology* in 1988 evaluating a theory that "when an extraordinarily large number of dogs and cats are reported in the 'Lost and Found' section of the *San Jose Mercury News*, the probability of an earthquake striking the area increases significantly."

Earthquake prediction has taken long steps forward on the insights of plate tectonics but has also, on occasion, overstepped. Until instrumentation is reliably able to chart a developing temblor, predictors obviously have a moral responsibility to present their calculations shy of the specific. The mathematical equivalent of a forked stick will produce such absurdities as the large earthquake that did not occur as predicted in New Madrid, Missouri, on December 2, 1990. A USGS geologist and a physicist in the United States Bureau of Mines whose research included (among other things) the study of rocks cracking in a lab predicted three great earthquakes for specific dates in the summer of 1981, to take place in the ocean floor near Lima. The largest—9.9—was to be twenty times as powerful as any earthquake ever recorded in the world. A few hundred thousand Peruvians were informed that they would die. Nothing happened.

If you set stakes in a straight line across a valley glacier and come back a year later, you will see the curving manner in which the stakes have moved. If you drive fence posts in a straight line across the San Andreas Fault and come back a year later, almost certainly you will see a string line of fence posts—unless your fence is in the hundred miles north of the Cholame Valley. There the line will be offset slightly, no more than an inch or two. Another year after that a little more; and so forth. In its 740 miles of interplate abrasion, the San Andreas Fault is locally idiosyncratic, but nowhere more so than here in the Central

Creeping Zone. Trees move, streams are bent, sag ponds sag. In road asphalt, echelon fractures develop. Slivers drop as minigrabens. Scarplets rise. The fault is very straight through the Central Creeping Zone. It consists, however, of short (two to six miles), stepped, parallel traces, like the marks made on ice by a skater. Landslides occur frequently in the Central Creeping Zone, obscuring the fresh signatures of the creep.

"The creep is relatively continuous for 170 kilometers here and seems to account for nearly all of the movement," Moores remarked. "Creep is rare. Most fault movement is punctuated. The creep produces numerous small earthquakes. There are actual 'creep events,' wherein as much as five hundred meters of the fault zone will experience propagating creep in one hour." There were many oaks and few people living in the creep zone. The outcrops on the Pacific side of the fault sparkled with feldspar and mica—the granitic basement of the Gabilan Range. More than three thousand feet in elevation and close against the fault trace, the Gabilan Range creeps, too.

Jumping and creeping, the San Andreas Fault's average annual motion for a number of millions of years has been thirty-five millimeters. The figure lags significantly behind the motion of the Pacific Plate, whose travels, north by northwest, go a third again as fast. In the early days of plate tectonics, this incongruous difference was discovered after the annual motion of the Pacific Plate was elsewhere determined. The volcanic flows that crossed the San Andreas and were severed by the fault had not been carried apart at anything approaching the rate of Pacific motion. This became known as the San Andreas Discrepancy. If the Pacific Plate was moving so much faster than the great transform fault at its eastern edge, the rest of the motion had to be taken up somewhere. Movements along the many additional faults in the San Andreas were not enough to account for it. Other motions in the boundary region were obviously making up the difference.

With the development of hot-spot theory (wherein places like Hawaii are seen as stationary and deeply derived volcanic penetrations of the moving plates) and of other refinements of data on vectors in the lithosphere, the history of the Pacific Plate became clearer. About three and a half million years ago, in the Pliocene Epoch, the direction in which it was moving changed about eleven degrees to the east. Why this happened is the subject of much debate and many papers, but if you look at the Hawaiian Hot Spot stitching the story into the plate, you see, at least, that it did happen: there is an eleven-degree bend at Pliocene Oahu.

The Pacific Plate, among present plates the world's largest, underlies about two-thirds of the Pacific Ocean. North-south, it is about eight thousand miles long, and east-west, it is about six thousand miles wide. What could cause it to turn? Various events that occurred roughly three and a half million years ago along the Pacific Plate margins have been nominated as the cause. For example, the Ontong-Java Plateau, an immense basaltic mass in the southwest Pacific Ocean, collided with the Solomon Islands, reversing a subduction zone (it is claimed) and jamming a huge slab of the Pacific Plate under the North Fiji Plateau. The slab broke off. Suddenly released from the terrific drag on its southwest corner, the rest of the great northbound plate turned eleven degrees to the northeast. A number of coincidental collisions along the plate's western margin may have contributed to the change in vector. Additional impetus may have been provided by the subduction of a defunct spreading center at the north end of the plate. The extra weight of the spreading center, descending, may have tugged at the plate and given it clockwise torque. Whatever the cause, it's not easy to imagine a vehicle that weighs 345 quadrillion tons suddenly swerving to the right, but evidently that is what it did.

The tectonic effect on North America was something like the deformation that results when two automobiles sideswipe. Between the Pacific and North American Plates, the basic motion along the San Andreas Fault remained strike-slip and parallel. But as the Pacific Plate sort of jammed its shoulder against most of California a component of compression was added. This resulted in thrust faults and accompanying folds—anticlines and synclines. (Petroleum migrated into the anti-clines, rose into their domes, and was trapped.)

Earlier—about five million years before the present—the ocean spreading center known as the East Pacific Rise had propagated into North America at the Tropic of Cancer, splitting Baja off the rest of the continent and initiating the opening of the Gulf of California. (By coin-cidence, the walls of the Red Sea, which much resembles the Gulf of California, parted at the same time.) The splitting off of Baja was accompanied by very strong northward compression, which raised, among other things, the Transverse Ranges above Los Angeles, at the great bend of the San Andreas. That the Transverse Ranges were rising compressionally had been obvious to geologists long before plate tec-tonics identified the source of the compression. But not until the late 1980s did they come to see that compression as well as strike-slip motion accompanies the great fault throughout its length, as a result of the slight shift in the direction of the Pacific Plate three and a half million years ago. All these compressional aspects taken together—anticlines, synclines, and thrust faults in a wide swath from one end of California almost to the other—account for some of the missing motion in the San Andreas Discrepancy. The Los Angeles basin alone has been squeezed about a centimeter a year for two million two hundred thou-sand years. The sites of Laguna Beach and Pasadena are fourteen miles closer together than they were 2.2 million years ago. This has happened an earthquake at a time. For example, the Whittier Narrows earthquake of 1987 lessened the breadth of the Santa Monica Mountains and raised the ridgeline.

The Whittier Narrows hypocenter was in a deeply buried fault in a young anticline. Such faults tend to develop about ten miles down and gradually move toward the surface. Northward for five hundred miles, young anticlines on the east side of the San Andreas Fault are similar in nature—the products of deep successive earthquakes. Most are recent-ly discovered, and many more, presumably, remain unknown. They make very acute angles with the fault, like the wake of a narrow boat. When a temblor goes off like a hidden grenade, geologists often have not suspected the existence of the fault that has moved. The 6.5 earthquake at Coalinga in 1983 was that kind of surprise. It increased the elevation of the ridge above it by more than two feet.

In 1892, a pair of enigmatic earthquakes shook Winters, which is near Davis, in the Great Central Valley. Evidently, the earthquakes occurred on the same sort of blind thrust that is under Coalinga, but the Winters thrust is of particular interest because it is east of the Coast Ranges and fifty miles from the San Andreas. Yet it is apparently a product of the newly discovered folding and faulting that everywhere shadow the great fault. The Central Valley of California is about the last place in the world where virtually any geologist would look for an Appalachian-style fold-and-thrust belt. Without shame, Moores sketches one on a map of California; it goes up the west side of the valley almost all the way from the Tehachapi Range to Red Bluff and reaches eastward as far as Davis. He and his Davis colleague Jeff Unruh have been out looking for tectonic folds in the surreally flat country surrounding the university. This is a game of buff even beyond the heightened senses of the blind. They have found an anticline—an arch with limbs spread wide for many miles and a summit twenty-five feet high. They call it the Davis Anticline. It is a part of what Moores likes to describe as "the Davis campus fold-and-thrust belt." He is having fun, but the folds are not fictions. The anticline at Davis has developed in the past hundred thousand years. It is rising ten times as fast as the Alps.

On perhaps the weirdest geologic field trip I have ever been invited to observe, he and Unruh went out one day looking for nascent mountains in the calm-water flatness of the valley. There were extremely subtle differentiations. Moores said, "We are looking here on the surface for something that is happening five kilometers down—blind thrusts. Compressional stress extends to the center of the valley."

"Topography doesn't happen for nothing," Unruh said. "Soil scientists have long recognized that these valley rises are tectonic uplifts. Soils are darker in basinal areas. There's a fault-propagation fold in this part of the valley."

Moores later wrote to me:

> We continue to gather evidence. We have seen two seismic profiles that show a horizontal reflection, presumably a fault, that extends all the way from the Coast Ranges to the Sacramento River. Jeff has been working at stream gradients. The rationale is that where there is a sharp change in gradient on a flood plain there is a reason, and the reason here is uplift. The analysis fits the two areas of acknowledged uplift west of Davis pretty well, and seems to indicate a new north-trending zone of uplift that goes right through Davis itself. Maybe there was a reason why the Patwin Indians selected this particular spot on the banks of Putah Creek for this village, after all. It was a high spot in a swamp, and it was high because it is coming up!

The compressive tectonism associated with the plate boundary contributes to the total relative plate motion, but not much: the overall average is less than a centimeter a year. And that does not nearly close the numerical gap. Surprisingly, the rest of the missing motion seems to come from the Basin and Range, the country between Reno and Salt Lake City, wherein the earth's crust has been stretching out and breaking into blocks, which float on the mantle as mountains. The stretching has increased the width of the region by sixty miles in a few million years. Very-long-baseline interferometry has shown that the Basin and Range is spreading about ten millimeters a year in a direction west-northwest. This supplies enough of the total plate-boundary motion between the Gulf of California and Cape Mendocino to make up the difference in the San Andreas Discrepancy. If some Pacific Plate motion is coming from Utah, Utah is part of the plate boundary.

The westernmost range of the Basin and Range Province is the Sierra Nevada, which has risen on a normal fault that runs along the eastern base of the mountains. The fault has experienced enough earth-quakes to give the mountains their exceptional altitude. The most recent great earthquake there was in 1872. In a few seconds, the mountain range went up three feet. In the same few seconds, the Sierra Nevada also moved north-northwest twenty feet. That would help to fill in anybody's discrepancy.

A Wind-Storm
in the Forest

John Muir (1838–1914) came with his family from Scotland to Wisconsin when he was eleven. He traveled to California in 1868. In 1889 he began, with Robert Underwood Johnson, a campaign to establish a national park that would include the Yosemite Valley; as a result of their efforts the Yosemite, Sequoia, and General Grant National Parks were established. Muir's careful field journals became the basis of descriptive essays of the area, which in turn resulted in his first book, The Mountains of California *(1894), from which this depiction of a storm in the Yuba River Valley is taken.*

The mountain winds, like the dew and rain, sunshine and snow, are measured and bestowed with love on the forests to develop their strength and beauty. However restricted the scope of other forest influences, that of the winds is universal. The snow bends and trims the upper forests every winter, the lightning strikes a single tree here and there, while avalanches mow down thousands at a swoop as a gardener trims out a bed of flowers. But the winds go to every tree, fingering every leaf and branch and furrowed bole; not one is forgotten; the Mountain Pine towering with outstretched arms on the rugged buttresses of the icy peaks, the lowliest and most retiring tenant of the dell; they seek and find them all, caressing them tenderly, bending them in lusty exercise, stimulating their growth, plucking off a leaf or limb as required, or removing an entire tree or grove, now whispering and cooing through the branches like a sleepy child, now roaring like the ocean; the winds blessing the forests, the forests the winds, with ineffable beauty and harmony as the sure result.

After one has seen pines six feet in diameter bending like grasses before a mountain gale, and ever and anon some giant falling with a crash that shakes the hills, it seems astonishing that any, save the lowest thickset trees, could ever have found a period sufficiently stormless to establish themselves; or, once established, that they should not, sooner or later, have been blown down. But when the storm is over, and we behold the same forests tranquil again, towering fresh and unscathed in erect majesty, and consider what centuries of storms have fallen upon them since they were first planted,—hail, to break the tender seedlings; lightning, to scorch and shatter; snow, winds, and avalanches, to crush and overwhelm,—while the manifest result of all this wild storm-culture is the glorious perfection we behold; then faith in Nature's forestry is established, and we cease to deplore the violence of her most destructive gales, or of any other storm-implement whatsoever.

There are two trees in the Sierra forests that are never blown down, so long as they continue in sound health. These are the Juniper and the Dwarf Pine of the summit peaks. Their stiff, crooked roots grip the storm-beaten ledges like eagles' claws, while their lithe, cord-like branches bend round compliantly, offering but slight holds for winds, however violent. The other alpine conifers—the Needle Pine, Mountain Pine, Two-leaved Pine, and Hemlock Spruce—are never thinned out by this agent to any destructive extent, on account of their admirable toughness and the closeness of their growth. In general the same is true of the giants of the lower zones. The kingly Sugar Pine, towering aloft to a height of more than 200 feet, offers a fine mark to storm-winds; but it is not densely foliaged, and its long, horizontal arms swing round compliantly in the blast, like tresses of green, fluent algae in a brook; while the Silver Firs in most places keep their ranks well together in united strength. The Yellow or Silver Pine is more frequently overturned than any other tree on the Sierra, because its leaves and branches form a larger mass in proportion to its height, while in many places it is planted sparsely, leaving open lanes through which storms may enter with full force. Furthermore, because it is distributed along the lower portions of the range, which was the first to be left bare on the breaking up of the ice-sheet at the close of the glacial winter, the soil it is growing upon has been longer exposed to post-glacial weathering, and consequently it is in a more crumbling, decayed condition than the fresher soils farther up the range, and therefore offers a less secure anchorage for the roots.

While exploring the forest zones of Mount Shasta, I discovered the path of a hurricane strewn with thousands of pines of this species. Great and small had been uprooted or wrenched off by sheer force, making a clean gap, like that made by a snow avalanche. But hurricanes capable of doing this class of work are rare in the Sierra, and when we have explored the forests from one extremity of the range to the other, we are compelled to believe that they are the most beautiful on the face of the earth, however we may regard the agents that have made them so.

There is always something deeply exciting, not only in the sounds of winds in the woods, which exert more or less influence over every mind, but in their varied waterlike flow as manifested by the movements of the trees, especially those of the conifers. By no other trees are they rendered so extensively and impressively visible, not even by the lordly tropic palms or tree-ferns responsive to the gentlest breeze. The waving of a forest of the giant Sequoias is indescribably impressive and sublime, but the pines seem to me the best interpreters of winds. They are mighty waving goldenrods, ever in tune, singing and writing wind-music all their long century lives. Little, however, of this noble tree-waving and tree-music will you see or hear in the strictly alpine portion of the forests. The burly Juniper, whose girth sometimes more than equals its height, is about as rigid as the rocks on which it grows. The slender lash-like sprays of the Dwarf Pine stream out in wavering ripples, but the tallest and slenderest are far too unyielding to wave even in the heaviest gales. They only shake in quick, short vibrations. The Hemlock Spruce, however, and the Mountain Pine, and some of the tallest thickets of the Two-leaved species bow in storms with considerable scope and gracefulness. But it is only in the lower and middle zones that the meeting of winds and woods is to be seen in all its grandeur.

One of the most beautiful and exhilarating storms I ever enjoyed in the Sierra occurred in December 1874, when I happened to be exploring one of the tributary valleys of the Yuba River. The sky and the ground and the trees had been thoroughly rain-washed and were dry again. The day was intensely pure, one of those incomparable bits of California winter, warm and balmy and full of white sparkling sunshine, redolent of all the purest influences of the spring, and at the same time enlivened with one of the most bracing wind-storms conceivable. Instead of camping out, as I usually do, I then chanced to be stopping at the house of a friend. But when the storm began to sound, I lost no time in pushing out into the woods to enjoy it. For on such occasions nature has always something rare to show us, and the danger to life and limb is hardly greater than one would experience crouching deprecatingly beneath a roof.

It was still early morning when I found myself fairly adrift. Delicious sunshine came pouring over the hills, lighting the tops of the pines and setting free a stream of summery fragrance that contrasted strangely with the wild tones of the storm. The air was mottled with pine-tassels and bright green plumes, that went flashing past in the sunlight like birds pursued. But there was not the slightest dustiness, nothing less pure than leaves, and ripe pollen, and flecks of withered bracken and moss. I heard trees falling for hours at the rate of one every two or three minutes; some uprooted, partly on account of the loose, water-soaked condition of the ground; others broken straight across, where some weakness caused by fire had determined the spot. The gestures of the various trees made a delightful study. Young Sugar Pines, light and feathery as squirrel-tails, were bowing almost to the ground; while the grand old patriarchs, whose massive boles had been tried in a hundred storms, waved solemnly above them, their long, arching branches streaming fluently on the gale, and every needle thrilling and ringing and shedding off keen lances of light like a diamond. The Douglas Spruces, with long sprays drawn out in level tresses, and needles massed in a gray, shimmering flow, presented a most striking appearance as they stood in bold relief along the hilltops. The madroños in the dells, with their red bark and large glossy leaves tilted every way, reflected the sunshine in throbbing spangles like those one so often sees on the rippled surface of a glacier lake. But the Silver Pines were now the most impressively beautiful of all. Colossal spires 200 feet in height waved like supple goldenrods chanting and bowing low as if in worship, while the whole mass of their long, tremulous foliage was kindled into one continuous blaze of white sun-fire. The force of the gale was such that the most steadfast monarch of them all rocked down to its roots with a motion plainly perceptible when one leaned against it. Nature was holding high festival, and every fiber of the most rigid giants thrilled with glad excitement.

I drifted on through the midst of this passionate music and motion, across many a glen, from ridge to ridge; often halting in the lee of a rock for shelter, or to gaze and listen. Even when the grand anthem had swelled to its highest pitch, I could distinctly hear the varying tones of individual trees,—Spruce, and Fir, and Pine, and leafless Oak,—and even the infinitely gentle rustle of the withered grasses at my feet. Each was expressing itself in its own way,—singing its own song, and making its own peculiar gestures,—manifesting a richness of variety to be found in no other forest I have yet seen. The coniferous woods of Canada, and the Carolinas, and Florida, are made up of trees that resemble one another about as nearly as blades of grass, and grow close together in much the same way. Coniferous trees, in general, seldom possess individual character, such as is manifest among oaks and elms. But the

California forests are made up of a greater number of distinct species than any other in the world, And in them we find, not only a marked differentiation into special groups, but also a marked individuality in almost every tree, giving rise to storm-effects indescribably glorious.

Toward midday, after a long, tingling scramble through copses of hazel and ceanothus, I gained the summit of the highest ridge in the neighborhood, and then it occurred to me that it would be a fine thing to climb one of the trees to obtain a wider outlook and get my ear close to the Aeolian music of its top-most needles. But under the circumstances the choice of a tree was a serious matter. One whose instep was not very strong seemed in danger of being blown down, or of being struck by others in case they should fall; another was branchless to a considerable height above the ground, and at the same time too large to be grasped with arms and legs in climbing, while others were not favorably situated for clear views. After cautiously casting about, I made choice of the tallest of a group of Douglas Spruces that were growing close together like a tuft of grass, no one of which seemed likely to fall unless all the rest fell with it. Though comparatively young, they were about 100 feet high, and their lithe, brushy tops were rocking and swirling in wild ecstasy. Being accustomed to climb trees in making botanical studies, I experienced no difficulty in reaching the top of this one, and never before did I enjoy so noble an exhilaration of motion. The slender tops fairly flapped and swished in the passionate torrent, bending and swirling backward and forward, round and round, tracing indescribable combinations of vertical and horizontal curves, while I clung with muscles firm braced, like a bobolink on a reed.

In its widest sweeps my tree-top described an arc of from twenty to thirty degrees, but I felt sure of its elastic temper, having seen others of the same species still more severely tried—bent almost to the ground indeed, in heavy snows—without breaking a fiber. I was therefore safe, and free to take the wind into my pulses and enjoy the excited forest from my superb outlook. The view from here must be extremely beautiful in any weather. Now my eye roved over the piny hills and dales as over fields of waving grain, and felt the light running in ripples and broad swelling undulations across the alleys from ridge to ridge, as the shining foliage was stirred by corresponding waves of air. Oftentimes these waves of reflected light would break up suddenly into a kind of beaten foam, and again, after chasing one another in regular order, they would seem to bend forward in concentric curves, and disappear on some hillside, like sea-waves on a shelving shore. The quantity of light reflected from the bent needles was so great as to make whole groves appear as if covered with snow, while the black shadows beneath the trees greatly enhanced the effect of the silvery splendor.

Excepting only the shadows there was nothing somber in all this wild sea of pines. On the contrary, notwithstanding this was the winter season, the colors were remarkably beautiful. The shafts of the pine and libocedrus were brown and purple, and most of the foliage was well tinged with yellow; the laurel groves, with the pale undersides of their leaves turned upward, made masses of gray; and then there was many a dash of chocolate color from clumps of manzanita, and jet of vivid crimson from the bark of the madroños, while the ground on the hillsides, appearing here and there through openings between the groves, displayed masses of pale purple and brown.

The sounds of the storm corresponded gloriously with this wild exuberance of light and motion. The profound bass of the naked branches and boles booming like waterfalls; the quick, tense vibrations of the pine-needles, now rising to a shrill, whistling hiss, now falling to a silky murmur; the rustling of laurel groves in the dells, and the keen metallic click of leaf on leaf—all this was heard in easy analysis when the attention was calmly bent.

The varied gestures of the multitude were seen to fine advantage, so that one could recognize the different species at a distance of several miles by this means alone, as well as by their forms and colors, and the way they reflected the light. All seemed strong and comfortable, as if really enjoying the storm, while responding to its most enthusiastic greetings. We hear much nowadays concerning the universal struggle for existence, but no struggle in the common meaning of the word was manifest here; no recognition of danger by any tree; no deprecation but rather an invincible gladness as remote from exultation as from fear.

I kept my lofty perch for hours, frequently closing my eyes to enjoy the music by itself, or to feast quietly on the delicious fragrance that was streaming past. The fragrance of the woods was less marked than that produced during warm rain, when so many balsamic buds and leaves are steeped like tea; but, from the chafing of resiny branches against each other, and the incessant attrition of myriads of needles, the gale was spiced to a very tonic degree. And besides the fragrance from these local sources there were traces of scents brought from afar. For this wind came first from the sea, rubbing against its fresh, briny waves, then distilled through the redwoods, threading rich ferny gulches, and spreading itself in broad undulating currents over many a flower-enameled ridge of the coast mountains, then across the golden plains, up the purple foothills, and into these piny woods with the varied incense gathered by the way.

Winds are advertisements of all they touch, however much or little we may be able to read them, telling their wanderings even by their scents alone. Mariners detect the flowery perfume of land-winds far at sea, and sea-winds carry the fragrance of dulse and tangle far inland, where it is quickly recognized, though mingled with the scents of a thousand land-flowers. As an illustration of this, I may tell here that I breathed sea-air on the Firth of Forth, in Scotland, while a boy; then was taken to Wisconsin, where I remained nineteen years; then, without in all this time having breathed one breath of the sea, I walked quietly, alone, from the middle of the Mississippi Valley to the Gulf of Mexico, on a botanical excursion, and while in Florida, far from the coast, my attention wholly bent on the splendid tropical vegetation about me, I suddenly recognized a sea-breeze, as it came sifting through the palmettos and blooming vine-tangles, which at once awakened and set free a thousand dormant associations, and made me a boy again in Scotland, as if all the intervening years had been annihilated.

Most people like to look at mountain rivers, and bear them in mind; but few care to look at the winds, though far more beautiful and sublime, and though they become at times about as visible as flowing water. When the north winds in winter are making upward sweeps over the curving summits of the High Sierra, the fact is sometimes published with flying snow-banners a mile long. Those portions of the winds thus embodied can scarce be wholly invisible, even to the darkest imagination. And when we look around over an agitated forest, we may see something of the wind that stirs it, by its effects upon the trees. Yonder it descends in a rush of waterlike ripples, and sweeps over the bending pines from hill to hill. Nearer, we see detached plumes and leaves, now speeding by on level currents, now whirling in eddies, or, escaping over the edges of the whirls, soaring aloft on grand, upswelling domes of air, or tossing on flame-like crests. Smooth, deep currents, cascades, falls, and swirling eddies, sing around every tree and leaf, and over all the varied topography of the region with telling changes of form, like mountain rivers conforming to the features of their channels.

After tracing the Sierra streams from their fountains to the plains, marking where they bloom white in falls, glide in crystal plumes, surge gray and foam-filled in boulder-choked gorges, and slip through the woods in long, tranquil reaches—after thus learning their language and forms in detail, we may at length hear them chanting all together in one grand anthem, and comprehend them all in clear inner vision, covering the range like lace. But even this spectacle is far less sublime and not a whit more substantial than what we may behold of these storm-streams of air in the mountain woods.

We all travel the milky way together, trees and men; but it never occurred to me until this storm-day, while swinging in the wind, that trees are travelers, in the ordinary sense. They make many journeys, not extensive ones, it is true; but our own little journeys, away and back again, are only little more than tree-wavings—many of them not so much.

When the storm began to abate, I dismounted and sauntered down through the calming woods. The storm-tones died away, and, turning toward the east, I beheld the countless hosts of the forests hushed and tranquil, towering above one another on the slopes of the hills like a devout audience. The setting sun filled them with amber light, and seemed to say, while they listened, "My peace I give unto you."

As I gazed on the impressive scene, all the so-called ruin of the storm was forgotten, and never before did these noble woods appear so fresh, so joyous, so immortal.

The Santa Ana

Joan Didion (b. 1934), a native of the Sacramento Valley, is an esteemed writer of essays and fiction, including the novels River Run *(1963) and* Play It as It Lays *(1970). She lived for many years in the Los Angeles area, and much of her nonfiction is about life there. This piece, originally published in the* Saturday Evening Post, *was collected in* Slouching Towards Bethlehem *(1968).*

There is something uneasy in the Los Angeles air this afternoon, some unnatural stillness, some tension. What it means is that tonight a Santa Ana will begin to blow, a hot wind from the northeast whining down through the Cajon and San Gorgonio Passes, blowing up sandstorms out along Route 66, drying the hills and the nerves to the flash point. For a few days now we will see smoke back in the canyons, and hear sirens in the night. I have neither heard nor read that a Santa Ana is due, but I know it, and almost everyone I have seen today knows it too. We know it because we feel it. The baby frets. The maid sulks. I rekindle a waning argument with the telephone company, then cut my losses and lie down, given over to whatever it is in the air. To live with the Santa Ana is to accept, consciously or unconsciously, a deeply mechanistic view of human behavior.

I recall being told, when I first moved to Los Angeles and was living on an isolated beach, that the Indians would throw themselves into the sea when the bad wind blew. I could see why. The Pacific turned ominously glossy during a Santa Ana period, and one woke in the night troubled not only by the peacocks screaming in the olive trees but by the eerie absence of surf. The heat was surreal. The sky had a yellow cast, the kind of light sometimes called "earthquake weather." My only neighbor would not come out of her house for days, and there were no lights at night, and her husband roamed the place with a machete. One day he would tell me that he had heard a trespasser, the next a rattlesnake.

"On nights like that," Raymond Chandler once wrote about the Santa Ana, "every booze party ends in a fight. Meek little wives feel the edge of the carving knife and study their husbands' necks. Anything can happen." That was the kind of wind it was. I did not know then that there was any basis for the effect it had on all of us, but it turns out to be another of those cases in which science bears out folk wisdom. The Santa Ana, which is named for one of the canyons it rushes through, is a *foehn* wind, like the *foehn* of Austria and Switzerland and the *hamsin* of Israel. There are a number of persistent malevolent winds, perhaps the best known of which are the mistral of France and the Mediterranean sirocco, but a *foehn* wind has distinct characteristics: it occurs on the leeward slope of a mountain range and, although the air begins as a cold mass, it is warmed as it comes down the mountain and appears finally as a hot dry wind. Whenever and wherever a *foehn* blows, doctors hear about headaches and nausea and allergies, about "nervousness," about "depression." In Los Angeles some teachers do not attempt to conduct formal classes during a Santa Ana, because the children become unmanageable. In Switzerland the suicide rate goes up during the *foehn*, and in the courts of some Swiss cantons the wind is considered a mitigating circumstance for crime. Surgeons are said to watch the wind, because blood does not clot normally during a *foehn*. A few years ago an Israeli physicist discovered that not only during such winds, but for the ten or twelve hours which precede them, the air carries an unusually high ratio of positive to negative ions. No one seems to know exactly why that should be; some talk about friction, and others suggest solar disturbances. In any case the positive ions are there, and what an excess of positive ions does, in the simplest terms, is make people unhappy. One cannot get much more mechanistic than that.

Easterners commonly complain that there is no "weather" at all in southern California, that the days and the seasons slip by relentlessly, numbingly bland. That is quite misleading. In fact the climate is characterized by infrequent but violent extremes; two periods of torrential subtropical rains which continue for weeks and wash out the hills and send subdivisions sliding toward the sea; about twenty scattered days a year of the Santa Ana, which, with its incendiary dryness, invariably means fire. At the first prediction of a Santa Ana, the Forest Service flies men and equipment from northern California into the southern forests, and the Los Angeles Fire Department cancels its ordinary non-firefighting routines. The Santa Ana caused Malibu to burn the way it did in 1956, and Bel Air in 1961, and Santa Barbara in 1964. In the winter of 1966–67 eleven men were killed fighting a Santa Ana fire that spread through the San Gabriel Mountains.

Just to watch the front-page news out of Los Angeles during a Santa Ana is to get very close to what it is about the place. The longest Santa Ana period in recent years was in 1957, and it lasted not the usual three or four days but fourteen days, from November 21 until December 4. On the first day 25,000 acres of the San Gabriel Mountains were burning, with gusts reaching 100 miles an hour. In town, the wind reached Force 12, or hurricane force, on the Beaufort Scale; oil derricks were toppled and people ordered off the downtown streets to avoid injury from flying objects. On November 22 the fire in the San Gabriels was out of control. On November 24 six people were killed in automobile accidents, and by the end of the week the *Los Angeles Times* was keeping a box score of traffic deaths. On November 26 a prominent Pasadena attorney, depressed about money, shot and killed his wife, their two sons, and himself. On November 27 a South Gate divorcee, twenty-two, was murdered and thrown from a moving car. On November 30 the San Gabriel fire was still out of control, and the wind in town was blowing eighty miles an hour. On the first day of December four people died violently, and on the third the wind began to break.

It is hard for people who have not lived in Los Angeles to realize how radically the Santa Ana figures in the local imagination. The city burning is Los Angeles's deepest image of itself; Nathanael West perceived that, in *The Day of the Locust*; and at the time of the 1965 Watts riots what struck the imagination most indelibly were the fires. For days one could drive the Harbor Freeway and see the city on fire, just as we had always known it would be in the end. Los Angeles weather is the weather of catastrophe, of apocalypse, and, just as the reliably long and bitter winters of New England determine the way life is lived there, so the violence and the unpredictability of the Santa Ana affect the entire quality of life in Los Angeles, accentuate its impermanence, its unreliability. The wind shows us how close to the edge we are.

Great Basin Desert

Nurslings of the Sky

Mary Austin (1868–1934) moved to California after graduating from college in Illinois in 1888, and soon moved to the high desert country of the Owens River Valley in Inyo County, between Death Valley and the eastern base of the Sierra Nevada. She would memorialize the region in her first and most enduring book (of thirty-five), The Land of Little Rain *(1903), in which this essay appeared.*

Choose a hill country for storms. There all the business of the weather is carried on above your horizon and loses its terror in familiarity. When you come to think about it, the disastrous storms are on the levels, sea or sand or plains. There you get only a hint of what is about to happen, the fume of the gods rising from their meeting place under the rim of the world; and when it breaks upon you there is no stay nor shelter. The terrible mewings and mouthings of a Kansas wind have the added terror of viewlessness. You are lapped in them like uprooted grass; suspect them of a personal grudge. But the storms of hill countries have other business. They scoop watercourses, mature the pines, twist them to a finer fibre, fit the firs to be masts and spars, and, if you keep reasonably out of the track of their affairs, do you no harm.

They have habits to be learned, appointed paths, seasons, and warnings, and they leave you no doubt about their performances. One who builds his house on a waterscar on the rubble of a steep slope must take chances. So they did in Overtown who built in the wash of Argus water, and at Kearsarge at the foot of a deep, treeless swale. After twenty years Argus water rose in the wash against the frail houses, and the piled snows of Kearsarge slid down at a thunder peal over the cabins and the camp, but you could conceive that it was the fault of neither the water nor the snow.

The first effect of cloud study is a sense of presence and intention in storm processes. Weather does not happen. It is the visible manifestation of the Spirit moving itself in the void. It gathers itself together under the heavens; rains, snows, yearns mightily in wind, smiles; and the Weather Bureau, situated advantageously for that very business, taps the record on his instruments and going out on the street denies his God, not having gathered the sense of what he has seen. Hardly anybody takes account of the fact that John Muir, who knows more of mountain storms than any other, is a devout man.

Of the high Sierras choose the neighborhood of splintered peaks about the Kern and Kings river divide for storm study, or the short, wide-mouthed cañons opening eastward on high valleys. Days when the hollows are steeped in a warm, winey flood the clouds came walking on the floor of heaven, flat and pearly gray beneath, rounded and pearly white above. They gather flock-wise, moving on the level currents that roll about the peaks, lock hands and settle with the cooler air, drawing a veil about those places where they do their work. If their meeting or parting takes place at sunrise or sunset, as it often does, one gets the splendor of the apocalypse. There will be cloud pillars miles high, snow-capped, glorified, and preserving an orderly perspective before the unbarred door of the sun, or perhaps more ghosts of clouds that dance to some pied piper of an unfelt wind. But be it day or night, once they have settled to their work, one sees from the valley only the blank wall of their tents stretched along the ranges. To get the real effect of a mountain storm you must be inside.

One who goes often into a hill country learns not to say: What if it should rain? It always does rain somewhere among the peaks; the unusual thing is that one should escape it. You might suppose that if you took any account of plant contrivances to save their pollen powder against showers. Note how many there are deep-throated and bell-flowered like the penstemons, how many have nodding pedicels as the columbine, how many grow in copse shelters and grow there only. There is keen delight in the quick showers of summer cañons, with the added comfort, born of experience, of knowing that no harm comes of a wetting at high altitudes. The day is warm; a white cloud spies over the cañon wall, slips up behind the ridge to cross it by some windy pass, obscures your sun. Next you hear the rain drum on the broad-leaved hellebore, and beat down the mimulus beside the brook. You shelter on the lee of some strong pine with shut-winged butterflies and merry, fiddling creatures of the wood. Runnels of rainwater from the glacier-slips swirl through the pine needles into rivulets; the streams froth and rise in their banks. The sky is white with cloud; the sky is gray with rain; the sky is clear. The summer showers leave no wake.

Such as these follow each other day by day for weeks in August weather. Sometimes they chill suddenly into wet snow that packs about the lake gardens clear to the blossom frills, and melts away harmlessly. Sometimes one has the good fortune from a heather-grown headland to watch a rain-cloud forming in mid-air. Out over meadow or lake region begins a little darkling of the sky—no cloud, no wind, just a smokiness such as spirits materialize from in witch stories.

It rays out and draws to it some floating films from secret cañons. Rain begins, "slow dropping veil of thinnest lawn"; a wind comes up and drives the formless thing across a meadow, or a dull lake pitted by the glancing drops, dissolving as it drives. Such rains relieve like tears.

The same season brings the rains that have work to do, ploughing storms that alter the face of things. These come with thunder and the play of live fire along the rocks. They come with great winds that try the pines for their work upon the seas and strike out the unfit. They shake down the avalanches of splinters from sky-line pinnacles and raise up sudden floods like battle fronts in the cañons against towns, trees, and boulders. They would be kind if they could, but have more important matters. Such storms, called cloud-bursts by the country folk, are not rain, rather the spillings of Thor's cup, jarred by the Thunderer. After such a one the water that comes up in the village hydrants miles away is white with forced bubbles from the wind-tormented streams.

All that storms do to the face of the earth you may read in the geographies, but not what they do to our contemporaries. I remember one night of thunderous rain made unendurably mournful by the houseless cry of a cougar whose lair, and perhaps his family, had been buried under a slide of broken boulders on the slope of Kearsarge. We had heard the heavy detonation of the slide about the hour of the alpenglow, a pale rosy interval in a darkling air, and judged he must have come from hunting to the ruined cliff and paced the night out before it, crying a very human woe. I remember, too, in that same season of storms, a lake made milky white for days, and crowded out of its bed by clay washed into it by a fury of rain, with the trout floating in it belly up, stunned by the shock of the sudden flood. But there were trout enough for what was left of the lake next year, and the beginning of a meadow about its upper rim. What taxed me most in the wreck of one of my favorite cañons by cloud-burst was to see a bobcat mother mouthing her drowned kittens in the ruined lair built in the wash, far above the limit of accustomed waters, but not far enough for the unexpected. After a time you get the point of view of gods about these things to save you from being too pitiful.

The great snows that come at the beginning of winter, before there is yet any snow except the perpetual high banks, are best worth while to watch. These come often before the late bloomers are gone and while the migratory birds are still in the piney wood. Down in the valley you see little but the flocking of blackbirds in the streets, or the low flight of mallards over the tulares, and the gathering of clouds behind Williamson. First there is a waiting stillness in the wood; the pine-trees creak although there is no wind, the sky glowers, the first rock by the water borders. The noise of the creek rises insistently and falls off a full note like a child abashed by sudden silence in the room. This changing of the stream tone following tardily the changes of the sun on melting snows is most meaningful of wood notes. After it runs a little trumpeter wind to cry the wild creatures to their holes. Sometimes the warning hangs in the air for days with increasing stillness. Only Clark's crow and the strident jays make light of it; only they can afford to. The cattle get down to the foothills and ground-inhabiting creatures make fast their doors. It grows chill, blind clouds fumble in the cañons; there will be a roll of thunder, perhaps, or a flurry of rain, but mostly the snow is born in the air with quietness and the sense of strong white piñons softly stirred. It increases, is wet and clogging, and makes a white night of midday.

There is seldom any wind with first snows, more often rain, but later, when there is already a smooth foot or two over all the slopes, the drifts begin. The late snows are fine and dry, mere ice granules at the wind's will. Keen mornings after a storm they are blown out in wreaths and banners from the high ridges sifting into the cañons.

Once in a year or so we have a "big snow." The cloud tents are widened out to shut in the valley and an outlying range or two and are drawn tight against the sun. Such a storm begins warm, with a dry white mist that fills and fills between the ridges, and the air is thick with formless groaning. Now for days you get a hint of the neighboring ranges until the snows begin to lighten and some shouldering peak lifts through a rent. Mornings after the heavy snows are steely blue, two-edged with cold, divinely fresh and still, and these are times to go up to the pine borders. There you may find floundering in the unstable drifts "tainted wethers" of the wild sheep, faint from age and hunger; easy prey. Even the deer make slow going in the thick fresh snow, and once we found a wolverine going blind and feebly in the white glare.

No tree takes the snow stress with such ease as the silver fir. The star-whorled, fan-spread branches droop under the soft wreaths—

droop and press flatly to the trunk; presently the point of overloading is reached, there is a soft sough and muffled drooping, the boughs recover, and the weighting goes on until the drifts have reached the midmost whorls and covered up the branches. When the snows are particularly wet and heavy they spread over the young firs in green-ribbed tents wherein harbor winter loving birds.

All storms of desert hills, except wind storms, are impotent. East and west of the Sierras they rise in nearly parallel ranges, desertward, and no rain breaks over them, except from some far-strayed cloud or roving wind from the California Gulf, and these only in winter. In summer the sky travails with thunderings and the flare of sheet lightnings to win a few blistering big drops, and once in a lifetime the chance of a torrent. But you have not known what force resides in the mindless things until you have known a desert wind. One expects it at the turn of the two seasons, wet and dry, with electrified tense nerves. Along the edge of the mesa there it drops off to the valley, dust devils begin to rise white and steady, fanning out at the top like the genii out of the fisherman's bottle. One supposes the Indians might have learned the use of smoke signals from these dust pillars as they learn most things direct from the tutelage of the earth. The air begins to move fluently, blowing hot and cold between the ranges. Far south rises a murk of sand against the sky; it grows, the wind shakes itself, and has a smell of earth. The cloud of small dust takes on the color of gold and shuts out the neighborhood, the push of the wind is unsparing. Only man of all folk is foolish enough to stir abroad in it. But being in a house is really much worse; no relief from the dust, and a great fear of the creaking timbers. There is no looking ahead in such a wind, and the bite of the small sharp sand on exposed skin is keener than any insect sting. One might sleep, for the lapping of the wind wears one to the point of exhaustion very soon, but there is dread, in open sand stretches sometimes justified, of being over blown by the drift. It is hot, dry, fretful work, but by going along the ground with the wind behind, one may come upon strange things in its tumultuous privacy. I like these truces of wind and heat that the desert makes, otherwise I do not know how I should come by so many acquaintances with furtive folk. I like to see hawks sitting daunted in shallow holes, not daring to spread a feather, and doves in a row by the prickle-bushes, and shut-eyed cattle, turned tail to the wind in a patient doze. I like the smother of sand among the dunes, and finding small coiled snakes in open places, but I never like to come in a wind upon the silly sheep. The wind robs them of what wit they had, and they seem never to have learned the self-induced hypnotic stupor with which most wild things endure weather stress. I have never heard that the desert winds brought harm to any other than the wandering shepherds and their flocks. Once below Pastaria Little Pete showed me bones sticking out of the sand where a flock of two hundred had been smothered in a bygone wind. In many places the four-foot posts of a cattle fence had been buried by the wind-blown dunes.

It is enough occupation, when no storm is brewing, to watch the cloud currents and the chambers of the sky. From Kearsarge, say, you look over Inyo and find pink soft cloud masses asleep on the level desert air; south of you hurries a white troop late to some gathering of their kind at the back of Oppapago; nosing the foot of Waban, a woolly mist creeps south. In the clean, smooth paths of the middle sky and highest up in air, drift, unshepherded, small flocks ranging contrarily. You will find the proper names of these things in the reports of the Weather Bureau—cirrus, cumulus, and the like—and charts that will teach by study when to sow and take up crops. It is astonishing the trouble men will be at to find out when to plant potatoes, and gloze over the eternal meaning of the skies. You have to beat out for yourself many mornings on the windy headlands the sense of the fact that you get the same rainbow in the cloud drift over Waban and the spray of your garden hose. And not necessarily then do you live up to it.

Santa Barbara

The Storm

Jane Hollister Wheelwright (b. 1905) wrote about growing up on the historic 39,000-acre Hollister Ranch, a land of mountains, mesas, arroyos, and seacoast in Santa Barbara County, in The Ranch Papers: A California Memoir *(1988). She and her daughter, Lynda Wheelwright Schmidt, both of whom were Jungian analysts, collaborated on* The Long Shore: A Psychological Experience of the Wilderness *(1991).*

A deluge during the night made planning for the day useless. By morning two inches of rain had fallen; as the forecast had predicted, a two-inch sheet of water laid out on 39,000 acres. In the middle of the morning, over leisurely cups of coffee, I thought of my good luck the day before in escaping back to the ranch in mid-afternoon despite the prevailing dark and forbidding mood. I also relished revisioning the scene encountered on the way, especially the Mexican cattle gathered on the mesas in all their odd shapes and colors—many more than in the early morning. Some of them were milling in bunches on the road in continuous restless movements. Others seemed even more vigorous than in the morning: now grabbing at food on the trot, rudely pulling grass up by the roots and quickly, neatly, nibbling yellow mustard flowers. They were demonstrating what had happened to the yellow effect on the range that year. Individual animals taking their stand on the road held their own against me, making butting gestures at the car.

The last of the cattle from high back country over the home canyon poured down the precipitous fronting hills, high tailing it through the heavy sage, kicking, jumping, sliding. Like the others in the early morning they were wildly, dangerously playful. They were also moving to the mesas where the great blue herons had gone the day before in anticipation of rain. These birds always knew; they were truly reliable weather forecasters.

In the night, rain and wind slapped against the board and batten of the superintendent's little house. The eucalyptus over our heads whirled round in violent, erratic, mad dances. Distant breakers and still more distant thunder added to the confusion. Rain, wind, and breakers combined their fury in a roaring turmoil throughout the night. There was some comfort in this pandemonium, for without a doubt it ensured a good year of plenty for beasts, plants, and man.

Listening to the storm gave me time to reminisce about our seacoast. The breakers, whatever their intensity, are indicators of the state of things. They also convey messages from distant lands—taking up the pressures from foreign storms thousands of miles away to spend them against our cliffs. The ocean limits the surrounding elements with its one mighty voice. So alive, it is like a faithful companion, a protector in the night. The power of the moon, too, had been reflected in the wide tidal swings.

That night, violence was only a variation on the theme—the ocean's other side. It comforted me in my snug hideout, promoting sleep.

The rain finally ceased by daybreak. But the minus tide would not turn from its extra high until late morning, so there was no use venturing out. The superintendent advised against a ride because the horse could never make it on the soaked trails. Reluctant to offer advice, he said in a near whisper: "Let the ground settle itself down a bit before riding to the beach." The ground had a life of its own? A familiar note—animism perhaps—but it seemed more like the natural feeling of a man intimate with the place.

Later in the day, being impatient, I had decided to go ahead on horseback and find out what he meant. The oozing ground, swollen and shifting in the saturating water, was treacherously undermined. Old Roan slipped and slid, his feet going in four directions at times. It was strange to see a horse so helpless. The old feelings of terra firma, the solid reliability taken for granted, all that one associates with the ground underfoot, were no more. There were no little islands of safety. That was my first conscious encounter with hostile land. It reminded me of bottomless bogs and quicksand experienced long ago in small estuaries formed by our larger creeks. I looked back with more awareness to the day our Indian pony sank to her belly, my brother and I hauling on the reins, forcing her to fight her way out. We were too young to fully grasp the horror of that predicament.

I could not remember having experienced a quarter of a mile like this—and it was all because I wanted a safe ride on the beach. The earth clung in masses to my shoes, sticking in heavy lumps of adobe we called "gumbo mud." I nearly gave up.

The ocean was not much more inviting. It churned and swirled and reared. Muddy runoff had turned it to a light dull brown. Mud still flowed from every stream, out of every culvert and indentation in the land. It streamed out of scalloped crests topping the banks as hundreds of tiny streams seeped down their fronts.

A broad continuous band of yellow foamed as breakers and swells piled up. There was not a square inch of quiet water anywhere; the tide had turned only because the tide book said it would. Nevertheless there was a thin telltale strip of raised sand, no longer reached by the waves. Storm pressures were still driving up the water. In all this turmoil, the small snipe scuttled along the ebb of the surf, scratching whatever was left exposed, hustling just out of reach of the incoming waves. A natural law was in control; they were tiny atoms of order within the unruly, law-breaking elements.

To the west the sky was heavy gray with ominous black masses of clouds directly in the line of our progress. A cold and wettish wind came from that quarter like a spear thrust. Was a second storm brewing? Better not think about it. There was the blue sky to the south and east, which promoted wishful thinking for one bent on a long ride.

White cotton clouds hovered over the range, but they were rolled back on themselves by the wind. Down the coast, eastward and as far as the rounded green hills of the Alegria Canyon, the background was gray and almost blotted out. The perfect, almost rounded hilltops that always so pleased the senses now stood out sharply green against the gray.

Earlier storms had denuded the beach at the headlands. There was nothing but rock underfoot, and the deluge of the night before had scraped them clean. The exposed ledge, which extended from the high yellow earth banks until it dipped out of sight in the wild water, had a curious, chipped look, as though leveled off by chisel strokes. Centuries of wave action had done that.

Old Roan preferred the ledge to the sand dune, into which he tended to sink. He sniffed suspiciously at the smaller deposits in the rock. With frank disapproval he cleared them in wide, unexpected lunges. He spooked at the tiny earth slides from above and shied at every insignificant pebble rolling down the bank. He had a special distaste for the minute cave-ins on the small sandy banks of streams traversing the beach. His jumping and snorting finally got to me, infecting me with uneasy feelings and foreboding. The horse seemed particularly focused on something in the high, saturated cliffs. He continually pulled away from them. Landslides? Strangely he did not fuss at all at the piles of debris and mounds of kelp on the shining, slippery rock underfoot, nor did he mind the splashing waves.

Old Roan never stopped trying to double back for home and get out of the situation. He had more sense that I, who exerted all possible pressure to keep him moving forward. On hindsight, I am sure he was wary of the black horizon that should have been disturbing me.

Around the next headland, and past more rock ledges, we edged along a narrow pass against the bank where the waves were still smashing at the bits of white sand that were left there. Underfoot it was soft but not impassable; but Old Roan only snorted louder than ever.

Suddenly, the cold wind in our faces doubled in force, and with no warning clouds blacked out the sun and everything around us. Single fat raindrops fell in the bitter stinging cold, and then came the downpour. My mackintosh, which was made for fishing, not riding, only came to my knees. The horse slowed to a standstill in spite of my forcing. We endured for some minutes—then somehow the rain was no longer wet. It had turned into large hailstones that bounced off both of us.

Pandemonium hit the breakers. The streams of water flowing out of banks swelled to twice what they had been, new ones broke out everywhere and from places never before even associated with water. Breakers darkened into deep brown with the mud. The earth, rocks, water, and mud broke loose as though there were no moorings left in the world. Over it all were the wild cries of shorebirds. The drenching continued, intermittently relieved by hail. My shoes filled with water and my jeans were soaked from the knees down. The horse dripped water; his ears drooped dejectedly.

There was one alternative to our predicament: turn back and try to reach home. But I was not in my right mind; this was perhaps my last chance to face out a storm—to indulge in what few people ever feel anymore.

Horses in pasture back their rumps into a storm when it drives too hard; it is warmer that way. It was, and Old Roan calmed down a little. We hugged the bank to escape the whipping wind despite the eerie sense that something high up should not be trusted. Old Roan's suspicious behavior had undermined me—or possibly my own sensitivity was sharpening. Without the slightest warning a torrent broke out at our feet where it didn't belong. Old Roan recoiled and so did I. A long, wide, solid streak rushed across the clean gray sand into the yellow ocean foam. That kind of mud contamination of the ocean and beach confuses a lifelong sense of difference between sand and earth, in spite of their common origin.

We would have done better on the sheltered side of the next headland. Where we stood was too much in line with the gale, but to move at all was arduous. The horse seemed to agree with me; it was better to stay put, in spite of the beating.

The wait gave me time to register a mixture of feelings. There was first the foolish one for not having noted the black warnings in the west; but over and above that was the exhilaration that came from bearing out the crisis to its end. To be undefeated—so far—felt good. The sense of having endured in so wild a situation made me part of nature, part of life. It was a chance to look out at nature from inside her. It was reassuring, too, to find out once more that a bitter cold soaking does no real harm. I was able also to forget for a while the endless manmade devices in one's daily city life that are designed to prevent one from being fully alive. Overall was the need to experience the violence of the wild once more, perhaps for the last time, and, if possible, take at least some of it with me.

The drenching may have lasted half an hour and was followed, again with no warning, by a blazing hot, glaring sun. The shorebirds, particularly the killdeer and the willets, which had been screeching throughout the squall, were suddenly silenced. A solitary great blue heron still faced the direction of the storm, but this time with his neck pulled in. Snipe flew low over the foam. Many tiny beach flies stung me. The impact of their minute, solid bodies had the force of hailstones. They swarmed out of nowhere to be in the hot sun that was playing on the steaming banks.

From time to time black clouds gathered threateningly to the west, announced by alarmed cries of the birds. Now that the storm had subsided, I could look around, and the wetting no longer mattered because of the heat.

Red-winged blackbirds were already dotting the sand. They were out of place, like the vultures I had seen once on the beach at La Paz. Their conspicuous markings and shrub-loving characteristics did not fit that setting. They were like people flocking to the beach on an unexpectedly sunny day in winter. The glistening green-black birds, with their startling red wing spots edged in yellow, sang ineffectually and incongruously against the breakers. Their songs were an odd contrast to the killdeer alarums—thin and shrill, synchronized and percussive. White gulls were flying low over my head in a slow, relaxed, orderly formation, enjoying the hot sun and the sudden quiet.

It was already past noon. In the east, great white clouds followed in force. One dark rain cloud, apparently in the process of releasing some of its load, loomed up again in the west like a gigantic hand. The thick wrist rose on the horizon and the fingers reached into the clear blue sky. It was the mysterious signal to Elijah: *"Behold, there ariseth a little cloud out of the sea like unto a man's hand. The heaven was black with clouds and wind, and there was a great rain."* We were directly in its path yet still in the hot sun. The atmosphere was clear, the visibility nearly perfect. Like a magnet the clarity of the air drew close what was around us—the oil platform stood out clearly. Visibility also heralds a storm; yet what about the thorough scrubbing we had just had!

Beyond the San Augustine Canyon's cove, the headland had melted into a confusion of yellow earth—into shifts and slides loosened by the saturating water. One mass that had slipped was still leaning on the cliff face. Caves, cracks, and holes opened high up in the precarious jumble. Piles of earth were strewn over the sand. Old bench marks from ancient ocean levels on the cliff still barely showed. Much of the coastline had been chewed off and washed out to sea. All in all, as on land, it gave off a sense of impermanence and insecurity.

Old familiar sand dunes normally piled high against banks and cliffs were gone, leaving only small sand deposits here and there in crevices and corners out of reach of the onslaught of waves. The cement flume for the pipes laid out to sea for oil and gas was exposed, forming a barrier across the beach. Two days earlier it had been out of sight, submerged.

Flocks of godwit, their light brown color warm in the sun against the white and gray of the other birds, were maneuvering on the beach. The warm color tucked under their brown wings blazed into red when they flew. Cousins of the curlew, they stalked around like miniature storks with their necks pulled in.

We continued on up the beach in the direction of Point Conception nearly as far as Little Cojo Cove. Large rocks stuck out of the sand and shallow water in a strange wild alignment. Old Roan once more sniffed and snorted and tried to turn back. His fear unnerved me. The minus tide, by now receded to its low ebb, left the tall, glistening black rocks boldly silhouetted. No longer just the remains of an ancient submerged rock stratum, they seemed to fulfill a mysterious purpose. Black shapes, strangely reminiscent of the eerie menhirs of Brittany, jutted from the flattened breakers. Ocean water churned white at their bases. The largest rock of all, a boulder, was set apart from the series. It barely surfaced, its bald top glistening. To this Old Roan said no, and he circled around it warily, snorting loudly. He would not be forced. For such a stable, sensible horse, his fear and distrust of the rock surprised me. But I was sympathetic—it was indeed the head of a submerged monster.

Looking for giant limpets I dismounted and examined another rock in the shallow water. I had to reach the rock in the infrequent intervals between the biggest waves. Climbing up, holding the reins with my free hand, I caught several limpets before they clamped down with their forty-pound thrust. The knapsack for the shells somehow had to be kept from falling into the water. It was a balancing stunt on the slippery surface, made more so by thousands of tiny jets of water from sea anemones. There was always the danger of being washed off. The suspicious roan knew I was out of my head. His complaints were continuous. Each breaking wave sent him swinging round and round the rock. The deep water splashed over most of the rock and welled up to his cinch band. He could have reared, falling back on his reins, and broken free, leaving me to walk the seven miles home.

But by then we had both had enough. As we set out for home, relief showed in every movement of my horse. His ears pricked forward and there was a spring in his gait. His anticipation of home promised a long, peaceful journey for me. My only concern lay in the threat from the black cloud looming in the distance and moving toward us. The visibility again increased suddenly. Small details in the superstructure of the oil platform brightened. Out at sea, a freighter's bow and stern were visible. Its middle section appeared as though it were below the water, meaning the ship was beyond the horizon.

The rain cloud to the west came inexorably toward us, but, by some undeserved luck, it came only as far as the breaker line at our feet and then quickly veered back out to sea. It swung back and forth a second and a third time. Its abortive charges gave me, finally, some feeling of community.

The willets refused to fly away unless we came right up to them. They seemed only mildly afraid of us. In flight they revealed striking black and white markings—broad black velvet appliqued to a background of white. The few times they left the sand they flew in long sweeps over the breakers and came in to land not far in front of us. They always kept in the same flight pattern. Finally, at the end of the cove, they doubled back and settled in peace behind us.

At three, and right on time, I heard the familiar relaxed jiggedy-jog of the orange-colored train, "The Daylight," as it slipped over the rail joints. When it came into sight without the usual fanfare and fuss, it looked caught by surprise. Its engine sounded a very long dragged-out "Ooo-oo" at each crossing. It chugged along languidly for a crack train; it seemed to belong there, and did not jar the feeling of the coast in the slightest. The noises it made recalled my childhood when we had no other way of telling time, and the sound of a whistle in the distance meant we were hopelessly late for lunch.

Puffy mounds of pure white foam, left by the outgoing tide, skidded slightly on the wet sand as we approached the home canyon. But behind us, our constant companion was the great black hand of rain, looming against the surrounding sky of clear bright blue. Its wrist still resting on the western horizon, the long, dark fingers of the hand now stretched directly overhead, angling across and far down the coast in the high wind. Out at sea, rain fell at intervals in dark, thick, slanting streaks from the cloud's fingers.

The afternoon sun was low in the west, lighting up the mist upon rows of churning breakers, like charging herds of phantom horses, their manes flowing in the wind. The mist had refracted the light in a way that intensified and magnified everything. The softening effect of the mist enhanced the brilliant green of the long, thin fringe of grass topping the cliffs and banks.

Over to the east, there were a few low-lying black and troubled clouds. The hand never left us. Overhead its fingers continued to stretch from out of the west and veer seaward. Far out to sea, a few clouds, lit by the sun, piled up gracefully like miniature castles and small towers. The shapes were delicate whirlwinds that pirouetted; otherwise, the sky was cloudless. Dark green seaweed showed in the minus tide, and streamers of green brightened the brown kelp. The sparkling foam bubbled and popped on the sand as the sun lowered almost to the sea's horizon. The foam scudded a bit in the slight wind; some of it slid out on the tide. In it were yellow and pink and green lights that shone like diamonds.

By five o'clock it was quiet enough to hear the small birds in the brush on the low banks. Only the breakers stirred. All else was serene in the long shadows. The horizontal evening light brought out the white of the churning water, making it glow in the mist that was blown out to sea from the turmoil.

Big shorebirds were very much in evidence. Waiting as though performing a stately dance, they jutted their necks out and back like East Indian dancers. Among them were round-bodied black turnstones, black and white with long black vests. The little snipe, shining white and no longer so drab as they had appeared in the stormy overcast, were busy pecking their supper.

Creeks tumbled out of the large culverts under the track's right-of-way. By then I was walking to get the stiffness out of my bones, so in order to cross and stay dry I had to remount Old Roan each time we came to a stream. My saddle was weighted down with a sack of abalone shells, and my knapsack had to be treated gently, because it was full of frail shells. With my stiffness, mounting became a chore. After the first sprightly move toward home, Old Roan resumed his jumping each time a pebble rolled down the cliff. He grunted at the few tiny mudballs and cave-ins made by the streams rushing across the sand to meet the incoming tide. At each crossing he lowered his muzzle, sniffed at the water, groaned, and sighed miserably. But as yet, no complaints about the ocean. Apparently he was not going to forgive me for the morning's huddle against the cliff.

One last look to the west in the path of the setting sun revealed miles of churning breakers, their mist and foam lifted high. It was a lovely vista, tender and luminous, and infinite. The broad band of moving white water along the breaker line swept gracefully with the curve of the coast. It extended all the way to the sun, which now rested on the water. Breaker beyond breaker beyond breaker were topped, softened and lighted.

We were ushered around the last headland by the few remaining rays of the sun not yet lost to the sea's depths. They were exactly at the point of being cut off by the horizon, but in the last moment the rays lit the small, smooth pebbles scattered over the wet sand, making each one a tiny lantern in the black. The shore was carpeted with softly glowing lights, like those of fireflies.

It was dark on land where we climbed up at the home canyon. The big clouds behind the sentinel hills of the Bulito were a mysterious smoke color. They were massed and softened at first sight, and rounded. In no time, they took on something of the seashells below them, more salmon than pink.

It was hard to let go of the sight in order to open the stiff gate at the tracks, but I had to hurry because black night was about to descend. Twilight is very brief at this latitude.

A last look at the sea was barely possible but essential. The familiar abalone colors had surfaced and the sea had calmed. It was as though it were content at last to be put to bed by night.

The drama that was there that day was something to talk about; yet, paradoxically, there was a stronger need to be silent. It was too personal a matter to discuss, and the others sensed this when I reached the house. The superintendent merely said, "We thought about you during the cloudburst." No questions were asked. They somehow knew the experience on the beach was part of a personal farewell to the land of my beginning.

Santa Barbara

After the Fire

Margaret Millar (1914–1994) was one of the premier suspense writers of her day. She was also an active environmentalist, and the author of a nonfiction paean to birding, The Birds and the Beasts Were There *(1967), which contains this description of the aftermath of the devastating Coyote fire in the hills above Santa Barbara.*

Fire . . . is a natural condition of life in the chaparral regions of southern California, and an essential condition if vegetation is to remain young and vigorous. Without an occasional clearing out, the underbrush gets so thick and high that deer and other mammals can't penetrate it and ground-dwelling birds have trouble foraging. When this happens the chaparral, normally rich in wildlife, becomes incapable of supporting its usual share. Fire occurring at twenty- to twenty-five-year intervals is a benefit, a cleaning-out of dead and diseased wood and groundcover. (Before any nature lover sets off into the hills with a pack of matches, it should be noted that more frequent fires result in the destruction of chaparral, and its conversion to a different and less interesting type of vegetation.)

Some forty or more plant species are grouped together under the name chaparral. Chaparral is the Spanish word for scrub oak; it also

349

means a short, stocky person, and perhaps this gives, to someone who has never seen it, a better idea of chaparral. Chaparral is short, stocky, tough vegetation, capable of withstanding a yearly drought of six months or more.

Throughout the centuries a number of ways have evolved for chaparral plants to survive burning. Some, like green-bark ceanothus, sprout new leaves directly from the "dead" stumps. Some have woody crowns or burls at ground level, like toyon, or underground, like Eastwood manzanita, which is back to full size in a few years. Others have seeds with a hard coat that must be split open by fire, or else soft-coated seeds which need very high temperatures to trigger their internal chemistry. Among the plants with seeds requiring fire in order to germinate are some of the most dominant and important in the chaparral group of this region—chamise, big berry manzanita, laurel sumac, hoary leaf ceanothus, big pod ceanothus, sugar bush, and lemonade bush. All but chamise are frequently used in cultivated gardens.

After the Coyote fire I hiked around the burned areas, observing as a bird watcher, not a botanist. But I couldn't help noticing that greenery started to reappear almost as soon as the earth had cooled. This applied especially to a certain vine, rather similar to a grapevine, which spread along the ground, as lush a green as ever graced a rain forest, and wrapped its tendrils around the blackened stumps of trees and shrubs. This was chilicothe, or wild cucumber. Its appearance had been neither delayed nor hastened by the fire, by the rain that followed, or by any external circumstances at all. When its cycle of growth was ready to begin again, it began: everything necessary for the complete process—leaves, flowers, fruit, seeds—was contained in a giant tuber buried underground.

An example of the chilocothe's self-containment and independence of the outside world was accidentally provided by the local Botanic Garden. To show the public the size of the tubers, one weighing about fifty pounds was dug up and placed in the information center. At Christmas time it started sprouting, and within the next few weeks it went through its entire growth cycle while in a display case. Again the following year, still in the display case, it grew leaves and tendrils, it flowered and fruited and went to seed. It was only during this second cycle that the tuber becomes noticeably smaller and wrinkled as its water content decreased.

The emergence of the chilicothe was unimportant as far as food or shelter for wildlife was concerned. Yet it appeared to be a signal for the forest to come alive again. After a December rainfall of four and a half inches, oaks that looked ready for the woodpile and seemed to be still standing only because nobody had leaned against them, suddenly burst out with a cluster of leaves here, and a cluster there. No two trees re-foliated in quite the same way. These native oaks are accustomed to fires and make strong comebacks, as do the sycamores. Not so the pines, which lack the regenerative powers of the other species. The pines that looked dead were dead. Although a few of them put out new needles at the top, these soon withered and dropped, and nothing further happened.

Such debility on the part of the tree itself must, in order to account for the species' survival through centuries of periodic fires, be compensated for by the durability of the seed or the seed's protective device. Some pines, such as Bishop, knobcone, and to a certain extent Monterey, are equipped with closed cones which open and drop their seeds only when exposed to very high temperatures. There is a stand of Bishop pines near Santa Barbara which passers-by assume to be a state or county planting because the trees are all exactly the same size. The actual reason is that the seeds all germinated after the same fire.

During the Coyote fire the eucalyptus trees, especially the most widely planted variety, blue gum, burned very quickly. This was partly because of their natural oil content, which caused a great deal of black smoke, and partly because they were very dry. The deep underground water which carried many large trees through the summer drought was unavailable to the shallow-rooted eucalyptus. But their comeback was also quick. In fact, the adaptation of these imports from Australia to

California fire provided one of the oddest sights of the spring and summer. Normally, eucalyptus leaves grow like other leaves, out of branches and twigs. When the branches and twigs, however, were consumed by fire, the leaves grew instead out of the trunk of the tree. They looked like telephone poles which had suddenly started to sprout leaves from top to bottom.

Certain trees took a long time to show signs of regeneration. These included the redwoods in the center of the Botanic Garden and the olive trees on the slopes of a canyon adjoining the Botanic Garden. The grove had been planted for the commercial milling of oil in the 1880s, about the time the first daily newspaper was established in Santa Barbara and the first free library and reading room was opened. The olive oil project was abandoned when cheap Mexican labor became scarce. One of the methods used to keep the workers on the job would be frowned on by present-day union officials; whenever the braceros gave evidence of wanting a siesta, a barrel of wine, carried on a donkey-drawn sled, passed between the rows of trees, and the braceros were bribed with booze on a considerably more generous scale than the British seamen with once-a-day grog.

This olive grove, left untended for years and with a heavy growth of underbrush between the trees, was severely damaged by the fire. The underbrush was the main reason for the destruction, not, as some people believed, the oil content of the wood or leaves. When I walked through the area a week after the fire ended, all the trees looked dead, and continued to do so for a long time. Yet on a visit in mid-January, sixteen months after the fire, I noticed that nearly every blackened stump was showing some greenery at the base. The heavy rains in November and December had caused the various kinds of grasses to grow thick and tall, and there were birds everywhere: house finches, white-crowned sparrows, golden-crowned sparrows, and lesser gold-finches foraged in flocks, with the sparrows providing the dinner music, assisted by two or three invisible wrentits. The brown towhees took part with an occasional chink, reminding me of grade school monotones who are allowed to accompany their musical classmates by "playing" percussion pie plates or cake tins. Dozens of quail, securely hidden, ticked and talked, discussing the intruder among themselves without bothering to lower their voices. They made it plain that they considered me a yark and a kookquat; since I didn't know what a yark or a kookquat was, I couldn't very well contradict them.

The same visit provided an unexpected bonus, a pair of black-chinned sparrows, male and female, resting on the burned branch of an olive tree. These birds are normally seen only during the late spring and summer in stands of chamise-dominant chaparral in the mountains or foothills. Finding them in January near the city limits was highly irregular. Perhaps the Coyote fire had something to so with their appearance, since the species is known to be partial to burn areas where the new vegetation is only half grown.

On my next visit to the olive grove in mid-July, most of the trees gave evidence that they would recover completely in time. Branches growing out of the woody crown were as long as six feet and covered with silver-green leaves.

Even without the braceros and the wine wagon to keep them on the job, there will someday be another crop of olives for the white-crowned sparrows, robins, and California thrashers.

The forest was turning green again. For residents of the fire areas the change was gradual. For those who only visited from time to time it was incredibly fast and far, from death to life. At the higher altitudes the white-bark ceanothus had a fresh growth of the tough, wiry stems and sharp spikes that kept predators away from such guests as the green-tailed towhee and the mountain quail. Closer to sea level the green-bark ceanothus was performing a similar function for the lazuli bunting and California quail, the wrentit and lark sparrow.

Soon manzanita apples would again be ripening for the cedar waxwings, toyon berries for the purple finches, and mistletoe for the phainopeplas. Oak buds were already appearing for the band-tailed pigeons, and there was promise of a fresh crop of chaparral currants for the hermit thrushes, mountain cherries for the Townsend solitaires, nightshade for the grosbeaks. Through the picture window beside my chair I watched the mountains recover from the fire, each day bringing a new patch of green that turned to violet when the sun set.

As each day of recovery came and went, and each new flight of birds landed on the ledge to feed, I was continually reminded of a letter John Keats sent to a friend in 1817.

"The setting Sun will always set me to rights," he wrote, "or if a Sparrow come before my Window I take part in its existence and pick about the Gravel."

Afterword

Coming into the Watershed

Gary Snyder (b. 1930) is a native Californian who grew up in the Pacific Northwest but returned to do graduate work at the University of California at Berkeley in East Asian languages. After some years in Japan he returned in 1969 to build a homestead in the Sierra foothills and teach at UC Davis. His poetry collections include Turtle Island, *awarded the 1975 Pulitzer Prize, and what may be his chief work,* Mountains and Rivers without End *(1996). In 1990 Snyder and his neighbors formed the Yuba Watershed Institute, which comanages 1,800 acres of timberland with the Bureau of Land Management near Nevada City. This essay, first presented as a talk for the California Studies Center at California State University–Sacramento as part of their 1992 conference "Dancing at the Edge," was published in* A Place in Space *(1995).*

I had been too long in the calm Sierra pine groves and wanted to hear surf and the cries of sea birds. My son Gen and I took off one February day to visit friends on the north coast. We drove out of the Yuba River canyon and went north from Marysville—entering that soulful winter depth of pearly tule fog—running alongside the Feather

River and then crossing the Sacramento River at Red Bluff. From Red Bluff north the fog began to shred, and by Redding we had left it behind. As we crossed the mountains westward from Redding on Highway 299 we paid special attention to the transformations of the landscape and trees, watching to see where the zones would change and the natural boundaries could be roughly determined. From the Great Valley with its tules, grasses, valley oak, and blue oak we swiftly climbed into the steep and dissected Klamath range with its ponderosa pine, black oak, and manzanita fields. Somewhere past Burnt Ranch we were in the redwood and Douglas fir forests—soon it was the coastal range. Then we were descending past Blue Lake to come out at Arcata.

We drove on north. Just ten or fifteen miles from Arcata, around Trinidad Head, the feel of the landscape subtly changed again—much the same trees, but no open meadows, and a different light. At Crescent City we asked friends just what the change between Arcata and Crescent City was. They both said (to distill a long discussion), "You leave 'California.' Right around Trinidad Head you cross into the maritime Pacific Northwest." But the Oregon border (where we are expected to think "the Northwest" begins) is still many miles farther on.

So we had gone in that one afternoon's drive from the Mediterranean-type Sacramento Valley and its many plant alliances with the Mexican south, over the interior range with its dry pine-forest hills, into a uniquely Californian set of redwood forests, and on into the maritime Pacific Northwest: the edges of four major areas. These boundaries are not hard and clear, though. They are porous, permeable, arguable. They are boundaries of climates, plant communities, soil types, styles of life. They change over the millennia, moving a few hundred miles this way or that. A thin line drawn on a map would not do them justice. Yet these are the markers of the natural nations of our planet, and they establish real territories with real differences to which our economies and our clothing must adapt.

On the way back we stopped at Trinidad Head for a hike and a little birding. Although we knew they wouldn't be there until April, we walked out to take a look at the cliffs on the head where tufted puffins nest. For tufted puffins, this is virtually the southernmost end of their range. Their more usual nesting ground is from southeastern Alaska through the Bering Sea and down to northern Japan. In winter they are far out in the open seas of the North Pacific. At this spot, Trinidad, we could not help but feel that we touched on the life realm of the whole North Pacific and Alaska. We spent that whole weekend enjoying "liminality," dancing on the brink of the continent.

I have taken to watching the subtle changes of plants and climates as I travel over the West. We can all tell stories, I know, of the drastic changes we have noticed as we ranged over this or that freeway. This vast area called "California" is large enough to be beyond any one individual's ability (not to mention time) to travel over and to take it all into the imagination and hold it clearly enough in mind to see the whole picture. Michael Barbour, a botanist and lead author of *California's Changing Landscapes*, writes of the complexity of California: "Of the world's ten major soils, California has all ten. . . . As many as 375 distinctive natural communities have been recognized in the state. . . . California has more than five thousand kinds of native ferns, conifers, and flowering plants. Japan has far fewer species with a similar area. Even with four times California's area, Alaska does not match California's plant diversity, and neither does all of the central and northeastern United States and adjacent Canada combined. Moreover, about 30 percent of California's native plants are found nowhere else in the world."

But all this talk of the diversity of California is a trifle misleading. Of what place are we speaking? What is "California"? It is, after all, a recent human invention with hasty straight-line boundaries that were drawn with a ruler on a map and rushed off to an office in D.C. This is another illustration of Robert Frost's line, "The land was ours before we were the land's." The political boundaries of the western states were established in haste and ignorance. Landscapes have their own shapes and structures, centers and edges, which must be respected. If a relationship to a place is like a marriage, then the Yankee establishment of a jurisdiction called California was like a shotgun wedding with six sisters taken as one wife.

California is made up of what I take to be about six regions. They are of respectable size and native beauty, each with its own makeup, its own mix of bird calls and plant smells. Each of these propose a slightly different lifestyle to the human beings who live there. Each led to different sorts of rural economies, for the regional differences translate into things like raisin grapes, wet rice, timber, cattle pasture, and so forth.

The central coast with its little river valleys, beach dunes and marshes, and oak-grass-pine mountains is one region. The great Central Valley is a second, once dominated by swamps and wide shallow lakes and sweeps of valley oaks following the streams. The long mountain ranges of the Sierra Nevada are a third. From a sort of Sonoran chaparral they rise to arctic tundra. In the middle elevations they have some of the finest mixed conifer forests in the world. The Modoc plateau and volcano country—with its sagebrush and juniper—makes a fourth. Some of the Sacramento waters rise here. The fifth is the northern coast with its deep interior mountains—the Klamath region—reaching (on the coast) as far north as Trinidad Head. The sixth (of these six sisters) consists of the coastal valleys and mountains south of the Tehachapis, with natural connections on into Baja. Although today this region supports a huge population with water drawn from the Colorado River, the Owens Valley, and the great Central Valley, it was originally almost a desert.

One might ask, What about the rest? Where are the White Mountains, the Mojave Desert, the Warner Range? They are splendid places, but they do not belong with California. Their watersheds and biological communities belong to the Great Basin or the lower Colorado drainage, and we should let them return to their own families. Almost all of core California has a summer-dry Mediterranean climate with (usually) a fairly abundant winter rain. More than any thing else, this rather special type of climate is what gives our place its fragrance of oily aromatic herbs, its olive-green drought-resistant shrubs, and its patterns of rolling grass and dark forest.

I am not arguing that we should instantly redraw the boundaries of the social construction called California, although that could happen some far day. But we are becoming aware of certain long-range realities, and this thinking leads toward the next step in the evolution of human citizenship on the North American continent. The usual focus of attention for most Americans is the human society itself with its problems and its successes, its icons and symbols. With the exception of most Native Americans and a few non-natives who have given their hearts to the place, the land we all live on is simply taken for granted—and proper relation to it is not considered a part of "citizenship." But after two centuries of national history, people are beginning to wake up and notice that the United States is located on a landscape with a severe, spectacular, spacy, wildly demanding, and ecstatic narrative to be learned. Its natural communities are each unique, and each of us, whether we like it or not—in the city or countryside—lives in one of them.

Those who work in resource management are accustomed to looking at many different maps of the landscape. Each addresses its own set of meanings. If we look at land ownership categories, we get (in addition to private land) the Bureau of Land Management, national forest, national park, state park, military reserves, and a host of other public holdings. This is the public domain, a practice coming down from the historic institution of the commons in Europe. These lands, particularly in the arid West, hold much of the water, forest, and wildlife that are left in America. Although they are in the care of all the people, they have too often been managed with a bent toward the mining or logging interests and toward short-term profits.

Conservationists have been working since the 1930s for sustainable forestry practices and the preservation of key blocks of public land as wilderness. They have had some splendid success in this effort, and we are all indebted to the single-minded dedication of the people who are behind every present-day wilderness area that we and our children walk into. Our growing understanding of how natural systems work brought us the realization that an exclusive emphasis on disparate parcels of land ignored the insouciant freeness of wild creatures. Although individual islands of wild land serving as biological refuges are invaluable, they cannot by themselves guarantee the maintenance of natural variety. As biologists, public managers, and the involved public have all agreed, we need to know more about how the larger-scale natural systems work, and we need to find "on-the-ground" ways to connect wild zone to wild zone wherever possible. We have now developed the notion of biological corridors or connectors. The Greater Yellowstone Ecosystem concept came out of this sort of recognition. Our understanding of nature has been radically altered by systems theory as applied to ecology, and in particular to the very cogent subdisciplines called island biogeography theory and landscape ecology.

No single group or agency could keep track of grizzly bears, which do not care about park or ranch boundaries and have necessary, ancient territories of their own that range from late-summer alpine huckleberry fields to lower-elevation grasslands. Habitat flows across both private and public land. We must find a way to work with wild ecosystems that respects both the rights of landowners and the rights of bears. The idea of ecosystem management, all the talk now in land management circles, seems to go in the right direction. Successfully managing for the ecosystem will require as much finesse in dealing with miners, ranchers, and motel owners as it does with wild animals or bark beetles.

A "greater ecosystem" has its own function and structural coherence. It often might contain or be within a watershed system. It would usually be larger than a county, but smaller than a western U.S. state. One of the names for such a space is "bioregion."

A group of California-based federal and state land managers who are trying to work together on biodiversity problems recently realized that their work could be better accomplished in a framework of natural regions. Their interagency "memorandum of understanding" calls for us to "move beyond existing efforts focused on the conservation of individual sites, species, and resources . . . to also protect and manage ecosystems, biological communities, and landscapes." The memorandum goes on to say that "public agencies and private groups must coordinate resource management and environmental protection activities, emphasizing regional solutions to regional issues and needs."

The group identified eleven or so such working regions within California, making the San Francisco Bay and delta into one, and dividing both the Sierra and the valley into northern and southern portions. (In landscapes as in taxonomy, there are lumpers and splitters.) Since almost 50 percent of California is public domain, it is logical that the chiefs of the BLM, the Forest Service, California Department of Fish and Game, California Department of Forestry, State Parks, the Federal Fish and Wildlife Service, and such should take these issues on, but that they came together in so timely a manner and signed onto such a far-reaching plan is admirable.

Hearing of this agreement, some county government people, elected officials, and timber and business interests in the mountain counties went into a severe paranoid spasm, fearing—they said—new regulations and more centralized government. So later in the fall, an anonymous circular made its way around towns and campuses in northern California under the title "Biodiversity or New Paganism?" It says that "California Resource Secretary Doug Wheeler and his self-appointed bioregional soldiers are out to devalue human life by placing greater emphasis on rocks, trees, fish, plants, and wildlife." It quotes me as having written that "those of us who are now promoting a bioregional consciousness would, as an ultimate and long-range goal, like to see this continent more sensitively redefined, and the natural regions of North America—Turtle Island—gradually begin to shape the political entities within which we work. It would be a small step toward deconstruction of America as a superpower into seven or eight natural nations—none of which have a budget big enough to support missiles." I'm pleased to say I did write that. I'd think it was clear that my statement is not promoting more centralized government, which seems to be a major fear, but these gents want both their small-town autonomy and the military-industrial state at the same time. Many a would-be westerner is a rugged individualist in rhetoric only, and will scream up a storm if tak-en too far from the government tit. As Mark Reisner makes clear in *Cadillac Desert*, much of the agriculture and ranching of the West exists by virtue of a complicated and very expensive sort of government wel-fare: big dams and water plans. The real intent of the circular (it urges people to write the state governor) seems to be to resist policies that favor long-range sustainability and the support of biodiversity, and to hold out for maximum resource extraction right now.

As far as I can see, the intelligent but so far toothless California "bioregional proposal" is simply a basis for further thinking and some degree of cooperation among agencies. The most original part is the call for the formation of "bioregional councils" that would have some stake in decision making. Who would be on the bioregional council is not spelled out. Even closer to the roots, the memorandum that started all this furor suggests that "watershed councils" would be formed, which, being based on stream-by-stream communities, would be truly local bodies that could help design agreements working for the preservation of natural variety. Like, let's say, helping to preserve the spawning grounds for the wild salmon that still come (amazingly) into the lower Yuba River gravel wastelands. This would be an effort that would have to involve a number of groups and agencies, and it would have to include the blessing of the usually development-minded Yuba County Water Agency.

The term "bioregion" was adopted by the signers to the Mem-orandum on Biological Diversity as a technical term from the field of biogeography. It's not likely that they would have known that there were already groups of people around the United States and Canada who were talking in terms of bioregionally oriented societies. I doubt they would have heard about the first North American Bioregional Congress held in Kansas in the late eighties. They had no idea that for twenty years communitarian ecology-minded dwellers-in-the-land have been living in places they call "Ish" (Puget Sound and lower British Columbia) or "Columbiana" (upper Columbia River) or "Mesechabe" (lower Mississippi) or "Shasta" (northern California), and all of them have produced newsletters, taken field trips, organized gatherings, and at the same time participated in local politics.

That "bioregion" was an idea already in circulation was the bad, or good, luck of the biodiversity agreement people, depending on how you look at it. As it happens, the bioregional people are also finding "watershed councils" to be the building blocks of a long-range strategy for social and environmental sustainability.

A watershed is a marvelous thing to consider: this process of rain falling, streams flowing, and oceans evaporating causes every molecule of water on earth to make the complete trip once every two million years. The surface is carved into watersheds—a kind of familial branching, a chart of relationship, and a definition of place. The watershed is the first and last nation whose boundaries, though subtly shifting, are unarguable. Races of birds, subspecies of trees, and types of hats or rain gear often go by the watershed. For the watershed, cities and dams are ephemeral and of no more account than a boulder that falls in the river or a landslide that temporarily alters the channel. The water will always be there, and it will always find its way down. As constrained and polluted as the Los Angeles River is at the moment, it can also be said that in the larger picture that river is alive and well under the city streets, running in giant culverts. It may be amused by such diversion. But we who live in terms of centuries rather than millions of years must hold the watershed and its communities together, so our children might enjoy the clear water and fresh life of this landscape we have chosen. From the tiniest rivulet at the crest of a ridge to the main trunk of a river approaching the lowlands, the river is all one place and all one land.

The water cycle includes our springs and wells, our Sierra snowpack, our irrigation canals, our car wash, and the spring salmon run. It's the spring peeper in the pond and the acorn woodpecker chattering in a snag. The watershed is beyond the dichotomies of orderly/disorderly, for its forms are free, but somehow inevitable. The life that comes to flourish within it constitutes the first kind of community.

The agenda of a watershed council starts in a modest way: like saying,

"Let's try and rehabilitate our river to the point that wild salmon can successfully spawn here again." In pursuit of this local agenda, a community might find itself combating clear-cut timber sales upstream, water-selling grabs downstream, Taiwanese drift-net practices out in the North Pacific, and a host of other national and international threats to the health of salmon.

If a wide range of people will join in on this effort—people from timber and tourism, settled ranchers and farmers, fly-fishing retirees, the businesses and the forest-dwelling new settlers—something might come of it. But if this joint agreement were to be implemented as a top-down prescription, it would go nowhere. Only a grass-roots engagement with long-term issues can provide the political and social stability it will take to keep the biological richness of California's regions intact.

All public land ownership is ultimately written in sand. The boundaries and management categories were created by Congress, and Congress can take them away. The only "jurisdiction" that will last in the world of nature is the watershed, and even that changes slightly over time. If public lands come under greater and greater pressure to be opened for exploitation and use in the twenty-first century, it will be the local people, the watershed people, who will prove to be the last and possibly most effective line of defense. Let us hope it never comes to that.

The mandate of the public land managers and the Fish and Wildlife people inevitably directs them to resource concerns. They are proposing to do what could be called "ecological bioregionalism." The other movement, coming out of the local communities, could be called "cultural bioregionalism." I would like to turn my attention now to cultural bioregionalism and to what practical promise these ideas hold for fin-de-millennium America.

Living in a place—the notion has been around for decades and has usually been dismissed as provincial, backward, dull, and possibly reactionary. But new dynamics are at work. The mobility that has characterized American life is coming to a close. As Americans begin to stay put, it may give us the first opening in over a century to give participatory democracy another try.

Daniel Kemmis, the mayor of Missoula, Montana, has written a fine little book called *Community and the Politics of Place* (Norman: University of Oklahoma Press, 1990). Mr. Kemmis points out that in the eighteenth century the word *republican* meant a politics of community engagement. Early republican thought was set against the federalist theories that would govern by balancing competing interests, devise sets of legalistic procedures, maintain checks and balances (leading to hearings held before putative experts) in place of direct discussion between adversarial parties.

Kemmis quotes Rousseau: "Keeping citizens apart has become the first maxim of modern politics." So what organizing principle will get citizens back together? There are many, and each in its way has its use. People have organized themselves by ethnic background, religion, race, class, employment, gender, language, and age. In a highly mobile society where few people stay put, thematic organizing is entirely understandable. But place, that oldest of organizing principles (next to kinship), is a novel development in the United States.

"What holds people together long enough to discover their power as citizens is their common inhabiting of a single place," Kemmis argues. Being so placed, people will volunteer for community projects, join school boards, and accept nominations and appointments. Good minds, which are often forced by company or agency policy to keep moving, will make notable contributions to the neighborhood if allowed to stay put. And since local elections deal with immediate issues, a lot more people will turn out to vote. There will be a return of civic life.

This will not be "nationalism" with all its dangers, as long as sense of place is not entirely conflated with the idea of a nation. Bioregional concerns go beyond those of any ephemeral (and often brutal and dangerous) politically designated space. They give us the imagination of "citizenship" in a place called (for example) the great Central Valley, which has valley oaks and migratory waterfowl as well as humans among its members. A place (with a climate, with bugs), as Kemmis says, "develops practices, creates culture."

Another fruit of the enlarged sense of nature that systems ecology and bioregional thought have given us is the realization that cities and suburbs are a part of the system. Unlike the ecological bioregionalists, the cultural bioregionalists absolutely must include the cities in their thinking. The practice of urban bioregionalism ("green cities") has made a good start in San Francisco. One can learn and live deeply with regard to wild systems in any sort of neighborhood—from the urban to a big sugar-beet farm. The birds are migrating, the wild plants are looking for a way to slip in, the insects in any case live an untrammeled life, the raccoons are padding through the crosswalks at 2:00 A.M., and the nursery trees are trying to figure out who they are. These are exciting, convivial, and somewhat radical knowledges.

An economics of scale can be seen in the watershed/bioregion/city-state model. Imagine a Renaissance-style city-state facing out on the Pacific with its bioregional hinterland reaching to the headwaters of all the streams that flow through its bay. The San Francisco/valley rivers/Shasta headwaters bio-city region! I take some ideas along these lines from Jane Jacobs's tantalizing book *Cities and the Wealth of Nations* (New York: Random House, 1984), in which she argues that the city, not the nation-state, is the proper locus of an economy, and then that the city is always to be understood as being one with the hinterland.

Such a non-nationalistic idea of community, in which commitment to pure place is paramount, cannot be ethnic or racist. Here is perhaps the most delicious turn that comes out of thinking about politics from the standpoint of place: anyone of any race, language, religion, or origin is welcome, as long as they live well on the land. The great Central Valley region does not prefer English over Spanish or Japanese or Hmong. If it had any preference at all, it might best like the languages it heard for thousands of years, such as Maiduor Miwok, simply because it's used to them. Mythically speaking, it will welcome whoever chooses to observe the etiquette, express the gratitude, grasp the tools, and learn the songs that it takes to live there.

This sort of future culture is available to whoever makes the choice, regardless of background. It need not require that a person drop his or her Buddhist, Jewish, Christian, animist, atheist, or Muslim beliefs but simply add to that faith or philosophy a sincere nod in the direction of the deep value of the natural world and the subjecthood of nonhuman beings. A culture of place will be created that will include the "United States," and go beyond that to an affirmation of the continent, the land itself, Turtle Island. We could be showing Southeast Asian and South American newcomers the patterns of the rivers, the distant hills, saying, "It is not only that you are now living in the United States. You are living in this great landscape. Please get to know these rivers and mountains, and be welcome here." Euro-Americans, Asian Americans, African Americans can—if they wish—become "born-again" natives of Turtle Island. In doing so we also might even (eventually) win some respect from our native American predecessors, who are still here and still trying to teach us where we are.

Watershed consciousness and bioregionalism is not just environmentalism, not just a means toward resolution of social and economic problems, but a move toward resolving both nature and society with the practice of a profound citizenship in both the natural and the social worlds. If the ground can be our common ground, we can begin to talk to each other (human and nonhuman) once again.

> California is gold-tan grasses, silver-gray tule fog,
> olive-green redwood, blue-gray chaparral,
> silver-hue serpentine hills.
> Blinding white granite,
> blue-black rock sea cliffs.
> —Blue summer sky, chestnut brown slough water, steep purple city
> streets—hot cream towns. Many colors of the land, many colors
> of the skin.

Abbey, Edward. *The Best of Edward Abbey*. San Francisco: Sierra Club Books, 1988.

———. *Confessions of a Barbararian: Selections from the Journals of Edward Abbey, 1951–1989*. Boston: Little, Brown, 1994.

———. *The Journey Home: Some Words in the Defense of the American West*. New York: E. P. Dutton, 1977.

Austin, Mary. *The Flock*. Boston: Houghton Mifflin, 1906.

———. *Isidro*. Boston: Houghton Mifflin, 1905.

———. *The Land of Little Rain*. Boston: Houghton Mifflin, 1903.

Brewer, William H. *Up and Down California in 1860*. Edited by Francis P. Farquhar. New Haven: Yale University Press, 1930; repr. Berkeley: University of California Press, 1940.

Chase, J. Smeaton. *California Coast Trails*. Boston: Houghton Mifflin, 1913.

———. *California Desert Trails*. Boston: Houghton Mifflin, 1919.

———. *Yosemite Trails*. Boston: Hougton Mifflin, 1911.

Chatham, Russell. *The Angler's Coast*. Livingston, Mont.: Clark City Press, 1990.

———. *Dark Waters*. Livingston, Mont.: Clark City Press, 1988.

Daniel, John. *All Things Touched by Wind*. Anchorage: Salmon Run Press, 1994.

———. *Common Ground*. Lewiston, Idaho: Confluence Press, 1988.

———. *The Trail Home: Nature, Imagination, and the American West*. New York: Pantheon Books, 1992.

Darlington, David. *Angels' Visits: An Inquiry into the Mystery of Zinfandel*. New York: Henry Holt, 1992.

———. *In Condor Country.* Boston: Houghton Mifflin, 1987.

———. *The Mojave: A Portrait of the Definitive American Desert.* New York: Henry Holt, 1996.

Didion, Joan. *Play It as It Lays.* New York: Farrar, Straus & Giroux, 1970.

———. *Run River.* New York: Ivan Obolensky, 1963.

———. *Slouching Towards Bethlehem.* New York: Farrar, Straus & Giroux, 1968.

Duane, Daniel. *Caught Inside: A Surfer's Year on the California Coast.* New York: North Point Press, 1996.

———. *Lighting Out: A Vision of California and the Mountains.* St. Paul: Graywolf Press, 1994.

Ehrlich, Gretel. *Islands, the Universe, Home.* New York: Viking Press, 1991.

———. *The Solace of Open Spaces.* New York: Viking Press, 1985.

Fisher, M. F. K. *Last House: Reflections, Dreams, and Observations, 1943–1991.* New York: Pantheon Books, 1995.

———. *Stay Me, Oh Comfort Me: Journal and Stories, 1933–1941.* New York: Pantheon Books, 1993.

———. *To Begin Again: Stories and Memoirs, 1908–1929.* New York: Pantheon Books, 1992.

Flanner, Hildegarde. *At the Gentle Mercy of Plants: Essays and Poems.* Santa Barbara: John Daniel, 1986.

———. *Brief Cherishing: A Napa Valley Harvest.* Santa Barbara: John Daniel, 1985.

———. *A Vanishing Land.* Portola Valley, Calif.: No Dead Lines, 1980.

Gilliam, Harold. *Creating Carmel: An Enduring Vision.* Salt Lake City: Peregrine Smith Books, 1992.

———. *Island in Time: The Point Reyes Peninsula.* San Francisco: Sierra Club Books, 1962.

———. *The San Francisco Experience.* New York: Doubleday, 1972.

Goddard, Pliny E. "The Creation." *University of California Publications in American Archaeology and Ethnology* 184, no. 2 (1909). Reprinted in *Folk Tales of the North American Indians,* edited by Stith Thompson. North Dighton, Mass.: JG Press, 1995.

———. *Indians of the Southwest.* New York: American Museum of Natural History, 1913.

Houston, James D. *California Heartland: Writing from the Great Central Valley* (with Gerald Haslam). Santa Barbara: Capra Press, 1978.

———. *Californians: Searching for the Golden State.* New York: Alfred A. Knopf, 1982.

———. *Continental Drift*. New York: Alfred A. Knopf, 1978.

———. *In the Ring of Fire: A Pacific Basin Journey*. San Francisco: Mercury House, 1997.

———. *Running West*. New York: Crown Publishers, 1989.

Kerouac, Jack. *Big Sur*. New York: Viking Press, 1962.

———. *The Dharma Bums*. New York: Viking Press, 1958.

———. *On the Road*. New York: Viking Press, 1957.

———. *Selected Letters, 1940–1956*. Edited by Ann Charters. New York: Viking Press, 1995.

LeConte, Joseph. *Autobiography*. Edited by William Dallam Arms. New York: D. Appleton, 1903.

———. *A Journal of Ramblings Through the High Sierra of California by the "University Excursion Party."* San Francisco: Frances & Valentine, 1875.

London, Jack. *Burning Daylight*. New York: Macmillan, 1910.

———. *Jack London's California: The Golden Poppy and Other Writings*. Edited by Sol Noto. New York: Beaufort Books, 1986.

——— *Novels and Stories*. Library of America, 2 vols. New York: Literary Classics of the United States, 1982.

———. *The Valley of the Moon*. New York: Macmillan, 1913.

Lopez, Barry. *Crossing Open Ground*. New York: Scribner's, 1988.

———. *Crow and Weasel*. New York: Random House, 1991.

———. *Field Notes: The Grace Notes of the Canyon Wren*. New York: Alfred A. Knopf, 1994.

———. *Of Wolves and Men*. New York: Scribner's, 1978.

Masumoto, David Mas. *Country Voices: An Oral History of a Japanese-American Family Farm Community*. Del Rey, Calif.: Inaka Countryside Publications, 1987.

———. *Epitaph for a Peach: Four Seasons on My Family Farm*. San Francisco: HarperCollins West, 1995.

———. *Harvest Son*. New York: W. W. Norton, 1998.

McKinney, John. *A Walk Along Land's End: Discovering California's Unknown Coast*. San Francisco: HarperCollins West, 1995.

———. *Walking the California Coast: One Hundred Adventures Along the California Coast*. San Francisco: HarperCollins West, 1994.

———. *Walking California's State Parks*. San Francisco: HarperCollins West, 1994.

McPhee, John. *Assembling California*. New York: Farrar, Straus & Giroux, 1993.

Millar, Margaret. *The Birds and the Beasts Were There*. New York: Random House, 1967.

Miller, Henry. *The Air-Conditioned Nightmare*. New York: New Directions, 1945.

———. *Big Sur and the Oranges of Hieronymous Bosch*. New York: New Directions, 1957.

———. *The Henry Miller Reader*. Edited by Lawrence Durrell. New York: New Directions, 1959.

Miller, Joaquin. *Memorie and Rime*. New York: Funk & Wagnals, 1884.

———. *Life Amongst the Modocs: Unwritten History*. London: Bentley, 1873.

Muir, John. *The Mountains of California*. New York: Century, 1894.

———. *My First Summer in the Sierra*. Boston: Houghton Mifflin, 1911.

———. *The Yosemite*. New York: Century, 1912.

Nabhan, Gary Paul. *The Desert Smells like Rain: A Naturalist in Papago Indian Country*. San Francisco: North Point Press, 1982.

———. *Gathering the Desert*. Tucson: University of Arizona Press, 1985.

———. *The Geography of Childhood (Why Children Need Wild Places)* (with Stephen Trimble). Boston: Beacon Press, 1994.

Nunn, Kem. *The Dogs of Winter*. New York: Scribner's, 1997.

———. *Pomona Queen*. New York: Pocket Books, 1992.

———. *Tapping the Source*. New York: Delacorte Press, 1984.

Powell, Lawrence Clark. *California Classics: The Creative Literature of the Golden State*. Los Angeles: Ward Ritchie Press, 1971.

———. *Fortune and Friendship: An Autobiography*. New York: Bowker, 1968.

———. *The Little Package*. New York: World, 1964.

Snyder, Gary. *Mountains and Rivers Without End*. Washington, D.C.: Counterpoint, 1996.

———. *A Place in Space: Ethics, Aesthetics, and Wilderness*. Washington, D.C.: Counterpoint, 1995.

———. *The Practice of the Wild*. New York: Farrar, Straus & Giroux, 1990.

Stegner, Wallace. *American Places* (with Page Stegner). New York: E. P. Dutton, 1983.

———. *American West as Living Space*. Ann Arbor: University of Michigan Press, 1987.

———. *Angle of Repose*. New York: Doubleday, 1971.

———. *Where the Bluebird Sings to the Lemonade Springs: Living and Writing in the West*. New York: Random House, 1992.

Steinbeck, John. *The Grapes of Wrath*. New York: Viking Press, 1939.

———. *The Long Valley*. New York: Viking Press, 1938.

———. *The Pastures of Heaven*. New York: Brewer, 1932.

———. *To a God Unknown*. New York: Ballou, 1933.

————. *Tortilla Flat.* New York: Covici, Friede, 1935.

Stevenson, Robert Louis. *Silverado Journal.* Edited by J. E. Jordan. San Francisco: Book Club of California, 1954.

————. *The Silverado Squatters.* London: Chatto & Windus, 1883.

Twain, Mark. *Autobiography.* 2 vols. New York: Harper, 1924.

————. *Roughing It.* New York: Harper & Bros., 1906.

Wallace, David Rains. *Bulow Hammock: Mind in a Forest.* San Francisco: Sierra Club Books, 1989.

————. *The Klamath Knot: Explorations of Myth and Evolution.* San Francisco: Sierra Club Books, 1972.

————. *The Untamed Garden and Other Personal Essays.* Columbus: Ohio State University Press, 1986.

Watkins, T. H. *On the Shore of the Sundown Sea.* San Francisco: Sierra Club Books, 1973.

————. *Time's Island: The California Desert.* Salt Lake City: Gibbs Smith, 1989.

————, ed. (with Patricia Byrnes). *The World of Wilderness: Essays on the Power and Purpose of Wild Country.* Boulder, Colo.: Roberts Rinehart, 1995.

Wheelwright, Jane Hollister. *The Long Shore: A Psychological Experience of the Wilderness* (with Lynda Wheelwright Schmidt). San Francisco: Sierra Club Books, 1991.

————. *The Ranch Papers: A California Memoir.* San Francisco: Lapis Press, 1988.

Wilson, Darryl Babe. "Grampa Ramsey and the Great Canyon." In *Blue Dawn, Red Earth: New Native American Storytellers,* edited by Clifford E. Trafzer. New York: Doubleday, 1996.

————. "Before There Was Something, There Was Nothing: The Creation." In *The Sound of Rattles and Clappers: A Collection of New California Indian Writing,* edited by Greg Sarris. Tucson: University of Arizona Press, 1994.

Zwinger, Ann. *A Desert Country near the Sea: A Natural History of the Cape Region of Baja California.* New York: HarperCollins, 1983.

————. *Land Above the Trees: A Guide to American Alpine Tundra.* New York: Harper & Row, 1972.

————. *Run, River, Run: A Naturalist's Journey Down One of the Great Rivers of the American West.* New York: HarperCollins, 1972.

————. *Yosemite: Valley of Thunder.* New York: HarperCollins, 1996.

Zwinger, Susan. *Stalking the Ice Dragon: An Alaskan Journey.* Tucson: University of Arizona Press, 1991.

————. *Still Wild, Always Wild: A Journey into the Desert Wilderness of California* (with photographs by Jeff Garton). San Francisco: Sierra Club Books, 1997.

ACKNOWLEDGMENTS

"Death Valley," from *The Journey Home* by Edward Abbey. © 1977 by Edward Abbey. Used by permission of Dutton Signet, a division of Penguin Books USA Inc. and Don Congdon Associates, Inc.

"Into the Valley," from *Up and Down California in 1860–1864* by William H. Brewer, edited by Francis Farquhar. © 1949 by The Regents of the University of California. Reprinted by permission of the University of California Press.

"A Certain Moment," from *Angler's Coast* by Russell Chatham. © by Russell Chatham. Reprinted by permission of Clark City Press, 1990.

"Desert Walking," from *The Trail Home* by John Daniel. © 1992 by John Daniel. Reprinted by permission of Pantheon Books, a division of Random House, Inc.

"In Condor Country," from *In Condor Country* by David Darlington. © 1987 by David Darlington. Reprinted by permission of Frederick Hill Associates Literary Agency.

"The Santa Ana," from "Los Angeles Notebook," in *Slouching Towards Bethlehem* by Joan Didion. © 1968 and renewed by Joan Didion. Reprinted by permission of Farrar, Straus & Giroux, Inc.

"Climbing Half Dome," © 1994 by Daniel Duane. Reprinted from *Lighting Out* with the permission of Graywolf Press, St. Paul, Minnesota, and Ellen Levine Literary Agency.

"Santa Rosa" reprinted by permission from the July/August 1996 issue of *Islands* magazine. © 1966 by Islands Publishing Company. All rights reserved.

"Spirits of the Valley" reprinted from *Stay Me, Oh Comfort Me* by M. F. K.

Fisher. © 1992 by M. F. K. Fisher. Reprinted by permission of Pantheon Books, a division of Random House, Inc., and Lescher & Lescher, Ltd.

"A Vanishing Land, " from *A Vanishing Land* by Hildegarde Flanner. © 1980 by John Monhoff. Reprinted by permission of John Monhoff and No Dead Lines.

"A Mount for All Seasons," from *The San Francisco Experience* by Harold Gilliam. © 1972 by Harold Gilliam. Used by permission of Doubleday, a division of Bantam Doubleday Dell Publishing Group, Inc.

"Continental Drift," from *Continental Drift* by James D. Houston. © 1988 by James D. Houston. Reprinted by permission of author.

"A Reflection on White Geese," from *Crossing Open Ground* by Barry Lopez. © 1988 by Barry Holstun Lopez. Reprinted by permission of Sterling Lord Literistic, Inc.

"Climbing Matterhorn Peak," from *The Dharma Bums* by Jack Kerouac. © 1958 by Jack Kerouac, renewed by Stella Kerouac and Jan Kerouac. Used by permission of Viking Penguin, a division of Penguin Books USA Inc.

"Lost Coast" (abridged). Reprinted by permission of author.

"The San Andreas Discrepancy," from *Assembling California* by John McPhee. © 1993 by John McPhee. Reprinted by permission of Farrar, Straus & Giroux, Inc., and Macfarlane Walter & Ross, Toronto.

"Winter's Fog," from *Epitaph for a Peach* by David Mas Masumoto. © 1995 by David Mas Masumoto. Reprinted by permission of HarperCollins Publishers, Inc.

"After the Fire," from *The Birds and Beasts Were There* by Margaret Millar. © 1967 by Margaret Millar, renewed 1995 by The Margaret Millar Charitable Remainder Unitrust u/a 1/12/82. Reprinted by permission of Harold Ober Associates Incorporated.

"Big Sur," from *Big Sur and the Oranges of Hieronymus Bosch* by Henry Miller. © 1957 by New Directions Publishing Corp. Reprinted by permission of New Directions Publishing Corp.

"The Palms in Our Hands," from *Gathering the Desert* by Gary Paul Nabhan. © 1985 by Gary Paul Nabhan. Reprinted by permission of the University of Arizona Press.

"Tapping the Source" by Kem Nunn. Reprinted by permission of author.

"Where the Mountains Meet the Sea," from *The Little Package* by Lawrence Clark Powell. © 1964 by Lawrence Clark Powell. Reprinted by permission of author.

"Remnants" by Wallace Stegner. From *American Places* by Wallace Stegner;

originally published in *Country Journal*, December 1979. © 1979 by Wallace Stegner. Reprinted by permission of Brandt & Brandt Literary Agents, Inc.

"Flight," from *The Long Valley* by John Steinbeck. © 1938, renewed © 1966 by John Steinbeck. Used by permission of Viking Penguin, a division of Penguin Books USA Inc.

"The Fourth Dimension," from Chapter One (abridged) of *The Klamath Knot* by David Rains Wallace. © 1972 by Sierra Club Books. Reprinted by permission of Sierra Club Books.

"The Sundown Sea," © 1973 by T. H. Watkins. Reprinted by permission of author.

"The Storm," © 1988 by Jane Wheelwright Hollister. Reprinted by permission of author.

"Grampa Ramsey and the Great Canyon" first appeared in *News from Native California* (Malcolm Margolin, editor) and was collected in *Blue Dawn, Red Earth* (Clifford E. Trafzer, editor), published by Doubleday, 1996. Reprinted by permission of author.

"Trumpets of Light," excerpt from *Yosemite: A Valley of Thunder* by Ann Zwinger. © 1996 by Tehabi Books, Inc. Reprinted by permission of Tehabi Books.

"Overlooking Carrizo Gorge," excerpt from *Still Wild, Always Wild* by Susan Zwinger. © 1997 by Susan Zwinger. Reprinted by permission of Sierra Club Books.

Designer:	Nola Burger
Compositor:	Integrated Composition Systems, Inc.
Text:	10/15 Janson
Display:	Janson and Futura Heavy
Printer and Binder:	BookCrafters, Inc.